MISOGYNY

The New Activism

GAIL UKOCKIS

OXFORD
UNIVERSITY PRESS

Oxford University Press is a department of the University of Oxford. It furthers
the University's objective of excellence in research, scholarship, and education
by publishing worldwide. Oxford is a registered trade mark of Oxford University
Press in the UK and certain other countries.

Published in the United States of America by Oxford University Press
198 Madison Avenue, New York, NY 10016, United States of America.

© Oxford University Press 2019

Library of Congress Cataloging-in-Publication Data
Names: Ukockis, Gail L., 1962– author.
Title: Misogyny: the new activism / Gail Ukockis.
Description: New York: Oxford University Press, 2019. | Includes
bibliographical references and index.
Identifiers: LCCN 2018024109 (print) | LCCN 2018037527 (ebook) |
ISBN 9780190876357 (updf) | ISBN 9780190876364 (epub) |
ISBN 9780190876340 (hardback)
Subjects: LCSH: Misogyny. | Women—Psychology. | BISAC: SOCIAL SCIENCE /
Feminism & Feminist Theory.
Classification: LCC HQ1233 (ebook) | LCC HQ1233 .U56 2019 (print) |
DDC 303.3/85082—dc23
LC record available at https://lccn.loc.gov/2018024109

9 8 7 6 5 4 3 2 1

Printed by Sheridan Books, Inc., United States of America

This book is dedicated to my brothers Francis, Timothy, and Martin because they taught me the enduring power of male friendship.

CONTENTS

PREFACE

"I am going to depress the hell out of you!" That was what I used to declare on the first day of my policy classes. In my view, policy is the response to ongoing problems such as poverty, racism, and climate change. Without studying the problems first, one cannot work for social change.

However, the point of this book is not to depress the hell out of you. Instead of spending money on such a grim book, you would be better off buying a decent bottle of wine or some gourmet chocolate. Yes, women's rights have suffered severe setbacks in the recent past. The resurgence of feminism, though, has energized a wide range of people all over the world. If you are concerned about the status of women, you are certainly not alone.

Do you identify yourself as a feminist? I don't care as long as you buy or at least read this book. Friends advised me to avoid the use of "feminist" in the title because it might scare off some folks. The crisis facing women today is too urgent to squabble over the "F" word. If you want to fight misogyny without calling yourself a feminist, go for it. Maybe call your-self an anti-misogynist instead, I don't care. We still need you.

Honestly, the fact that I have written two books about women's issues has resulted in my new identity as a Scary Feminist. When I tell somebody about my books, I get that double-take—but you don't *look* like a Scary Feminist. I do not snarl, nor do I show any fangs. Hell, I even wear a bra. In fact, I actually smile and joke around a lot. Sometimes their surprised reaction is as extreme as if I had just grown an-other head. But you're a nice person, that look says.

Once at a holiday gathering, a friend introduced me to the group. "This is Gail. She's writing a book about women's issues but she's not a feminist."

I had to correct her. "Um, actually I am a feminist."

"Well, you know what I mean! You don't hate men or an-ything like that."

One part of me wanted to mention the pair of scissors I carried around to castrate men, but I behaved myself. Instead, I meekly agreed that I did not hate men or anything like that.

As a Scary Feminist, I should have a solid understanding of deconstructivist post-humanism or whatever. My primary identity, though, is not "feminist" but "writer/activist" with a keen awareness of social injustice. The oppression of women is only one aspect of these injustices. Interrelationships have always intrigued me, such as HIV prevention as related to gender dynamics—will or won't he put on a condom?

My intellectual background is diverse. My senior honor thesis was on T. S. Eliot's "The Wasteland" ("April is the cruelest month"). In my 20s, I had pursued a doctorate in history. During those four years of graduate school, I co-authored a book about public works in Colorado (yes,

I wrote the chapter on sewers!) and wrote my thesis about the Vietnam War. Then I spent 10 years in the business world working for finance and insurance companies. To rescue my brain from "cubicle psychosis," I wrote novels that never got published.

When I had entered the social work field in my late 30s, I had no idea of what my specialty would be. I ended up writing my dissertation on HIV/AIDS after a field placement in that area. It just happened. Like my interest in HIV/ AIDS, the women's issues textbook emerged because of life circumstances. When I first started teaching at a small university, I was lucky enough to develop my own course in women's issues that covered US and global concerns. Unable to find a textbook to match my course, I wrote my own. Teaching and writing about feminism, of course, have strengthened my belief that gender equality is critical in today's world. Still, I probably never would have written that book if I had been teaching at a larger school with its own women's studies faculty.

During my social work career, I have also worked with several populations: homeless persons, TANF/welfare recipients, and HIV-positive persons. After a stint in gerontology, now I am a drug counselor at a medication-assisted treatment clinic. Obviously, these experiences have deepened my commitment to fighting injustices such as misogyny.

What is misogyny anyway? I simply define it as the hatred of women. (Don't worry, Chapter 1 has a more in-depth discussion of this concept.) Unfortunately, the word sounds too much like "massage" as in "massage therapy." When I would tell people that I was writing a book against misogyny, I would sometimes get the stink eye. To all the massage therapists and clients out there—it's cool, I have nothing against you.

You may wonder why you should even be buying this book when that bottle of wine looks quite tempting. When I was writing this book in 2017, I could not decide between the songs "I Wanna Be Sedated" or "Comfortably Numb." As one Facebook post stated, "These days if a clown invited me into the woods, I would just go." When it comes to political depression, I get it. Whimpering under a pillow can be one way to cope with the recent political chaos.

Time's up! (Okay, I misquoted Oprah here.) Get out of bed or off the couch and exercise your rights! We have work to do! You are going to be one kick-ass (or genteel) advocate for women now!

But where do we even begin? That question is why I wrote this book. Thoughtful activism, not random actions, will help us to fight misogyny.

Read. Discuss. Plan your actions. And remember: leave the massage therapists alone—unless they are misogynistic, of course.

ACKNOWLEDGMENTS

Writing this book has been both a joyful and aggravating experience. Many thanks to my friends and family who boosted my endeavors this past year. At Oxford University Press, the editors Dana Bliss and Andrew Dominello have been wonderful. Dana Bliss was the one who had suggested this book idea, so I hope that he is satisfied with the result.

Since its inception, the book project has involved several in-depth conversations with individuals and groups. These community members helped me to develop my concepts and provided me with striking insights. Without the folks listed here, the book would have been sparser and less relevant. Thank you!

- Members of COUNT (Central Ohio United Non-Theists) group who had a discussion on masculinity: five men and three women
- Shirley Curtis, social worker in rural Ohio

- Students from my social work classes at Sinclair Community College and Wright State University
- Cara Iacovetta, artist
- Larry Meyers, retired mental health professional
- Anjel Stough-Hunter (sociology professor) and her friends
- Kari Higgins, social worker
- Laura Gaines, social worker
- Julie Hart, sociology professor and peace activist
- Phil Hart, carpenter
- Michel Coconis, social worker and hell-raiser
- Miriam Potocky, social work professor
- Deona Hooper, activist
- Vickie Deisner, animal rights activist
- Ellen Muncy, hair stylist
- Dan O'Kane, corporate recruiter
- Joseph Ukockis, graduate student
- Paul Morgal, student
- Michele Blackford, social worker
- Julia D'Agostino, social worker
- Dorothy Martindale and Colleen Dempsey, National Association of Social Workers
- Robin Mama, social work professor
- Susan Wismer, Sexual Assault Response Network of Central Ohio
- Laura Hancock, journalist
- Ed Norwood, IT
- Writing group at Delaware Library

MISOGYNY

INTRODUCTION

I'm a Feminist—Now What?

THE RESURGENCE OF MISOGYNY

During an August weekend in 2017, White supremacists marched through the streets of Charlottesville, Virginia. Called "Unite the Right," these neo-Nazis chanted slogans such as "blood and soil" and "Jews will not replace us!" One of the White supremacists deliberately rammed his car into a crowd of counterprotesters, an act of mindless violence that killed Heather Heyer. Instead of acknowledging her death as a tragedy, though, the editor of the *Daily Stormer* "excoriated her appearance and called her a 'drain on society.' [He] also noted Heyer's marital and parental status, calling her a 'fat, childless, 32-year-old slut,' claiming that her failure to marry and have children meant that she had 'no value' "[1].

Meanwhile, popular entertainment, such as *Game of Thrones,* includes so many rape scenes that female stunt performers have a new specialty: rape choreography. Because "filmmakers still rely on (often unnecessary) rape scenes as a catalyst for movie and TV plots," rape choreography has become a booming business. "Rape choreographer isn't exactly a desirable position (it takes an emotional toll to reenact sexual assault all day)"—especially if the director insists on 10 to 12 takes instead of a few[2].

"Misogyny" (hatred of women) is a word that belongs in the dustbin of history but still appears in our current society. For decades, the word "sexism" seemed sufficient to describe the demeaning treatment of females. One typical definition of sexism is "prejudice or discrimination based on sex or gender, especially against women and girls"[3]. Sexism can be subtle, such as a man talking over a woman during a business meeting.

In contrast, the word "misogyny" is a much stronger word than "sexism" because it is simply defined as hatred of women. Although the overlap between sexism and misogyny is obvious, misogyny implies an overt and violent aspect. Intimate partner violence (also called domestic violence), sexual assault, street harassment, and judging a female merely on her appearance are but some examples of misogyny. In the historical context, many religions and philosophers have justified this oppression of women.

Hillary Clinton, who has been the target of extreme misogyny, defines the difference between sexism and misogyny this way:

> A note here on terminology. Others might have a different view, but here's how I see the distinction between sexism and misogyny. When a husband tells his wife, 'I can't quite explain why and I don't even like admitting this, but I don't want you to make more money than me, so please don't take that amazing job offer,' that's sexism. He could still love her deeply and be a great partner in countless ways. But he holds tight to an idea that even he knows isn't fair about how successful a woman is allowed to be.

Sexism is all the big and little ways that society draws a box around women and says, 'You stay in there.' . . . We can all buy into sexism from time to time, often without even noticing it. Most of us try to keep an eye out for those moments and avoid them or, when we do misstep, apologize and do better next time.

(But) misogyny is something darker. It's rage. Disgust. Hatred. It's what happens when a woman turns down a guy at a bar and he switches from charming to scary. Or when a woman gets a job that a man wanted and instead of shaking her hand and wishing her well, he calls her a bitch and vows to do everything he can to make sure she fails. [4]

Later she said that both sexism and misogyny "are endemic in America. If you need convincing, just look at the YouTube comments or Twitter replies when a woman dares to voice a political opinion or even just share an anecdote from her own lived experience. People hiding in the shadows step forward just far enough to rip her apart"[5].

The resurgence of misogyny, sometimes called the "new misogyny," is part of a shifting mood in the United States that troubles many. The backlash against "political correctness" is one sign of this trend. Starting in the 1970s, mainstream culture tried to reduce the sexism and racism in their television shows and other venues. People like me began to realize that some behaviors and words were offensive, such as showing off Confederate flags at a high school that has several African American students. Some people, though, wanted to return to the "good old days" when racial epithets and crude sexism were the norm. In the late 1980s, the comedian Andrew Dice Clay gained notoriety for jokes such as these: "If my girlfriend brings home a nice looking friend of hers, I f*** her on principal. You know what I mean? Don't throw another bush in front of my face. What do you think I'm gonna do? Talk to it? I'm gonna bang it"[6]. The factor that made Clay so famous 20 years ago, his overt rejection of gender equality, has now become so commonplace that he would no longer stand out (Box 1.1).

Besides ridiculing political correctness, these misogynists are also using the Internet as a new weapon. Rape threats against female bloggers, revenge porn (i.e., ex-boyfriends posting nude pictures of women without their consent), men's sites that promote male superiority (e.g., Red Pill), and abuse of social media (e.g., Facebook posts) are creating a frightening place in the virtual world. "On the one hand, these online images and words are bringing awareness to a longstanding problem. On the other hand, the amplification of these ideas over social media networks is validating and spreading pathology"[7].

Another form of the new misogyny has been the sharp increase in the number of attacks on women's reproductive health. On the legislative level, state lawmakers have enacted hundreds of bills that restrict abortion rights[8]. The courts have also limited access to birth control, including the Supreme Court's decision to allow employers such as Hobby Lobby to prohibit insurance coverage of IUDs (intrauterine devices, a form of birth control) based on religious grounds[9]. Antiabortion activists have used guns, bombs, arson, and harassment to deny women their basic health care[10].

Despite this new misogyny, though, we can remain optimistic because so many persons are speaking out and refusing to back down. One example is the comedian Amy Schumer, who is the topic of the first case study.

BOX 1.1

LIFE BEFORE WOMEN'S LIBERATION: "HE MADE ME FEEL SO SMALL"

Recently, a woman in her 70s approached me about this book. She said, "Well, I've been harassed but it was such a little deal. Not like what those poor women have had to deal with."

Based on her age, I guessed that she had seen much more overt sexism than me. She had been "just a secretary" because that was the only position allowed women at that company in the late 1960s. We agreed that in those days, many "secretaries" actually ran companies but never got the credit or the money. The incident she told me was not that shocking: a married man had asked her out to dinner.

"There I was, a small-town girl from Ohio in the big city of New York, and a married man asked me out! I was so floored!"

Shocked, she was up all night trying to figure out what to say to him. When she went to him the next day, she said that she would not go out with him because he was a married man. In those days, that took some courage.

"Then he said, 'It was only dinner. We both have to eat, right?' He made it sound like I was crazy for thinking anything else. He tried to turn it around on me, like I was an idiot. And he made me feel so small."

That line struck me: "He made me feel so small." Those words capture the essence of harassment, whether a minor incident like hers or a more serious situation. We talked about how his inappropriate request had belittled her because she had been in a professional role that was ignored. Even though she was "just a secretary," she was proud of her work. He seemed to see only a young woman he could hit on.

"I did not know what to do." In those days, of course, she had had two options: quit or put up with it. Nobody in power would have listened to her story back then.

After I got her permission to write about this conversation, she said she was embarrassed to even mention that story because it was so minor. The fact that she had remembered it this vividly after 50 years, though, proves that it had affected her. "He made me feel so small." Nobody wants to remember humiliating moments like these.

FIRST CASE STUDY: AMY SCHUMER AND THE HECKLER

In 2016, Schumer was performing her stand-up comedy act in Stockholm when a heckler shouted out, "Show us your tits!" She did a good job handling the situation by calling him on stage and humiliating him. By the way, his T-shirt read, "I love pussy"[11]. This incident illustrates some key points of misogyny, described next.

Silencing of Women

Historically, society told women to shut up or be punished. Patriarchal (male-dominated) societies must silence women to further their oppression. The heckler, then, was merely continuing the centuries-old tradition of trying to diminish a strong woman's power.

Instead of conforming to the ideal of the meek woman, Schumer is bold enough to stand on a stage to do live comedy. She has the nerve not to diminish herself by insulting her own appearance. Although the film industry still cranks out male-dominated movies with few female protagonists, women like Schumer are claiming their space by standing alone on the stage.

One early female comedian, Phyllis Diller, had to resort to self-deprecation to be allowed on stage. A typical joke was: "My photographs don't do me justice—they look just like me"[12]. Another one was: "I once wore a peekaboo blouse. People would peek and then they'd boo"[13]. Diller's humor was an effective defense in her time, but it is fortunate that women have other options than self-deprecation to get noticed now.

Public Sphere Versus Private Sphere

One cannot get more public than flying to another country to perform a comedy show. In contrast to modern women working outside the home and demanding respect as politicians, traditional women must stay in the private sphere. Home represents purity and modesty. Some Catholic religious orders such as the Carmelites find holiness in the convent, far from the corrupt world. In some Muslim societies, females must obey the purdah restrictions about wearing veils and having a male escort whenever they step outside the house. The Victorians invented the housewife ideal, which stressed the Angel of the House avoiding the sinful temptations of the public sphere.

Traditional societies, then, only allow men to venture into the public sphere. One common punishment for women who violate this norm—even in modern societies—is street harassment. The heckler's shout to Schumer about her body parts sounds like what a "catcaller" would yell out to a girl or woman. Whether a man is ordering a female to "smile" or invading her personal space, he is punishing her for entering the public sphere without a male escort. As Illustration 1.1 shows, street harassment is nothing new.

ILLUSTRATION 1.1 Young girls running the gauntlet of men making remarks (sometimes vile). Location: New Bedford, Massachusetts—1912. Source: Library of Congress.

Sexual Harassment on the Job

One form of sexual harassment is a hostile work environment, which would apply to Schumer being heckled for being a woman. It is possible that the heckler could have called out, "Show us your junk!" to a male comedian, but it is more likely that the Schumer incident was gender-based harassment. Waitresses also report a high rate of sexual harassment from both customers and managers. They usually have to smile through gritted teeth to earn their tips and keep their jobs. The message of this harassment is clear: You don't belong here doing this job! Go back home to the kitchen!

Illustration 1.2 is a 1814 cartoon demonstrating that sexual harassment is nothing new. A woman running a lodging house is showing the man his room. He says, "My sweet honey, I hope you are to be let with the lodgins!" She answers: "No, sir, I am to be let alone."

Objectification

The heckler had tried to reduce Schumer to a mere body part, which is one aspect of objectification. This way of looking at women (or men, in some cases) could seem harmless. What is wrong with the classic ZZ Top song, "She's Got Legs, and She Knows How to Use Them?"

First, objectification also extends to female children. The average age of girls' breast development has gone down from 16.6 years in 1860 to 10.5 years in 2010[14]. If a 10-year-old child were accosted by a man on a street or called a slut by her classmates because of her breast size, she would be less able to handle this situation than an older girl. At any age, of

ILLUSTRATION 1.2 "Lodgings to Let"—1814 cartoon. Source: Library of Congress.

course, being harassed for breast size can be traumatic and even dangerous.

Objectification also relates to violence against women. If society regards any person as a thing instead of a person who deserves respect, then inexcusable acts become acceptable. Any car owner can choose to trash their car because it is theirs. Unfortunately, some people regard others as objects they are entitled to damage. If a man sees a fellow party guest who is passed out by a dumpster, he may objectify her so much that he only sees a body that he can molest (Box 1.2).

BOX 1.2

ANOTHER PERSPECTIVE ON OBJECTIFICATION

Does objectification only involve dehumanizing the person, or is there another dimension? One dimension of cruelty has emerged as a new topic—the recognition of the humanity of the victims. Paul Bloom, for example, writes about how this recognition can motivate people to be cruel to other humans. When European soccer fans make monkey noises at African players and throw bananas at them, "the whole point of their behavior is to disorient and humiliate. To believe that such taunts are effective is to assume that their targets would be ashamed to be thought of that way—which implies that, at some level, you think of them as people after all"[19].

The cruelties inflicted by misogynists, then, are cruelties that go far beyond objectification of the victims. Kate Manne (2017) writes about Elliot Rodgers, the young man who felt rejected by the sorority girls and decided to go on a shooting spree that killed six people. According to the manifesto he had taped before the murders, he appeared fully aware that he was killing humans.

> What is striking about these sentiments is that they not only presuppose but seem to *hinge* on the women's presumed humanity. . . . Rodger ascribes to these women subjectivity, preferences, and a capacity to form deep emotional attachments (love, as well as affection).

And he attributes to them agency, autonomy, and the capacity to be *addressed* by him. But far from being a pan-
acea for his misogyny, such recognition in fact seems to
have been its very precondition. Rodger wanted what
these women were not giving him; they subsequently
had a *"hold"* over him. He did not deny women's power,
independence, or the reality of their minds. Rather, he
hated and sought to punish them for evincing these
capabilities in ways which frustrated him, given his
sense of entitlement to their benefit. [20]

Mixed with the dehumanization, then, is the
pleasure of humiliating a person. As Bloom states, "A
lot of the cruelty we do to one another, the real savage,
rotten terrible things we do to one another, are in
fact because we recognize the humanity of the other
person"[21].

Beauty Bias

Objectification is related to beauty bias because appearance becomes the primary criterion for a female's worth.
Also called "appearance discrimination," beauty bias can
affect anybody. However, females consistently report a
higher level of dissatisfaction with their looks than males.
The harsh beauty standards relate to body size (hence the
new buzzword "fat-shaming," as in: I wish the mirror would
stop fat-shaming me), clothes, makeup, shoes, hair, skin,
and even eye shape. Noses could be smaller, while wrinkles
provide the horrifying evidence that one has not died at a
young age.

Using the male gaze, a man can judge a woman's looks and rate them from 1 to 10. If his eyes merely flick away, this indicates that she should be invisible because she is so unworthy of his attention. A lingering glance, then, indicates that a woman might be worth considering. Women also inflict the beauty bias against other women, a practice that starts in elementary school and continues for decades. For instance, I once had a client in her 80s who told me that the other women in the senior housing complex were insulting her long hair and telling her to cut it.

It takes guts for Schumer and other female celebrities to fight back against the beauty bias. When a male critic said something rude (and unprintable) about Schumer's "fatness," she tweeted a revealing picture of herself with these bold words: "I am a size 6 and have no plans of changing. This is it. Stay on or get off. Kisses!"[15]. Many would find it ludicrous that a size-6 person could actually be fat-shamed, so we can delight in her refusal to be diminished in any way.

SECOND CASE STUDY: ADVERTISING

Advertising is one form of propaganda, which is information used to persuade people (or to propagate a point of view.) The first advertisement that made me think, "Wow, that's sexist!" came out when I was just a kid. An airline ad showed a stewardess with the line: "I'm Cheryl. Fly me." Even a dim-witted child like me could figure out the sexual overtones of this "Coffee, tea, or me" motif. At the age of nine, I often saw a TV commercial with a husband saying to his friends: "My wife, I think I'll keep her." Ads for Virginia Slims associated smoking with liberated women who are both pretty

ILLUSTRATION 1.3 Flapper from 1920s. Source: Library of Congress.

and—surprise!—slim. The thin smoker ideal also appeared for decades as the essence of cool femininity. This 1920s ad of a flapper (Illustration 1.3) is fascinating because it resembles so many modern images. Who knows how many women died of lung cancer or emphysema because they tried to lose weight by smoking?

Of course, advertising has reinforced social standards for more than 100 years. The models were more buxom in this 1870 ad than today, but the "sex sells" message still resonates in Illustration 1.4.

The advertisements mandate that women should also be concerned about good housekeeping. Several ads promoted their cleaning products, including one from 1870 about "the Great Scrub Race" with sweepers and mops.

Although several other examples of misogynistic advertising are available, most people are probably already aware

ILLUSTRATION 1.4 Whiskey ad, *circa* 1870. Source: Library of Congress.

of ads that offended them. Even the advertising industry has admitted to pushing the limits on acceptability, as one writer from *Advertising Age* notes, "Most sexual ads portray women as objects of male fantasy and desire. These ads instruct women on how to look attractive to men, or they employ sexy women to represent successful goal attainment for men"[16].

Advertising as a form of propaganda, of course, can also be positive. Since the early 1970s, feminists have used slogans and posters that affected me as strongly as any corporate message. I grew up with "A woman's place is in the House . . . and Senate!" at a time when few women were running for national office. Slogans such as "The best man for the job . . . may be a woman!" made me consider several career options once reserved for men. This snarky statement also made me smile when I was a girl: "Whatever women do, they must do twice as well as men to be thought half as good—luckily, this is not difficult."

Other slogans from the women's liberation movement (also called the "second wave of feminism") include:

- A poster with a coffee pot that reads: "Make policy, not coffee"
- A poster with a loaf of bread that reads: "I swear it to you/On my common woman's head/The common woman is as common/As a common loaf of bread. . . . And will rise"
- An Italian poster with the slogan: *"Siamo tante, siamo donne, siamo stufe"* (We are many, we are women, we are fed up)"
- A quote from William Allen White: "My advice to the women of America is to raise more hell and fewer dahlias"
- "Wise women, strong, proud healers, midwives, creators, and builders—they misunderstood your soul for the gentleness within . . ."
- A quote from Susan B. Anthony: "Failure is impossible" [17]

Advertising the feminist message, then, can be a powerful counterbalance to the male-dominated propaganda machine that has told women to put up and shut up. Although it can be discouraging to encounter yet another media image that treats women as bimbos or some other stereotype, we can amplify our own message of woman-affirming principles.

ON BEING A SCARY RADICAL FEMINIST

I did not emerge from the womb crying out, "I am woman, hear me roar!" That song did not come out until I was a child, and frankly, I did not want to roar or make any fuss. Just getting by in a crazy, zigzag world was enough challenge for me. Occasionally, I would catch glimpses of how unfair the world was to women. Males were the only ones good enough to be "chefs" (women were merely "cooks"), while only males could be Catholic priests or doctors or politicians. If a woman wanted to be taken seriously, she had to pull her hair back into a severe bun, wear ugly glasses, and desexualize herself.

In this setting of the early 1970s, I saw an album cover that shocked me. John Lennon and the Plastic Ono Band had boldly stated in a song title that "Woman Is the Nigger of the World." The song lyrics noted that "We insult her every day on TV/And wonder why she has no guts or confidence." Based on a quote by Yoko Ono, this song disturbed me so much that I pushed the thought away. In my youth, I craved a world that was inherently fair. Few of us want to see the broad scale of injustice when we are young. I wanted to live in a just world that would not devalue or mock anyone. Because of my wishful thinking, I chose to minimize or even deny any signs of oppression. I wanted sexism to be over, so I pretended that it was ancient history (Box 1.3).

Sexism and misogyny, though, are not yet in the dustbin of history. I was never reluctant to be called a feminist, but I have been reluctant to be called a radical instead of a moderate. Now I have a better understanding of the song "Woman Is the Nigger of the World." Now is the time to look at the big picture of oppression and devise strategies to uproot the causes.

One protest sign in recent marches says: "I can't believe I still have to protest this s***." Yes, misogyny has experienced a resurgence that is as persistent as the most noxious weed. Activism for gender equality, though, has had its own

BOX 1.3

IN THE CONTEXT OF ONGOING RACISM, WAS THE SONG TITLE "WOMAN IS THE NIGGER OF THE WORLD" APPROPRIATE?

Kennedy's book, *Nigger: The Strange History of a Troublesome Word*, provides a framework for examining this question. "Over the years, *nigger* has become the best known of the American language's many racial insults, evolving into the paradigmatic slur. It is the epithet that generates epithets. That is why Arabs are called 'sand niggers,' Irish 'the niggers of Europe,' and Palestinians 'the niggers of the Middle East' "[22]. This derogatory term, then, signifies an oppressed class that deserves to be oppressed.

The song's lyrics about women being the "slave of slaves" reinforces the idea that racism and sexism are inextricably linked together. In fact, any oppression is connected to any other oppression. Women's rights and civil rights share a common history in the United States. The abolitionist movement to end slavery gave birth to the first wave of feminism (the women's suffrage movement). In the 1950s and 1960s, the civil rights movement foreshadowed the second wave of feminism. Hence, the song lyrics that connect women's subordination to slavery may have been controversial but could still be appropriate. Also, the song's coauthor Yoko Ono was an Asian woman who had certainly experienced racism herself.

resurgence that is more glowing and formidable that anything thrown at us.

One amusing aspect of this resurgent feminism is that people sometimes characterize people like me as a "radical feminist." For me, the word "radical" does not necessarily mean extremism but rather getting to the root of a social problem. For example, my first activist experience occurred in high school with the Nestlé boycott. I had opposed Nestlé's unethical practices to sell baby formula to mothers in developing countries, despite the babies being better off breastfed. The good news is that Nestlé finally ended the practice of sending sales representatives dressed as nurses to villages. The bad news is that corporations like Nestlé still inflict considerable harm to vulnerable populations in several countries. By focusing on a single problem instead of the entire system, I was no radical then. Now I am more interested in questioning the bigger picture, the structures of oppression.

Another reason that I smile at being considered a "radical feminist" is that it implies a high degree of anger and bitterness. I cannot deny that a news item can infuriate me, while the years of watching the same old rubbish can fill me with sullen resentment. The essence of any social activism, though, is a sense of hope. If I did not believe in positive social change, I would not be wasting my time writing this book. I believe in transformation because of my own changes. Socialized by a racist culture, I now work on confronting my own implicit biases. Having grown up in a heterosexist society with rigid gender roles, I am learning to embrace diversity.

Critics may use the term "radical feminist" as a way to dismiss those who are concerned about common decency. I do not oppose domestic violence because I am a feminist—I oppose it because I am a caring human. Also, I grew up in a violent household and had to struggle with the dark shadow it cast on my life. I do not oppose rape/sexual assault because I am a feminist—I oppose it because it is a horrifying type of violence. I do not support equal pay for equal work because I am a feminist—I support it because the pay gap violates my sense of fairness. I do not support access to reproductive health care because I am a feminist—I support it because health care is a basic human right.

Feminism, then, gives me a voice to express the positions that I would have had anyway. For me, feminism is not an ideology but rather a tool for social justice. As a decentralized movement with no hierarchy of leadership, "feminism" is not a structure that dictates to me what I should or should not believe. Critics sometimes quote (or misquote) a certain feminist as a method to attack all feminists. For example, one feminist recently said that transwomen were not really women. I do not agree with that statement, nor did I ever say that this woman represented me in any way. In this debate over the concept of gender, nobody should quote one or two people as the authorized spokesperson for all feminists.

As we enter the era of challenging the concept of gender itself, though, is a book promoting gender equality even relevant? One woman noted to me that the younger generation was promoting the nonbinary view of gender with its multiple variations: gender queer, gender fluid, androgynous, and others. The transgender rights movement is related to this social shift, but transgender persons do reinforce the binary view of gender (i.e., male-to-female and female-to-male). In this setting, is my call for gender equality obsolete?

Absolutely not. The social constructs of gender still exist and still exert a powerful influence on our lives. A parallel concept would be the idealistic notion that the United States is a postracial country. Before Obama became president, some were naïve enough to believe that racism only thrived in little pockets of this country. If the Obama haters (not the policy critics, but the people who simply hated Obama himself) are not enough proof of widespread racism, then the 2016 election is proof enough. One candidate gained political attention by promising to prove that Obama was not really born in the United States, then opened his campaign by calling Mexican immigrants rapists. Racism has become more overt and threatening than in recent decades.

Unfortunately, we do not live in a postgender world either. Society still categorizes us by our gender, then judges us by different standards. How often has a gender construct trapped us into a box? "I wish I didn't have to play sports to prove I'm not a wuss," a boy may say to himself. "I wish I didn't have to say how cute that baby is—he just spit on my blouse," a woman may say to herself while faking enthusiasm. After all, doesn't every female want to experience motherhood?

Because gender constructs and misogyny still exist, we cannot say that we live in a postgender world. The good news is that radical feminists also exist. Anybody who wants to uproot social injustice deserves the title of "radical." Although the term "feminism" has so much baggage attached, let us reclaim the word for what it is—a supporter of gender equality.

STRUCTURE OF THE BOOK

Simply put, the first seven chapters of this book describe the problem of misogyny, and the last three propose activist strategies. Hopefully, folks will get together to talk over the ideas in the book and then take some action. Reading is usually a solitary pleasure, but this book would also be ideal for discussion groups. The overlooked tradition of consciousness-raising groups during the early days of the women's liberation movement deserves credit for bringing the issues of rape and domestic violence out into the open. The perfect word for these consciousness-raising groups could be "synergy," but then I would sound like a computer engineer.

As Illustration 1.5 shows, the fight against misogyny is a fight for the future. This book provides a context for the resurgent misogyny that appears in the next six chapters. First, in Chapter 2 I propose a framework for misogyny, which includes three levels: gender violence, hate speech, and mainstream culture. This framework will show how not

ILLUSTRATION 1.5 Young girl with sign. Source: Shutterstock.

all misogynists are alike but how their language and actions often overlap.

The silencing of women is a theme that emerged from the observations of how female politicians (especially Hillary Clinton) were regarded by the media and the public. Since the 2016 election, another striking example of the silencing of women appeared in the news: numerous cases of sexual harassment and assault by powerful men. The second half of Chapter 3 reviews the #MeToo movement and its ongoing implications.

No discussion of today's feminism is complete without an overview of intersectionality, which Chapter 4 addresses. Our different identities (e.g., female, White, college-educated) provide us with either privilege or a source of oppression. Racism, sexism, ableism, classism, and other prejudices can intersect to amplify the impact of being excluded from full citizenship.

Chapter 5 explores the traits of masculinity, some of which are inherently toxic and some of which can become toxic if too extreme. For instance, self-reliance is an admirable trait, but too much self-reliance can lead to a male to avoid getting the medical or psychological help he needs to stay healthy or even alive.

Rape culture is another aspect of misogyny, which Chapter 6 delves into by looking at a culture that is embedded with rape. Instead of seeing sexual assault as only the act of a pathological attacker, we can look at the society that reinforces and even encourages this form of violence. Of course, rape culture is closely associated with toxic masculinity.

In case nobody has noticed, the issue of reproductive rights remains a polarizing issue in the United States. Chapter 7 considers the reproductive health debate from the context that women's bodies have historically caused revulsion instead of appreciation for their life-giving abilities.

The last part of the book, then, focuses on thoughtful activism in three ways. First, Chapter 8 describes the inner work of activism that includes looking at our own biases. Chapter 9 delves into the outer work of activism, especially with the section on tools such as writing and speaking. Lastly, Chapter 10 explains why "failure is impossible" because activism has worked before and feminism is experiencing a resurgence. Although misogyny still threatens our basic human rights, the push for progress is a powerful force.

One of the hardest aspects of writing this book has been deciding which issues to emphasize and which ones to leave for other writers to work on. For instance, the book is limited in scope by its emphasis on the United States instead of global issues. Although I had the opportunity to write about global women in my textbook (*Women's Issues for a New Generation: A Social Work Perspective*, Oxford, 2016), this book concentrates on the United States because of time and space limitations. Also, the list of topics in this book is by no means exhaustive because the book could not include every issue related to misogyny. Despite these limitations, though, I hope that this book will provide insights and inspiration for both new and experienced activists (Box 1.4).

ACTION STEPS

- At the first Women's March in 2017, Michael Moore's speech was striking because he urged everyone to call their Congresspersons every day. These calls count! The staff has to tabulate every call that comes in, so let

BOX 1.4

CASUAL INSULTS

When watching some Hallmark Christmas movies over the holidays, I found myself disturbed by the casual insults toward women in this venue that is usually considered wholesome. The first movie I had to stop watching showed a woman who is making out with a guy on the first date. She suddenly stops and says that she cannot have sex with him because that would put her in the "ho zone." In her view, women who express their desires on a first date deserved to be called names. This repetition of the ancient restrictions on women's sexuality saddened me.

Another casual insult appeared in a movie about a young assistant with a mean boss. Her friends commiserate with her, even to the point of calling that boss a "skank" for exerting her power. Obviously, the scriptwriters had intended to make the dialogues zip with modern slang. The inclusion of woman-shaming comments, though, demonstrates the power of the casual insult in the context of oppression.

I could not help comparing these insults with the casual use of the word "nigger" in the *Narrative of Frederick Douglass*, a book written before the Civil War. Slave owners and overseers used the term interchangeably with the word "slave," with the understanding that they could use any word they damn well pleased. The power of naming a subordinate group coincides with the power of cruelty. The word "nigger" during the slavery era merges with the images of cowhide whips and other instruments of torture. Verbal oppression and physical attacks, then, were inseparable in the era of treating humans as property.

Because I was socialized to regard the word "nigger" as completely unacceptable, I still flinch when I hear it used—even by African Americans. It is an ugly word that makes me think of a snarling overseer who spits out some chewing tobacco before beating a random slave. Whites sometimes ask why they can't use the word "nigger" when African Americans still use it. But the obvious question for Whites is: Why would you want to?

Why would anyone want to use "skank" and "ho" and "slut"? If only these words were as controversial as the word "nigger." I hate those words just as much because they also represent oppression to me: social punishment, sexual assault, and even murder. By their very nature, skanks and hos deserve to be touched, hassled, banged around, laughed at, gang-raped . . . the list goes on. The oppression goes on.

At the risk of being called the PC police or a snowflake, I suggest that we respond to the casual use of "skank" and similar insults with this simple message: "That is an ugly term to use. Do you have any idea of how damaging this kind of language can be?" Today it is the norm to use these terms as a joke, but norms can change. I am old enough to remember when parents blew cigarette smoke into their children's faces in restaurants and nobody said a thing. Not using seatbelts used to symbolize freedom and nonchalance, but now it only symbolizes stupidity. If we work on telling those in our social circles that disrespectful language is offensive, we can be role models for others.

Words have power to either build up or tear down. By acknowledging our own power to show respect to others, we can start changing some harmful norms.

us build up the numbers. The US Capitol Switchboard number is 202-224-3121. You can also find your representative on www.house.gov and your senators on www.senate.gov. The email systems are also useful. Keep your message direct and simple—one issue per call. Here is one sample: "I am a constituent and I am calling to oppose any further cuts to Planned Parenthood. This organization saves countless lives with cancer screenings and other essential health services. Planned Parenthood deserves more funding, not less." Persistence is the key. Remember, the US women's suffrage movement started in the 1790s, so it took more than a century for women to get the vote.

- At the second Women's March in 2018, the young singer/songwriter Halsey read a poem that stirred thousands. "A story like mine" shared stories about rape, abortion, and other realities of women's lives. Near the end of the poem, she encouraged us to act: "So love your neighbor/PLEASE treat her kindly/Ask her her story/Then shut up and listen"[18]. That line struck me—shut up and listen. The next step, of course, is to advocate on behalf of those who have been silenced. But first, shut up and listen.

Notes

1. Angyal, C. (2017). Heather Heyer was the alt-right's worst nightmare. Huffington Post. Retrieved from www.huffingtonpost.com/entry/heather-heyer-was-the-alt-rights-worst-nightmare_us_59946c02e4b04b193362484b

2. Davies, M. (2017). What is a "rape choreographer" and why do film sets need one? Jezebel. Retrieved from https://jezebel.com/what-is-a-rape-choreographer-and-why-do-film-sets-need-1797267080

3. Definition of "sexism" retrieved from the Brittanica website: www.britannica.com/topic/sexism

4. Clinton, H. R. (2017). *What happened.* New York, NY: Simon & Schuster, pp. 114–115.

5. Clinton, H. R. (2017). *What Happened.* New York, NY: Simon & Schuster, p. 115.

6. Andrew Dice Clay joke quoted on SComedy website. Retrieved from www.scomedy.com

7. Bumy, C., & Chemaly, S. (2014). The unsafety net: How social media turned against women. *The Atlantic.* Retrieved from www.theatlantic.com/technology/archive/2014/10/the-unsafety-net-how-social-media-turned-against-women/381261/

8. The Guttmacher Institute provides the latest information on reproductive rights. For state laws, the link is www.guttmacher.org/state-policy/explore/overview-abortion-laws

9. Richey, W. (2014). Hobby Lobby 101: Explaining the Supreme Court's birth control ruling. Christian Science Monitor website. Retrieved from www.csmonitor.com/USA/Politics/DC-Decoder/2014/0710/Hobby-Lobby-101-explaining-the-Supreme-Court-s-birth-control-ruling

10. The National Abortion Federation tracks the violent incidents against abortion providers. For the latest information, check out this link: https://prochoice.org/education-and-advocacy/violence/violence-statistics-and-history/

11. Lachener, J. (2016). Amy Schumer invites sexist heckler on stage, righteously shaming him in front of crowd.

The Mary Sue. Retrieved from www.themarysue.com/amy-schumer-wrecks-heckler/

12. Phyllis Diller joke quoted on Brainy Quote website. Retrieved from www.brainyquote.com/quotes/authors/p/phyllis_diller.htmlwww.brainyquote.com/quotes/authors/p/phyllis_diller.html

13. Phyllis Diller joke quoted on AZ Quote website. Retrieved from www.azquotes.com/author/3977-Phyllis_Diller

14. Chalabi, M. (2013). Why is puberty starting younger? The Guardian. Retrieved from www.theguardian.com/politics/2013/nov/04/why-is-puberty-starting-younger-precocious

15. Puchko, K. (2015). Amy Schumer tells fat shaming trolls where they can get off. Pajiba website. Retrieved from www.pajiba.com/celebrities_are_better_than_you/amy-schumer-tells-fat-shaming-trolls-where-they-can-get-off.php

16. Sex in advertising. (2003). Advertising Age. Retrieved from http://adage.com/article/adage-encyclopedia/sex-advertising/98878/

17. The Library of Congress website has a rich treasure of feminist posters and artifacts. Their website is www.loc.gov.

18. The Halsey poem was retrieved from this site: http://variety.com/2018/music/news/halsey-speech-new-york-city-womens-march-read-1202671345/

19. Bloom, P. (2017). The root of all cruelty. The New Yorker. Retrieved from www.newyorker.com/magazine/2017/11/27/the-root-of-all-cruelty

20. Manne, K. (2017). *Down girl: The logic of misogyny*. New York, NY: Oxford University Press, pp. 123–124.

21. Iling, S. (2017). Why humans are cruel: An interview with Paul Bloom. Vox. Retrieved from www.vox.com/science-and-health/2017/12/14/16687388/violence-psychology-human-nature-cruelty

22. Kennedy, R. (2002). *Nigger: The strange history of a troublesome word*. New York, NY: First Vintage Books, p. 22.

2

A CLOSER LOOK

AT MISOGYNY

INTRODUCTION

The look on this woman's face is haunting. This photograph (Illustration 2.1), taken in 1938 in a Pennsylvania
bar, demonstrates the no-win situation that this anonymous
woman and millions of others encounter several times in
their lives. For whatever reason, she had gone alone to the
bar. This scenario is similar to the 1983 gang rape in a New
Bedford, Massachusetts bar where witnesses watched the attack without stopping it. In both cases, the woman would
be blamed for going into a bar as if it implied consent to sex
with strangers. If she said no to the men, they would probably call her a tease or worse. Verbal and/or physical violence
could ensue. If she agreed to have sex with one of these men,
she would probably have been called a slut, whore, and all
the creative variations of the "worthless woman" theme. In
this tense setting, maybe she did not even have the power to
decide what happens next.

This picture, then, depicts the essence of misogyny: the
destructive power that men can have over women (Box 2.1).
Not all men are misogynistic, of course. Because many social
structures still support men who hurt women, though, the

ILLUSTRATION 2.1 *Shenandoah, Pennsylvania bar scene—1938?*
Source: Library of Congress.

"Not all men are like that" statement is irrelevant. Misogyny can appear in several forms, including sex trafficking (an example of gender violence), the manosphere (a forum for woman bashers), and sports culture (an example of how a mainstream institution can be affected by sexism).

GENDER VIOLENCE: SEX TRAFFICKING

Introduction

The first time I was mistaken for a prostitute, I was just a 15-year-old kid in downtown Denver. A sleazy guy came up to me and asked me how much I charged for "head." Later

---

BOX 2.1

LET'S BASH SEXUAL HARASSMENT
IN BARS

On a brighter note, a recent trend for bartenders is to intervene when they see a possible scenario like the one faced by this woman. Ontario has invested in the BASH (Bartenders Against Sexual Harassment) training program, while Washington, DC has created a Safe Bars initiative. Both programs stress bystander intervention for bartenders and servers if they see a patron at risk or a fellow employee[28] . These hopeful signs indicate that social structures such as the hospitality industry are willing to fight misogyny instead of condoning it.

I bragged to my friends about this encounter to show off my street smarts and even laughed about it, but it stopped being funny real fast. Since I later got a job at the downtown library, I was often near the red-light district of Colfax Avenue where men accosted me. These experiences made me angry at the pimps and I felt pity for the poor girls who had to endure the touch of these johns. Nobody had to tell me that sex work had a darker side—I saw it for myself at the age when I would have been most vulnerable to getting pimped.

Decades later, the public has learned more about human trafficking (which includes both labor and sex trafficking). Although many people may still call prostitution harmless, the evidence proves that a great deal of sex work is involuntary and damaging. Like other aspects of misogyny, capitalism is interwoven with the sale of women's bodies (Box 2.2).

Sex tourism has existed for decades, but it exploded into an international crisis when two major changes occurred in the 1990s: the rise of the Internet and the fall of the Soviet

---

BOX 2.2

THE GRIM STATISTICS OF HUMAN TRAFFICKING

- At least 20 million persons are victims of trafficking: one in four are children, and 58% are women and girls[29].
- Globally, about 4.8 million persons are victims of sex trafficking[30].
- One out of seven runaways likely became a child sex-trafficking victim, and many of these came from the foster care system[31].
- Although many advocates estimate that the average age of somebody entering prostitution is 12 to 14 years, this statistic is not based on solid evidence[32].
- Statistics about the money earned by sex traffickers are hard to obtain for obvious reasons. However, one study by the Urban Institute estimates that the underground sex industry in Atlanta generates $260 million a year. Globally, then, it would be safe to say that billions are made on an annual basis[33] .

Union. The Internet facilitated sex tourism, while crime rings forced thousands of East European and Russian women into the sex trade. For obvious reasons, it is difficult to research sex tourists themselves. One exceptional book is the journalist Victor Malarek's *The Johns: Sex for Sale and the Men Who Buy It* (2009).

> "Well, let me give you a little advice to keep you from making a fool of yourself. These girls all smile and make you think you're a king, acting all lovey-dovey . . . going gaga for you. They may seem sincere, but half of what they tell you is a life and the other half is a line. Don't fool yourself into thinking any one of them really thinks you're something special. These girls are nothing but a bunch of whores. . . ."
>
> "Look at them. Look at that one over there." He motioned with a beer bottle, pointing to a young woman in jeans and a yellow tank top. "I was here six months ago when she first hit the bar. She was sweet. I saw her with this guy . . . had to be three hundred and fifty pounds of whale blubber. He brings her a bag of goodies . . . make-up, perfume, chocolates, a staffed teddy bear. Like he's going to somehow make her think he's a nice guy and maybe get better service. Look at her now. She's jaded. She has what I call fish eyes."
>
> "Fish eyes?"
>
> "That hardened, dead look. It's what happens to most of these whores after they've been humped by so many fat, sloppy, ugly guys."
>
> "So there's no respecting these girls?" "I don't respect whores. I don't get sucked into the whine about them having to feed their families. I pay to f*** them. That's why I come down here." [1]

After I decided to research johns myself, I could not figure out the logistics of finding and interviewing johns. Then

I realized that the blogs of sex tourists and advertisements by the sex resorts were online. The information was in the public domain, an advantage for anyone concerned about confidentiality and other ethical questions.

The worst part about this research was the secondary trauma I experienced when I saw numerous pictures of girls—many who were obviously preteen. Most of the sex tourist blogs [2] had public and "members only" forums, so I decided to stay in the public forums for safety reasons (both computer and emotional). While I was in one public forum, I saw a picture of a girl being tortured. I exclaimed out loud in horror at this picture and still wish that I could unsee it. If a picture like that was in the public forum, what images existed in the "members only" forum?

Silencing of Women

After reading hundreds of sex tourists' blogs, I compiled a list of rules to summarize the men's demands on the females. What disturbed me most about their comments was the dark undertone because the men could complain anytime about a "chica." A pimp might then beat her up for not acting affectionate enough, or a proprietor may kick her out of the resort. The implicit threat in the comments was that the girls had to cuddle with the johns—or else.

Rules for the girls:

- Don't be pushy;
- Don't have an attitude;
- Don't be a clock watcher;
- Pretend to like sex;
- Get along with the other girls; and

- Always be willing to act bisexually (share a man with one or two others in the bed).

Public Sphere/Private Sphere

When feminists originated this concept of the two spheres, the assumption was that women were somewhat protected by their families in the private sphere. Economic security also appears as a given in this concept. In the poverty-stricken regions where sex tourism flourishes, though, the females may have had families who encouraged or even forced them into prostitution. Thus, the private sphere does not always protect the women as promised.

Jeffreys, author of *The Industrial Vagina: The Political Economy of the Global Sex Trade* (2008), writes about the power imbalance between the male customer and the prostitute (usually a female child). In their transaction, the power imbalance extends to the relationships between the prosperous countries and the developing countries—formerly the colonizer and the colonies[3]. The Caribbean resorts are not only reflections of colonialism but also an echo of slavery[4]. Countries such as Indonesia and Thailand have become so economically dependent on sex tourism that it would be catastrophic if the business ended.

Sex tourism, then, thrusts females into a sphere that is dominated by global capitalism, postcolonial exploitation, and modern slavery. Whether they like it or not, the sex workers must live in a world with little privacy. Anybody with an Internet connection can click a few keys to see photos of girls in provocative poses. Often the photo directories show not the face but a rear shot, with girls either kneeling or on all fours. The vulnerability of these girls is heartbreaking because the public sphere is so dangerous for them.

Objectification

"A classy woman is like a good bottle of wine." This sentiment could go unnoticed on a billboard because objectification is so prevalent in both sex tourism and mainstream advertising. Another quote from a resort website reads: "You can change companions every day. You can have as many as you can afford at any one time." One blogger wrote that he could not remember which girl he had been with the prior night because they all looked alike to him.

The sex tourists also found it difficult to tolerate Western women, probably because they resisted being objectified. One blogger was kicked out of a Pennsylvania bar for bothering women and wrote, "There are few things I find more enjoyable than putting bitchy chicks in their place." Another blogger wrote, "I'll get straight to it, online dating in America is useless. The girls are ugly, uneducated, and looking for a free diner [sic]."

According to the bloggers, the sex workers in their hometowns were not much better than the other women. Some sex workers were "expensive and not worth the money," while others were "too business like." Another blogger complained that the selection was only "junkies or fat girls." Others called the women "dirty filthy hos" and "street trash."

In contrast to these "bitchy chicks" and "street trash" were the girls at the sex resorts, girls who were described this way in the advertisements:

- She is one mysterious hot chick. . . . She may be shy at first but is very much accommodating and generous as you go along together.
- She is one great girlfriend experience you do not want to miss . . . she is the bombshell of your dreams.

- Sexy and subtle curves that will surely start up your engines is what you are going to get if you spend time with this temptress.

Objectification, then, appeared in the men's posts stating that they had to "clean out their pipes" on these vacations. However, the blogs also reveal a full recognition of the humanity of sex workers. In a complaint about the "street trash" back home, one man wrote: "There is minimal touching, no multiple positions, no kissing, these girls are just scam artists that hate their job." A vicious streak also runs through these comments about sex workers in general, as indicated by this typical quote: "He should of bent her over, f*d her then pay her 1500 [*sic*]." Mixed with the dehumanization, then, is the pleasure of humiliating a person.

Beauty Bias

Not surprisingly, the sex tourists feel entitled to demand that the workers be "hot." These men rated the "girls" from 1 to 10 for each body part, compulsively listing numbers as if they were sacred mantras. One man advised, "Although it's common courtesy to warm up with a 7 or 8 before you go directly to the 9's and 10's. . . ." Another man wrote, "Her face was only a 6, maybe a 7, but her body was a perfect 10!!" This graphic of faceless, nameless shapes captures the men's view of women (Illustration 2.2).

Fat-shaming is one prevalent theme on the sites. One blogger wrote about women in America: "Unless you are looking for a 40 year old woman who has kids and a flabby stomach. If this is the case, you need more help than I can offer." These men often complain about their "girls" gaining

ILLUSTRATION 2.2 Objectifying women. Entofolio.

weight: "Unfortunately, the Thai girls dancing on stage must have adopted a western diet as they were fat!"

Extreme ageism also appears on the sites, where many bloggers considering workers older than 25 years to be too old. One man complained that the hookers were "old and not that much good looking . . . though very cheap . . ." and another stated that he saw some "rather disgusting looking" workers in their mid 20s to 40s. None of the bloggers wrote about how their own actions had caused such damage to the women that they had prematurely aged. Instead, they turned their sights on "girls"—many who appeared far too young to be considered an adult.

The beauty bias also has a strong relationship with capitalism—and so does sex tourism in general. Not only is sexual access commodified, but so is the "Girlfriend Full Experience" product. A sex tourist can demand that a girl pretend to "love" him as if affection could be bought and sold. Indeed, forced prostitution/sex trafficking symbolizes the most toxic aspects of capitalism, especially the echoes of colonialism (White men preying on the Native women). Naturally, sex tourists do not live in a vacuum apart from the mainstream but are an integral part of our society. The next section will explore an overlapping culture of misogyny, the manosphere that includes the websites of men's rights activists, pickup artists (PUAs), and other groups that denigrate women.

WHY THE MANOSPHERE MATTERS

Capitalism on Steroids

In Thomas Hardy's Victorian novel *The Mayor of Casterbridge*, a destitute man sells off his wife and child to the highest bidder at a bar. When I first read about this story, I thought that the premise was highly unlikely. Then I found out about wife sales in British history—at least 300 times, a man sold off his wife at a cattle auction. Presented like livestock, the wife would wear a rope around her neck or waist[5]. British law allowed for husbands to have complete control and ownership over their civilly dead wives.

Wife sales no longer occur, but this attitude of hypercapitalism still affects modern society. One striking aspect of the manosphere (e.g., men's rights activists, PUAs, and men going their own way [MGTOW]) is how these men consider women as commodities instead of persons. Also, the men consider themselves to be commodities or buyers themselves. One compelling aspect of their argument is that both sexes have sexual market value (SMV). "A woman's value significantly depends on her fertility and beauty. A man's value significantly depends on his resources, intellect, and character"[6].

Competition for "hot babes" is also related to the capitalistic ideal of winners and losers. Besides being sexually assertive, PUAs should be willing to dominate their partners in a competition with other men (Box 2.3). The *Seduction Science* article "Fifteen Dominant Sex Moves for Hot Orgasmic Sex with Pretty 'Good Girls'" includes these moves: "Slam her against a door. . . . Pull her hair. . . . Push her face into the floor. . . . Pin her hands down. . . . Fuck her hard, fast, and deep. . . . Tie her hands together." Pulling her hair is also recommended for the "wall thump" move in which she is banged against the wall. Supposedly, such aggressiveness adds to a man's SMV[7].

Aggressive Behavior and Hostility Toward Women

In the world of the PUA, men can overcome their beta status (i.e., a chump who is taken advantage of) to emerge as alpha males by using "game" to get the hot babes. These tricks to get women into bed include "negging," a negative comment to throw off a woman's self-confidence. Besides negging, "kino" (kinesthetics) is the tactic of light touching. "The moment you start speaking to [a girl], touch her arm or shoulder to initiate kino. Don't touch her for longer than

BOX 2.3

THE TRADITIONAL HATRED TOWARD "LOOSE WOMEN"

In the world of the pickup artist, a woman should always be willing to have sex with the man but not with too many men. The ASD (anti-slut defense) "is a conscious or unconscious process that women, especially younger women, go through to avoid the perception of being 'slutty' or 'too easy.' . . . Before sex, anti-slut defense often manifests as token resistance put up by the woman to demonstrate that they resisted the sexual advances, which helps absolve them of their guilt of sex, which originates mostly from social programming. Post-sex ASD often involves justifications for the sex act: 'It just happened,' 'he wouldn't give up,' 'I was really drunk,' etc."[34].

Sluttiness, then, can reduce or even destroy a woman's sexual market value. Like a used car, she loses value as a commodity for every time she is driven. Although the historical use of the term "loose woman" probably referred to loose morals or loose clothes, it could also apply to the vagina's elasticity and size. Virgins and less experienced women allegedly have tighter vaginas than other women, especially mothers who have had vaginal births. This value set on tightness could be one reason that so many plastic surgeons are performing "vaginal rejuvenation" on women who want to tighten their vaginas.

The historical prejudice against loose women, then, has not died out yet. As discussed in Chapter 5, society still values a female's virginity as if it were a commodity.

a couple of seconds each time because it will come across as creepy"[8]. Like the men in the photograph at the beginning of this chapter, these men are certainly not respecting the woman's physical boundaries.

Hostility toward women also appears in the manosphere when men feel rejected by women and become disillusioned with the PUA culture. Some men who have faced enough rejection in the dating scene call themselves "incels" or involuntary celibates. Elliott Rodgers, who was mentioned in the first chapter, remains the most famous example of incels. This disturbed young man who went on a murderous rampage in 2014 after making a YouTube video and writing a manifesto. "You girls have never been attracted to me. . . . I don't know why you girls aren't attracted to me, but I will punish you for it." He went to a sorority house on the "day of retribution" to "slaughter every single spoiled, stuck-up blonde slut I see insider there"[9].

Rodgers' involvement with the PUAHate website, a venue for criticizing the PUA industry and women in general, stirred debate about how much the manosphere culture had influenced him. Although it is obvious that the manosphere was not the source of Rodgers' revenge fantasies, the angry language "reinforced Rodger's mindset, telling him, in effect, that he was perfectly right to be enraged at half the human race. Men's rights activists did not tell Rodger to kill—but in their writings, it seems like many of them wouldn't mind doing some killing of their own"[10].

The incels appeared in the news again in 2017, when Reddit banned the incel subreddit for inciting violence against women. This group of 40,000 members revered Rodger as "Saint Elliot." Another subreddit, called the Philosophy of Rape, was also banned. However, "creep shots" ("upskirts," which are pictures taken below a female's skirt) are still protected as free speech.

Incels often expressed anger toward women for playing with them. Incel Tears, a subreddit group, tracks the incel sites to monitor any misogynistic posts. For example, the "I want to murder a femoid" post explicitly describes a rape/murder fantasy. "For all the evil shit they've done to me, this would be the ultimate payback"[11].

Failing in the dating scene, then, can lead to a deep sense of outrage that can become dangerous. "These men got angry at the women that they see as depriving them of something they are entitled to"[12] . Countless movies show that even average-looking guys get the hot babes. *Out of His League*, for example, relates the story of a nice airport security officer who starts dating a strikingly attractive woman. The dowdy and overweight schmuck in *Hitch* is guaranteed a sunny future with a gorgeous and rich woman because—well, because. In real life, though, men may feel angry at these false promises and think about retaliation.

Men of the Manosphere, Can We Talk?

If MGTOW regard "women" (i.e., girlfriends) as a luxury but PUAs consider "women" (i.e., female sex partners) to be a necessity, how does that affect our society? Neither group regards "women" as an assortment of individuals with different personalities and lives. Instead, the entire manosphere seems to miss one essential point—we are all sharing the same planet and need to get along.

The men's rights movement had started as an advocacy group regarding fathers' rights in the family courts, so child support has remained a sore topic. Many men bemoan the lost era of the male breadwinner, a time of even worse wage inequity and limitations for women. Now the competition is between workers of both genders. Men who call themselves disposable because of feminism miss the point—the capitalist system itself is to blame for their economic insecurity. This dilemma parallels the White workers' antagonism toward immigrant workers, a destructive response to an inherently exploitative system.

In trying to make sense of social changes, for instance, the PUAs do not write angry statements about their rivals (i.e., the alpha males who get the girl) or the system itself. Instead, the PUAs save their venomous attacks against women for those within the system. Women are bitches and snobs who like to hurt men and show off their power. The PUAs seem to think that if only they could play the game better, they could succeed in the sexual marketplace. This is similar to a woman who competes in a male-based setting but does not argue with the unfair rules. Even overachievers who fail to achieve the success they deserve may tell themselves that they need to play the game better. Neither the PUAs nor those undervalued women want to admit that the problem is bigger than their personal stories, that the system itself needs to change (Box 2.4).

SPORTS CULTURE

Influence of Capitalism

Although I do not "get" sports, I do not scoff at sports fans (well, except for the face painters and the tailgaters who

BOX 2.4

CASE STUDY: HUGH HEFNER

One example of the mainstream being infused with misogyny is in the story of Hugh Hefner and his Playboy Empire. On the same weekend that Hugh Hefner died in 2017, a news report came out about a sex robot (i.e., a sex doll with artificial intelligence that can talk and even moan) being molested at a technology convention. It was humorous to think of somebody complaining about an object being objectified. "The doll's developer, Sergi Santos, from Barcelona, Spain complained, 'The people mounted Samantha's breasts, her legs and arms. Two fingers were broken. She was heavily soiled.' He added, 'People can be bad. Because they did not understand the technology and did not have to pay for it, they treated the doll like barbarians'"[35]. The thought of men (and maybe some women?) simulating aggressive sex with a robot can be disturbing, especially because experts predict that such robots will become popular.

Unfortunately, this robot developer cares more about his object than Hugh Hefner did about some of his women. Hefner treated the young women as simply interchangeable, easily replaceable, and eventually worthless. Although he showed kindness and generosity to several women, the sad truth is that he harmed countless others through his warped version of the sexual revolution.

Despite his support for birth control, he admitted to not using condoms and not worrying about sexually transmitted infections (STIs) because he denied they were ever a problem. Even at the height of the HIV/AIDS epidemic in 1994, he dismissed the risks because they "are very clearly defined and related to specific behavior." Perhaps he was implying that heterosexuals did not have to worry about HIV/AIDS[36] . We will never know how many people contracted an STI at the Playboy Mansion. Because his refusal to use condoms probably influenced his male guests to do the same, he knowingly risked the lives and health of numerous women.

Hefner's condomless existence corresponds with the silk pajamas, which signified the relaxed, pleasure-seeking male. In stark contrast is the uncomfortable attire of the Bunny with her tight-waisted outfit and high heels that punished her feet. A female Mansion guest would have to wear a clingy dress, a perfect hairstyle, and expensive cosmetics. A man could scowl or frown, but a woman would have to smile and giggle no matter how many times she got groped.

Hefner got to wear silk pajamas while some women had to keep sex toys between their legs for hours. His former bodyguard also reported that Hefner would watch girls have sex until they were too sore to walk. "Hef sometimes gave bonuses to the women because the sex acts were so painful." Breast implants were mandatory for some women in the late 1970s, despite the medical risks of the silicone implants bursting open. "I witnessed many women who had this done begging and crying to Hef to help them and he would put them back in the hospital and then discard these women. He didn't care. They were disposable"[37]. It would be impossible to calculate how many women decided to have breast implants and other plastic surgeries because of the Playboy culture.

Even worse than these stories were the allegations of rape and abuse at the Playboy Mansion. Bill Cosby, for instance, allegedly took a 15-year-old girl to the Mansion after getting her drunk. Hefner himself offered Quaaludes to a new girl, calling them "thigh openers"[38] . One controversial point is whether all of the sex that occurred in the Mansion was consensual. Former girlfriend Holly Madison said that group sex was mandatory twice a week, which indicates that some coercion was involved. Forbidden to work outside the home and dependent on his allowances, the girlfriends had few options but to obey.

If sexual abuse was never proved, emotional abuse was certainly apparent. One chilling quote by Madison, who went through a severe depression while at the Mansion, exemplifies Hefner's attitude toward women: "Hefner was withholding, treating her like she was stupid, and criticizing her looks. She wasn't allowed to wear red lipstick; he hated her short haircut, telling her, 'You look old, hard, and cheap'" (23).

Old, hard, and cheap. A bright young woman in her early 20s had done everything she could to please him (e.g., looking pretty and complying with his 9 p.m. curfew) but still was not good enough. This, then, is the essence of the Playboy culture: telling a woman that even if she plays by the rules, she will never be good enough. Some may want to romanticize Hefner's legacy, but I think he was nothing but a creep.

start partying hours before the game and the "Go Bucks" mantra in central Ohio). However, my bafflement at the raw emotions evoked by touchdowns or fumbles makes me an outsider. "Cool" women love sports as much as men, so they fit in snugly with the mainstream culture that values physical stamina and dexterous moves. In a football-mad city such as Columbus with its motif of scarlet and gray, people like me (both male and female) can sometimes feel disoriented and disengaged.

Last Thanksgiving, I was at a friend's house where her husband was watching an OSU-Michigan game. I sat down and said to myself, give this a chance. It can't be that bad. All I could see was men: players on the field acting out ancient rituals of male dominance, sportscasters behind a desk commenting on the coaches' decisions, and commercials dripping with testosterone and Axe spray. Sure, women were in the audience or in cheerleaders' costumes—but this was truly a man's world. As Illustration 2.3 shows, society honors the heroic male whose superiority is undisputed.

So what if football and many other sports still represent a fortress of masculinity? Perhaps modern society needs ceremonies like these to affirm virility—what is wrong with that? And does the topic of sports culture even belong in a book about misogyny?

First, the combination of capitalism and sports culture is both powerful and destructive. The amount of taxpayer support for the sports business can be staggering: $3 billion for NFL stadiums in 2015. As the president of the Taxpayers Protection Alliance stated,

> Unfortunately, beneath all of the glitz and glamour, these venues are nothing more than monuments to corporate welfare and taxpayer handouts. These stadiums have been built

ILLUSTRATION 2.3 *The Doak Walker statue on the campus of Southern Methodist University, Dallas, Texas. Source:* Library of Congress.

on the backs of taxpayers who had no or little say in the matter and in many cases have benefitted little or not at all. [13]

Another study that included more sports concluded that out of the $43 billion required to build and maintain sports facilities, the public had to pay for half of it. Even worse, the upkeep also cost the taxpayers—who have to pay about 75% of the total costs. Although some of these facilities are moneymakers for the local economy, the results are mixed. The Harvard researcher stated, "But with every great success story, you have a Minneapolis, a Chicago White Sox or a Washington Nationals . . . (with a new stadium) almost never" generating income for the city or even the neighborhood[14] . College football is another example of extravagant spending on sports, with academics overshadowed by this big business. For example, Ohio State University paid

$194 million to rebuild the stadium in 2001 and $42 million to upgrade it in 2017[15].

The huge financial costs of the sports culture, then, has implications for social justice. The billions of dollars paid by taxpayers to support the sports facilities could be better used for health care and other urgent needs. In the United States, poverty is more likely to affect women than men. For example, two-thirds of low-wage workers (earning $10.50 or less an hour) are women, even though most have high school degrees and are supporting their families[16]. When people sneer at low-income women who need public assistance, they are ignoring the barriers to those women's success, such as affordable child care and living wages. Instead, the anger directed toward "welfare queens" and "white-trash women" has nothing to do with the facts and everything to do with misogyny and classism.

Marginalization of Women

Besides the social justice dimension, the impact of the tax-supported sports culture on women is deep. Women are either bystanders or outsiders to this male-dominated sphere of influence, but rarely full participants. For example, women who have tried to break into sports broadcasting still face hostility. In a recent article with the subtle title of "Women in Sports Journalism Are Still Putting Up with a Lot of Bullshit," Moskovitz writes: "How many women ditch sports journalism because they decide, and understandably so, that it's not worth all the bullshit? Being called 'difficult' or 'shrill' or 'bitchy'. . . turning down unwanted advances. . . . The 'get back in the kitchen' emails; the 'shut up cunt' tweets; the harassment that comes, daily, from all sides"[17] .

After discussing the recent revelations of harassment by female sports journalists for the #MeToo campaign, a former newscaster writes: "There's a famous line every female inevitably learns when she enters the world of sports: *Check your dignity at the door.* . . . If you're extremely lucky you might even go an entire season without an incident that demeans or belittles you, makes you feel as if you barely exist"[18] .

Sports culture also marginalizes some female athletes. The advances made by Title IX, which required equal spending for male and female sports, have not achieved full equality for female athletes. For example, the minimum salary for the National Women's Soccer League is $6840 (below minimum wage), while that for the National Hockey League is $550,000. Similar male-dominated sports also have high salaries[19] . Despite the financial success of Serena Williams, female tennis players earn less prize money and even fewer endorsements[20] .

Besides unequal pay, female athletes sometimes have to wear inappropriate outfits. The beach volleyball players at the Rio Olympics in 2016, for example, had to wear bikinis as if they were not serious athletes. Illustration 2.4 shows the skimpy attire that the women wore during the competitions. The "sex sells" motif that is so prominent in capitalism, then, even appears in this venue when women's bodies are focused on athletic excellence instead of pleasing men.

Even worse than the sexualization of the female athlete is the sexual harassment by coaches and others in authority. This power balance can have a profound impact on a young girl's self-image—and her sports career. In "athlete domestic violence," in which most of the offenders are male and most of the victims are young females, there is "a (perceived) 'relationship' with a coach and can involve consenting age or

ILLUSTRATION 2.4 Women's volleyball at the Olympics.
Source: Shutterstock.

not. The dynamics develops regardless of age. Professional standards maintain that a 'romantic relationship' is never appropriate as the coach always has a structural power advantage over a competing athlete"[21] .

Social Implications of Sports Culture

Sports metaphors are almost unavoidable in our daily conversations: *Let's touch base* because *I need to take a rain check*. Fine, but *what is your game plan*? I don't know, but I will *try to hit it out of the ballpark*[22]. In fact, I find it hard to think of many metaphors that do not relate to sports— but maybe I should think outside the box to make sure that we are on the same page. Sports metaphors obviously add to the richness of our language, but a darker aspect of their use does exist.

A sporting match means that unless there is a draw, somebody wins and somebody loses. Even if a heartbreaking last-minute touchdown nudges a score to victory by one point, one team is deemed the champion. This ethos is harmless enough for entertainment purposes, but not for politics or diplomacy. For instance, news coverage of the 2016 Republican primary race stressed the "neck-to-neck" concept of horse racing but little in-depth analysis. Like politics, diplomacy has less need for the aggressive attitude of contact sports and more need for the concept of saving face. Allowing an opponent to retreat or lose without complete humiliation (or in wrestling terms, annihilation) is the essence of diplomacy. How many wars have countries avoided by the valuable skill of letting somebody save face?

The failure of diplomacy, then, can result in wars. One example of a sports-related military action is the massive bombing campaign by the United States against North Vietnam that was called Operation Linebacker. During the Iraq War, military operations had names such as Cotton Bowl and Cornhusker. Also, for decades the president's black box that contains the nuclear launch codes bears the name of "the football." Such a reckless mixture of destructive weapons and toxic masculinity should alarm any thoughtful person.

Another social implication of the sports culture is the prevalence of athletes' violence against women. Indeed, the association between college sports and rape is troubling. One recent study, for example, used an online survey of US college students. More than half of the male athletes (54.3%) reported using sexual coercion, a higher percentage than nonathletes (37.9%). "Among the *sexually coercive* behaviors were making a partner have sex without the use of a condom and using physical force or threats to commit rape"[23] . An expert on sexual assault on campus stated that he was not surprised because "Hostile masculinity is a predictor of sexual violence, and you're more likely to see that on an athletic team. If you have a norm among a group of men that is negative toward women, there can be an effect where they all drop to that lowest common denominator"[24] .

For rape victims who had been assaulted by college football players in a college town, the trauma of social rejection can be brutal. Krakauer (2016) writes of how the Missoula community responded to a high incidence of rape by football players. Between 2008 and 2012, the local police did little to investigate the hundreds of rape cases. The federal government had to intervene, with the Department of Justice pursuing 350 cases. One rape victim, pressured by her mother to sue the prosecutor, said, "Mom, they're football players and no one's gonna listen to me. They'll make my life hell"[25].

Juries may also favor the alleged attacker instead of the alleged victim if football is involved. The article title " 'But He's a Star Football Player!': How Social Status Influences Mock Jurors' Perceptions in a Sexual Assault Case" indicates the disadvantage that victims may encounter if they choose to file charges. The social status given to football players meant that the higher his team position, the less likely he would be blamed for rape[26].

In response to the gender violence related to sports, one Australian group has set up a Purple Armband campaign to highlight this problem. The online activism of fans has energized thousands to challenge the idea that sports culture must be violent. Fan advocacy, then, may be the new direction for those who love sports but hate violence[27].

ACTION STEPS

- Sex trafficking is a distressing reality, but international organizations such as the Polaris Project have answered the challenge to save lives. (Their website is www.polarisproject.org).
- On the local level, you may be living in a community with a coalition that is fighting trafficking. The Central Ohio Rescue and Restore Coalition, for example, exemplifies the multiple layers of response needed to be effective. The coalition meetings consist of social workers, health care workers, law enforcement, and other front-line personnel. Its committees include:
  - Public awareness (e.g., how to spot a trafficking victim at a highway rest stop);
  - Comprehensive services for survivors (e.g., jobs and housing);
  - Legislation/advocacy; and
  - Reducing the demand for the sex trade. (www.centralohiorescueandrestore.org)
- Legal reforms such as punishing the johns and pimps instead of the prostitutes can be an issue for advocacy. The Nordic Model, also called the Sex Buyer Law, does not regard prostitution as a victimless crime because of the likelihood that the prostitute had been coerced into the trade. Providing social services to the prostitutes, while criminalizing the johns and pimps, has greatly reduced the rate of prostitution in Scandinavia. After 10 years of the Sex Buyer Law in Sweden, street prostitution had been cut in half without an increase in other venues. This legal reform has reduced the

demand for prostitution, the key element to stopping the "world's oldest oppression." (CATW—Coalition Against Trafficking in Women—has the website www. catwinternational.org.)

- If you want to track the latest with the manosphere, the major websites are A Voice for men (www. avoiceformen.com) and the Red Pill thread on Reddit. Two helpful resources are:
  - We Hunted the Mammoth website, which monitors the postings (www.wehuntedthemammoth.com); and
  - The Southern Poverty Law Center, which records instances of hate speech on the manosphere (www. splcenter.org/).

Notes

1. Malarek, V. (2009). *The Johns: Sex for sale and the men who buy it.* New York, NY: Arcade Publishing, pp. 147–148
2. *Sex resorts:*
   Oxygenretreat.com
   Mywildvacation.com
   Fieldofdreamsresort.com
   DR Nights (Dominican Republic): www.drnights.com
   Viking's Exotic Resort: cat69.co/faq.html
   DR Sex Holidays: www.dominicanrepublicsexholidays.com
   Alexis Club: www.alexisclub.com
   Ripe Lady: www.ripelady.com
   Charlie's Angels: www. caribbeanlogue.com
   Tour 69: www.tour69.com/dominican-republic-adult-vacations
   Alternative Phuket: www.alternativephuket.com/destinations
   Advice sites:
   Travelsexguide.com
   Dexterhorn.com
   Worldsexguide.com—advice site for sex tourists

Punternet.com—British advice site (includes a section on Dangerous Punter Warnings for sex workers)

In Search of Chicas: www.insearchofchicas.org

Sexcations: www.sexcation-review.com

Godsofthailand.com: advice site for sex tourists

Sirmarjalot's Mongering Blog: The Confessions of a Sex Tourist at

sirmarjalot.wordpress.com

World Sex Archives (not a free site, so only looked at thousands of listings)

Mongerplanet.com

3. Jeffreys, S. (2009). *The industrial vagina: The political economy of the global sex trade*. New York, NY: Routledge

4. Kempado, K. (1999). Continuities and change: Five centuries of prostitution in the Caribbean. In Kempado, K. (Ed.), *Sun, sex, and gold: Tourism and sex work in the Caribbean*. Lanham, MD: Rowan & Littlefield, pp. 3–36

5. One article on wife sales in 19th-century England is on the Madeline Hunter website. Retrieved from www.madelinehunter.com/extras/history/tt_sellingwife.php

6. The Return of Kings website includes articles such as: "Feminists are hysterical because no man wants to rape them" Roosh V's quote retrieved from www.returnofkings.com/about

7. The Seduction Science website has several articles about male-dominated sex. The one quoted was retrieved from www.seductionscience.com/2009/dominant-sex-moves-for-the-bedroom/

8. The Pickup Artist Training (Natural Mastery with Women and Dating) includes videos and even a "university." The kino technique is described in this link: www.puatraining.com/blog/pick-up-artist-techniques-you-need-to-master

9. The quote from Rodgers' note is cited from an Intelligence Report called "War on Women" by the Southern Poverty Law Center's report on the Men's Rights Activists. Retrieved from www.splcenter.org/fighting-hate/intelligence-report/2014/war-women

10. Intelligence Report called "War on Women" by the Southern Poverty Law Center's report on the Men's Rights Activists. Retrieved from www.splcenter.org/fighting-hate/intelligence-report/2014/war-women

11. This March 28, 2018 post is typical of ones found on the Incel Tears subreddit. Retrieved from www.reddit.com/r/IncelTears/comments/87vxk2/gee_why_dont_women_like_him/

12. Professor Mary Anne Franks quoted in Hauser, C. (2017). Reddit bans "Incel" group for inciting violence against women. New York Times. Retrieved from www.nytimes.com/2017/11/09/technology/incels-reddit-banned.html

13. Waldron, D. (2015). Taxpayers have spent a 'staggering' amount of money on NFL stadiums. Huffington Post. Retrieved from www.huffingtonpost.com/entry/taxpayers-nfl-stadiums_us_55f08313e4b002d5c077b8ac

14. Lee, J. (2013). Taxpayers on the hook for stadium costs. USA Today. Retrieved from www.usatoday.com/story/news/nation-now/2013/11/25/stadiums-taxpayers/3663541/

15. Ohio State University website. Retrieved from https://news.osu.edu/news/2016/03/29/ohio-stadium-renovations-planned-for-2017-20/

16. National Women's Law Center website. Retrieved from https://nwlc.org/resources/chart-book-women-low-wage-workforce-may-not-be-who-you-think/

17. Moskovitz, D. (2017). Women in sports journalism are still putting up with a lot of bullshit. Deadspin. Retrieved from https://deadspin.com/women-in-sports-journalism-are-still-putting-up-with-a-1821584038

18. Olson, L. (2017). The #MeToo movement comes to sports, a reckoning long overdue. The Athletic. Retrieved from https://theathletic.com/192516/2017/12/21/the-metoo-movement-comes-to-sports-a-reckoning-long-overdue/

19. Fortier, S. (2015). The minimum pro female soccer salary is below the poverty line. Esquire. Retrieved from www.esquire.com/sports/news/a36233/womens-soccer-pay/

20. Cox, D. (2018). Why are female athletes still paid less than males? Al Jazeera. Retrieved from www.aljazeera.com/indepth/features/female-athletes-paid-males-180114100158659.html

21. Starr, K. (2013). Breaking down sexual abuse in sports. Huffington Post. Retrieved from www.huffingtonpost.com/katherine-starr/breaking-down-sexual-abus_b_2500956.html

22. The list of sports metaphors came from a list retrieved from https://themeltingthought2000.wordpress.com/2012/10/24/sports-metaphors-we-live-by/

23. 54 percent of US college athletes admit to raping their partners—survey. (2016). Reuters. Retrieved from www.rt.com/usa/345383-half-college-athletes-admitted-rape/

24. New, J. (2016). Sexual coercion among athletes. Inside Higher Education. Retrieved from www.insidehighered.com/news/2016/06/03/more-half-athletes-study-say-they-engaged-sexual-coercion?utm_content=buffer178ed&utm_medium=social&utm_source=twitter&utm_campaign=IHEbuffer

25. Krakauer, J. (2016). *Missoula: Rape and the justice system in a college town.* New York, NY: First Anchor Books, p. 49.

26. Pica, E., Sheahan, C., & Pozzulo, J. (2017). "But he's a star football player!": How social status influences mock jurors' perceptions in a sexual assault case. *Journal of Interpersonal Violence,* 0886260517713715.

27. Dimitrov, R. (2008). Gender violence, fan activism and public relations in sport: The case of "Footy Fans Against Sexual Assault." *Public Relations Review, 34*(2), 90–98.

28. The Washington, DC program: Carpenter, J. (2018). How bartenders fight harassment and workplace violence. CNN Money. Retrieved from http://money.cnn.com/2018/01/03/pf/bartenders-sexual-harassment/index.html

    The Ontario program. (2016). Bartenders and servers to receive sexual violence and harassment intervention training. Press release from Ontario Ministry of the Status of Women. Retrieved from https://news.ontario.ca/owd/en/2016/09/bartenders-and-servers-to-receive-sexual-violence-and-harassment-intervention-training.html

29. International Labor Organization. Website: www.ilo.org/global/topics/forced-labour/lang--en/index.htm

30. International Labor Organization. Website: www.ilo.org/global/topics/forced-labour/lang--en/index.htm

31. Graphic on missing children found on the National Center for Missing and Exploited Children website. Retrieved from www.missingkids.com/1in6

32. The 12–14 statistic was examined by PolitiFact. Retrieved from www.politifact.com/oregon/statements/2013/mar/02/diane-mckeel/Is-average-age-entry-sex-trafficking-between-12-an/

33. Coorlim, L., & Ford, D. (2017). Sex trafficking: The new American slavery. CNN. Retrieved from www.cnn.com/2015/07/20/us/sex-trafficking/index.html

34. The Pickup Artist (PUA) lingo website. Retrieved from www.pualingo.com

35. Frymorgen, T. (2017). Sex robot sent for repairs after being molested at tech fair. BBC. Retrieved from www.bbc.co.uk/bbcthree/item/610ec648-b348-423a-bd3c-04dc701b2985

36. Proffitt, S. (1994). Hugh Hefner: In the shadow of AIDS, examining what's left of the sexual revolution. Los Angeles Times. Retrieved from http://articles.latimes.com/1994-07-31/opinion/op-22019_1_hugh-hefner/2

37. Kimball, W. (2017). Working for Hugh Hefner sounds like a horror show of blood and semen and pelvic cheeseburgers. Jezebel. Retrieved from https://jezebel.com/working-for-hugh-hefner-sounds-like-a-horror-show-of-bl-1819036690

38. Aurthur, K. (2015). Holly Madison reveals the hell that is Playboy Mansion life. Buzzfeed. Retrieved from www.buzzfeed.com/kateaurthur/holly-madison-burns-it-down?utm_term=.iuJrLVaPw#.nl00N1a2z

3

SILENCING OF WOMEN

INTRODUCTION

Frances (Fanny) Wright, a British-born writer and activist, went on a US tour to speak out against slavery in 1829. She faced intense criticism for speaking out as a woman, as seen in this cartoon (Illustration 3.1). This example of trying to silence a woman parallels the current efforts to shut women up.

First, the picture shows her to be a preposterous figure. Ridicule is a powerful weapon to use against any political opponent because after one has laughed at somebody, it is hard to take them seriously. Calling her a gabbler adds to the claim that nothing she says could be of any importance.

The second point is that her critics would regard a female public speaker as violating the laws of nature. Those who argued against the women's suffrage movement stressed that giving women any political power violated God's laws. As recently as 2013, the Turkish president stated that equality between the sexes was "against nature"[1]. In this cartoon, the subordinate male who is holding her bonnet would also be unnatural because he should be the one in control. A female public speaker, then, was considered as abnormal as a goose dressed in a black dress.

A DOWNRIGHT GABBLER,
or a goose that deserves to be hissed

ILLUSTRATION 3.1 Fanny Wright: A downright gobbler. Source: Library of Congress.

As long as patriarchy has existed, it has tried to silence countless women such as Wright in several ways. Two themes have dominated the recent discourses about women's voices: women in politics and credibility. This quote from Malala Yousafzai, the Nobel Peace Prize winner who advocates for girls' education, captures the spirit of this chapter: "We realize the importance of our voices only when we are silenced"[2].

Lastly, the caption from the Library of Congress website includes this observation: "[Her] costume and the scene itself—with its table, water, candles, and acolyte-like attendant—seems intended to suggest an underlying parallel with liturgical rites"[3]. In 1829, it was indeed shocking for anybody—especially a woman—to critique religious institutions as did Wright. Her suggestion that children be sent to boarding schools to be educated outside the home outraged many who believed that she was trying to impose atheism on society. By rejecting blind faith in religions, advocating for the freedom and education for enslaved Americans, and promoting women's rights in an era when they had almost none, Wright must have appeared as a freak to many.

WOMEN IN POLITICS

Personal Attacks

Wright was not the first outspoken woman to be savaged by cartoonists. One of the first British women to publicly engage in politics was Georgiana, Duchess of Devonshire. In 1780, this high-born lady had the nerve to appear on stage with a Whig candidate. Her canvassing on his behalf led cartoonists to display her as a voluptuous temptress who even showed off her thighs and exchanged kisses for votes. Soon she had to drop her political activities to avoid further embarrassment[4].

Today we would call her situation a "slut-shaming" episode, with the deeper meaning of slut-shaming concerning social and political marginalization. For example, a left-wing blogger recently called Theresa May, the British Prime Minister, a "whore" after the special election fiasco. This could be flabbergasting to anyone who has seen May's demure clothes and manners—she is certainly not slutty.

However, calling her "whore" was parallel to calling a male opponent a "bastard" to delegitimize him. For centuries, illegitimate sons could not inherit property, find employment, or get married. On the fringes of society, bastards were often as disrespected as prostitutes. Today, of course, the insults hurled at males are "gay" or "limp dicked" because being not fully male means being not a full person.

Another aspect is that slut-shaming is a power ploy against women related to street harassment. Both practices intend to humiliate a female for simply existing. Usually directed against females without a male companion, street harassment can include insults and "compliments"— sometimes to the same woman when she is called an "ugly bitch" after she refuses to smile. If a female is walking independently in a public space, she is fair game to any male who chooses to comment on her appearance.

Besides slut-shaming, cartoonists and others who try to tear down females in politics also use the tactic of simply calling her ugly. Historian Amanda Vickery notes, "Women who have the temerity to speak out in public on the affairs of the day are unsexed. They become physically hideous"[5]. One antisuffragette cartoon, for instance, shows a woman who goes on a hunger fast and goes from ugly/fat to then ugly/skinny. Another example portrays Susan B. Anthony (Illustration 3.2) as a hatchet-faced virago who is almost as scary as a Stephen King villain.

Learning to Hate Hillary Clinton

The 2016 election provided many compelling examples of misogyny toward Hillary Clinton, the woman who won the popular vote but still lost. In my experience, I was amazed

ILLUSTRATION 3.2 Susan B. Anthony. Source: Library of Congress.

by the degree of hostility that Clinton engendered among moderates who were otherwise sensible about politics. Did she deserve all that visceral hatred? It would take weeks to systematically list the conspiracy theories, malicious insults, and other personal attacks on her. In the 2016 campaign, Clinton haters (not critics like me, but actual haters) also felt justified in laying into her with slogans such as "Trump that bitch!" and "Lock her up!"

The first consideration should be about how many of the personal attacks on Hillary Clinton were related to misogyny and how many to simple meanness against an opponent. Physical appearance is one factor. In history, of course, male politicians had sometimes received insults about their appearances. Even Lincoln had to deal with slurs about his looks—one Cabinet member called him a gorilla[6]. In the past, both Johnson and Nixon had noses that delighted the cartoonists. The only nonracist caricatures of Obama usually stressed his big ears, which were really not that big.

Since 1992 when Bill Clinton ran for president, people have launched personal attacks on his wife's hairstyle and other aspects of her looks. As this photo from the 1990s shows (Illustration 3.3), she had such a professional appearance that the mean-spirited remarks were baffling to many.

However, Trump-bashing had similarities to Hillary-bashing that are not necessarily related to misogyny. If Clinton was attacked for her physical appearance, so was Trump. His weight seemed to be fair game because of the numerous times he had called women fat. A sculptor even displayed a nude statue of him, complete with pot belly

ILLUSTRATION 3.3 First Lady Hillary Clinton presenting on health care reform in 1993. Source: Library of Congress.

and sagging buttocks. This humiliating portrayal of Trump seemed appropriate to many because of the feeling that he deserved it. Besides his body shape, how many times have Trump bashers also called him orange or mentioned his hair?

Another aspect of appearance is clothing, which has been a point of derision for Clinton bashers for decades. If she had decided on pantsuits as more practical and/or comfortable than skirts or dresses, this wardrobe choice should not even matter. Trump also has faced criticism for his clothes, from the too-long ties to the ill-fitting suits. Although people judge women much more harshly for their clothes than men, both genders must deal with cutting remarks about what they wear.

Besides physical appearance was the topic about one's gender identity, with Clinton being defeminized and Trump being demasculinized. Because Clinton is not afraid to show off her strength and intelligence, she has been called Killary, Shillary, a ballbreaker, and a lesbian (in this context, a deviant and perhaps defiant person who is not truly female). Clinton played the roles of mother and wife as well as any other woman, but her career ambitions inspired her critics to defeminize her. Similarly, Trump has had to deal with questions about his manliness. The assertion that his fingers are smaller than normal, which is associated with smaller penis size, even emerged in a Republican debate. Trump felt the need to boast about his physical attributes, thus indicating an anxiety about his masculine image. His chest-thumping foreign policy, public putdowns of women, and other macho behaviors could be related to the threat of feeling demasculinized.

Ageism is yet another ugly facet of the attacks on both Clinton and Trump. During the 2016 election, commentators questioned whether Trump or Clinton (who are about the same age) could be too old for the presidency. More than one website posted this preelection article: "These 11 Photos Prove Hillary Clinton Is a Tired Old Woman Who Should Never Be President"[7]. After Clinton's granddaughter was born, the Drudge Report called her "Grandma Hillary" as an insult. Nancy Pelosi, also a grandmother, had faced the same kind of contempt that no grandfather politician ever experienced.

By comparing the personal attacks on Clinton and Trump, then, it appears that neither candidate emerged unscathed. Several questions come to mind, including whether the American public insulted Clinton and Trump to the same extent or if Clinton faced worse treatment. After researching the multiple anti-Clinton themes, one must deduce that misogyny did play a role in the 2016 election. However, misogyny may or may not have been the primary cause of Hillary-bashing instead of being just another campaign tactic.

Besides these personal attacks, why else should we hate Hillary? Bill Clinton had certainly generated antagonism that went far beyond polite discourse, so her gender may not be the only facet of Hillary-bashing. Below is an incomplete list of accusations—obviously, many of them are libelous instead of factual. Many of the conspiracy theories in the list appear as absurd as the charge that Obama was the Antichrist who was setting up FEMA concentration camps. The reader can conclude which ones are associated with misogyny and which ones are not gender related.

- As a defense lawyer, she had defended child rapists;
- As the First Lady, she had tried to cram socialized medicine down the throats of Americans who would die from her nefarious schemes;

- As the First Lady, she had murdered Vince Foster (a White House counsel);
- Before she murdered Vince Foster, she had an affair with him;
- But wait, she really was a lesbian;
- As the wife of an adulterer, she should have divorced him;
- As the wife of a man accused of harassing and raping women, she was just as culpable as him because of her complicity;
- She was a Wall Street insider, as proved by the well-paid speeches she gave at Goldman Sachs;
- Every policy decision (e.g., NAFTA) made by President Clinton was also her fault because she was First Lady at the time;
- As Secretary of State, she had allowed the Libyan mob to attack the Benghazi embassy—or even orchestratedit;
- She created ISIS—no wait, she was part of a Muslim Brotherhood plot because the name of her State Department aide was Huma Abedin;
- She had single-handedly arranged to sell Uranium One to Russia in exchange for donations to the Clinton Foundation;
- She had used an email server that was not properly secured, thus prompting an FBI investigation;
- She was associated with a Satanic child-sex ring that met at a pizzeria; and
- As Secretary of State, she had planned to tax the billionaires to engineer a United Nations takeover of the United States[8].

Dinesh D'Souza exemplifies the venomous nature of Hillary-bashing. He even produced a documentary called *Hillary's America: The Secret History of the Democratic Party*. In his book with the same title he writes, "She is old, and mean, and even her laugh is a witch's cackle"[9]. He condemns her for supporting her husband: "She took on the task of prosecuting, discrediting, and destroying the women that spoke out against him"[10]. In D'Souza's view, "Hillary couldn't do it for him (Bill Clinton) in the bedroom"[11]. His policy critiques are subtle and nuanced: "Hillary's plan . . . is the enslavement of America. We have become serfs not of a plantation owner, but serfs of the progressive state"[12].

Misogyny, then, becomes apparent in some of the justifications for Hillary-bashing. Two other factors deserve consideration. First, the media coverage of Clinton's policy proposals in 2016 was appalling. Almost nobody covered her policy proposals, which were her strong point. According to one research study, "Not a single one of Clinton's policy proposals accounted for even 1% of her convention-period coverage; collectively, her policy stands accounted for a mere 4% of it. But she might be thankful for that: News reports about her stances were 71% negative to 29% positive in tone. Trump was quoted more often about her policies than she was." For example, Trump's accusation that she had created ISIS received more coverage than her own proposal to fight the Islamist State[13]. Also related was the email controversy used as a campaign issue: the media did not give the controversy the proper context but instead implied the "see, you can't trust her" message.

Another factor is the predatory behavior of the newsmen who had damaged Clinton's chances for electoral success. Matt Lauer, for example, had conducted back-to-back interviews with both Clinton and Trump in 2016. Commentators noted that he had spent about one-third of the interview asking Clinton repeated questions about the email issue and then spent little time on other issues. "He notoriously peppered and interrupted Mrs. Clinton with cold, aggressive, condescending questions hyper-focused on her emails, only to pitch softballs at Mr. Trump and treat him with gentle collegiality a half-hour later"[14]. Months later, NBC fired Lauer when sexual harassment allegations came to light. Charlie Rose had also showed signs of hostility to her as a woman as described by a blogger: "the tone of voice dripping with hate and condescension, the badgering, the dark facial expression as he leaned forward, the deep fear of the evil woman that seemed to hang in the background"[15]. A year after the interview, this highly respected journalist would lose his job because of allegations that he had harassed his female staff. Two other prominent men who had been disrespectful to Clinton, Mark Halperin and Glenn Thrush, also were fired for similar allegations.

On a broader scale, the entertainment industry and other venues are power structures that still silence women's voices. The title of Rebecca Traister's article, "Our National Narratives Are Still Being Shaped by Lecherous, Powerful Men," describes how we need to rethink what we are watching and reading. "The accused are men who help to determine what art gets seen and appreciated—and, crucially, paid for. They decide whose stories get brought to screens"[16].

Clinton's electoral loss, then, is not simply the story of one woman trying to break the glass ceiling. Complex factors affected the 2016 election, including the Russian interference in the election through social media and computer hacking. "On Twitter, as on Facebook, Russian fingerprints are on hundreds or thousands of fake accounts that regularly posted anti-Clinton messages. Many were automated Twitter accounts, called bots, that sometimes fired off identical messages seconds apart"[17]. When somebody says that they despise Clinton, then, it would be wise to ask where they got their information. Perhaps if the media had focused on her policy proposals and if the Russians had not interfered in the election, the Hillary bashers would be fewer in number (Box 3.1).

CREDIBILITY

When I was seven, I had a miniature doll in a plastic bubble that I took to school. A classmate had an identical doll and lost hers that day. She and the rest of the class accused me of stealing her doll. I had a severe speech impediment, so I could not articulate a proper defense. They took my doll away until the classmate found her missing doll later that day.

I am not relating this story to avoid paying for a therapy session, but to illustrate a major point about credibility: the lack of power. Not only did I have trouble communicating, but also I was less popular than the classmate with the missing doll. This kind of unequal situation leads to an injustice that may never be addressed. Why tell the truth when nobody would believe you anyway?

At the age of 10, I heard on the news that a congressperson suggested sending Canadian troops to the Mideast instead of American. I went to my older sister upstairs and repeated this idea to her. Assuming that I had made it up myself, she had snapped at me that it was the stupidest thing she

BOX 3.1

KEEPING SWEET—WHEN WOMEN OBEY THE PATRIARCHY

The term "keep sweet" became known when the story came out about a survivor of a polygamist cult. Rulon Jeffs, the patriarch of the Fundamentalist Latter Day Saints (FLDS) group, defined it this way: "I want you all to understand the continual use of the two words 'keep sweet' means keep the Holy Spirit of the Lord, until you are full of it. Only those who have it will survive the judgments of God which are about to be poured out"[30]. One survivor described it thus: "We were constantly told to 'keep sweet' and that 'perfect obedience produces perfect faith.' Behind these sugary slogans lay the impossible duty of living in complete obedience to the Prophet"[31].

"Keep sweet no matter what" is a phrase often seen on the plaques in FLDS homes. Hold in your emotions, obey God and the men who speak for him, and pray hard that you do not disturb the community's peace. Red was a forbidden color because—well, just because. Women should not cut their hair because it must stay long enough for wiping the feet of Jesus in heaven[32].

The Quiverfull movement also has a "keep sweet" theme in its patriarchal framework. This decentralized group of conservative Christians stresses the importance of families having as many children as possible— a quiverfull of arrows, as dictated by a Psalms verse.

According to an interview of a woman who grew up in a Quiverfull family, the adults and churches regarded their children as soldiers who needed strict discipline. Bill Goddard's Children's Institute, for example, trained children how to smile properly (at least three teeth showing) and how to raise their hands in a polite manner. The Pearls, authors of the controversial book, *How to Train Up Your Child*, held seminars on how to beat your child. One film clip shows Michael Pearl using a stick on a doll to demonstrate the best strokes, then chiding the parents to remember that "psychological terror" was also effective[33].

In this setting, the term "keep sweet" takes on ominous overtones. An authoritarian father who demands complete obedience from his children also has the God-given right to "train" his wife to submit to him. A blogger writes that "Disturbingly, this notion of submissiveness is somehow fixed to a notion of femininity—a package presented to these girls, tied up with religious guilt and obligation, that they must accept, whether willingly, guiltily, or painfully"[34]. Equating submission to femininity, then, can be one way to control women's thoughts because femininity is so valued in traditional societies.

The FLDS and Quiverfull groups, of course, are extreme examples of patriarchal control in the United States. However, the "keep sweet" concept does appear in mainstream society. People tell women to "smile" as if they did not have the right to their own facial reactions when they are out in public. At work, women must also "play nice" to be liked to achieve a good reputation. Researchers recently reported that "to be considered confident and influential at work," a woman had to appear prosocial. Unlike their male colleagues, then, women must achieve two impressions: being competent and being likable[35].

This quote from Pam Houston describes how women can lose their voices by keeping sweet: "I spent years acting and not acting a million particular ways because I thought it was what a man wanted from me. Worse even than that was when I dimmed myself down from 100 watts to 60 because that was all they could take"[36]. Fortunately, this writer and many other women have learned to raise their voices high.

had ever heard. I felt completely dismissed when she thought that I was too young to know what I was talking about.

These minor incidents came to mind during the coverage of Roy Moore's alleged behavior that was disclosed in late 2017. Several trustworthy sources confirmed Moore's preference for "dating" underage girls. In one case, Moore had allegedly said to a 16-year-old girl after he had assaulted her in his car: "You're just a child and I am the district attorney of Etowah County. If you tell anyone about this, no one will ever believe you"[18]. No wonder she did not report the incident for years. When the *Washington Post* published the allegation of a decades-old sexual encounter between Moore and a 14-year-old, a female columnist in the *National Review* (a conservative publication) wrote that Moore was a pedophile[19]. In the comments section below was this statement: "And now this ethically-obtuse virago Timpf [writer] insists we should take as Gospel the word of some conveniently unavailable, 3x divorced, 3x bankrupt, Payday Loan lowlife over a public servant with an impeccable personal and professional record otherwise we are all co-conspirators after the fact. Really? So sorry, pussy hat, shirt, pants and jockstrap wearer Timpf. It is YOU and your fellow testosterone-despising misanthropes who need to be removed from the public eye, not the honorable Roy Moore"[20].

The list of reasons that these women are not credible, then, includes:

- Age of the first young victim;
- Long gap between the alleged incidents and the public report;
- Columnist is an "ethically obtuse virago" (i.e., immoral bitch) for speaking out on behalf of the second victim;
- Columnist must be one of those crazy feminists (pussy hat);
- Columnist is crossing a gender line for speaking out (jockstrap);
- Columnist hates men;
- Second alleged victim is three times divorced (sign of personal failure);
- Second alleged victim is three times bankrupt (sign of irresponsibility); and
- Second alleged victim is too poor to be believed ("Payday loan lowlife").

This example shows that credibility is such a precious social commodity that we can take for granted if we are believed because of our race, social class, and so forth.

During the surge of sexual misconduct allegations in 2017, the people denying the alleged victims' credibility often stressed the motivations of money and attention. However, it became harder to dismiss the stories from wealthy and famous actresses such as Angelina Jolie.

Academic research on the credibility of women reveals that most articles focused on sexual harassment and sexual assault. For example, rape victims sometimes have confused memories about their traumas, so their inconsistent stories may appear as lies. *Rolling Stone Magazine* had published a story of a campus rape in 2014, only to retract it because of discrepancies in the alleged victim's story. However, one expert states: "Though we may never know what happened in this particular case, it's not uncommon for trauma survivors to have very fragmented recollections and difficulty with details. . . . This can sometimes lead to an incorrect retelling of the story"[21].

Credibility was also an issue for Anita Hill, who had to testify in front of a Senate committee in 1991 about Clarence Thomas' alleged sexual harassment; one writer called her "a little bit nutty and a little bit slutty"[22]. More than one senator accused her of being a deranged erotomaniac who had obsessed and fantasized about Thomas. Senator Alan Simpson had demanded to know why she had stayed in touch him later: "Why in God's name would you ever speak to a man like that the rest of your life?"[23].

Besides sexual misconduct, some researchers have focused on the limited credibility of immigrant women. One example of discredited immigrant women appeared in the 2012 debate about the Violence Against Women Act's reauthorization. Some politicians opposed the clause protecting immigrant women who feared being deported if they reported domestic violence. What if foreign brides were coming to the States just to fake abuse and get a visa? Since foreign brides seeking protection would have to show police and medical records to prove the abuse, that scenario appeared unlikely. However, one critic stated that "We have welcomed many scam artists into our country"[24].

Another reason for women's lack of credibility is the belief that women are inherently different than (and thus inferior to) men. One comment on a men's rights activist (MRA) site reads:

> You are hating women because you have the wrong expectations for them. Don't hate someone for something they CANNOT be. Women are, by nature, manipulative, attention-seeking, inconsistent, emotional, and hypergamous. Accept this truth. Once you do, you can game women for what they are . . . not what you want them to be. [25]

It would be a relief to dismiss bloggers like him as extreme outliers who do not represent any mainstream views. However, their opinions are but the latest manifestation of the traditional view of women as manipulative and devious. Sin began in the world because of Eve talking to the serpent and tempting Adam, thus causing centuries of suffering for humankind.

- Tertullian: And do you not know that you are Eve? God's sentence hangs still over all your sex and His punishment weighs down upon you. You are the devil's gateway; you are she who first violated the forbidden tree and broke the law of God. It was you who coaxed your way around him whom the devil had not the force to attack. With what ease you shattered that image of God: Man! Because of the death you merited, even the Son of God had to die. . . . Woman, you are the gate to hell and her gaping genitals the mouth to hell. [26]

- St. Augustine: What is the difference whether it is in a wife or a mother, it is still Eve the temptress that we must beware of in any woman. . . . I fail to see what use woman can be to man, if one excludes the function of bearing children. [27]

Delilah was another evil women because she had arranged to cut off Samson's hair, a God-given source of superhuman strength that symbolized his masculinity. The evil Salome danced before the king so that she could demand the head of John the Baptist on a platter. Historical examples of devious women also abound, such as Catherine d'Medici ordering assassinations and slaughters. No wonder that through the ages, theologians have warned humanity about women.

As late as 1999, a Christian pastor (James Fowler) stated that "The Holiness of God is not evidenced in women when they are brash, brassy, boisterous, brazen, head-strong, strong-willed, loud-mouthed, overly-talkative, having to have the last word, challenging, controlling, manipulative, critical, conceited, arrogant, aggressive, assertive, strident . . . "[28].

Traditional theologians, then, have argued for centuries that women are inherently evil. Distrust of women can also arise from a bone-deep aversion to females in all aspects of life. The book title, *Too Fat, Too Slutty, Too Loud: The Rise and Reign of the Unruly Woman* (Petersen, 2017), illustrates the reactions that some people may have to celebrities who break the rules of femininity. However, Peterson reminds us that women themselves may add to the public rejection of unruly women: "[T]he imperative against unruliness might be largely created by men, but . . . it's often enforced by women, whether in the form of mothers, best friends, peers, producers, or women reproducing judgment on unruly celebrities"[29]. As we examine how society strips women of their credibility, we must also examine our own role in the silencing of women (Box 3.2).

The silencing of women, then, appears in several venues, including politics. The lack of credibility is one major hurdle to gender equality. Credibility can remain elusive for several reasons. Children often lack credibility because they are only children. Unfortunately, adults can also lack credibility because of physical appearance, voice pitch, income level, sexual history, ethnic/racial background, and accusations of greed. Fortunately, movements such as the #MeToo campaign are making progress toward giving voice to women's lives.

ACTION STEPS

- Women must fight for both their own credibility *and* the credibility of other women. No matter your gender, though, you have probably been dismissed as not credible. Consider the possible reasons that this happened (e.g., race) and how you might react differently next time it happens.
- It is likely that you have dismissed somebody as not being credible based on their clothes, accents, or some other feature that gave you a bad impression. Think about a celebrity or somebody in your life whom you

BOX 3.2

THE EMPTY BARREL COMMENT

In October 2017, General John Kelly (Trump's Chief of Staff) called an African American congressperson an "empty barrel" and refused to apologize when it was proved that he had lied. "Oh, no. No. Never. Well, I'll apologize if I need to. But for something like that, absolutely not. I stand by my comments"[37]. The story began with Representative Frederica Wilson had criticized Trump for his alleged botched phone call to a war widow. Wilson, who had been in the car with the family, heard the call on speakerphone. Trump had reportedly told them, the fallen soldier "knew what he signed up for"[38].

Trump's allies shot back at her, accusing her of being a politically motivated liar. One such critic was Kelly. Without naming her, he implied that she was a grandstander for telling people about Trump's callous words to a Gold Star family. Kelly then added that she had boasted "in a long tradition of empty barrels making the most noise" about obtaining funding for a government building. And we were stunned, stunned that she'd done it. Even for someone that is that empty a barrel, we were stunned"[39]. This statement was an obvious lie, as proved by the video evidence of the ceremony.

The "empty barrel" comment, then, stirred up debates about a possible racist undertone. One factor could be his outrageous interpretation of the Civil War that reflects the White supremacist view of slavery and the real cause of that war. In discussing the conflict between the North and South, he talked about the "men and women of good faith" who followed their consciences—but nothing about the slaves themselves. (He did not explain how a person of conscience could even condone the horrors of slavery.) To render slaves invisible in this interpretation is to dehumanize millions of persons who were deemed as property.

Indeed, he had also dehumanized Wilson when he had called her an empty barrel. Instead of treating her as a person worthy of his respect, he had characterized her as an object worthy only of contempt. Few of us know anything about the "long tradition of empty barrels," but we do know about the long tradition of oppressing slaves and other persons of color.

Besides the racist tendency to erase people of color from the pages of history and the realm of politics, Kelly also showed a disrespectful attitude toward Wilson as a woman in that interview. Why should he ever apologize to her? She is only a woman, and in the good old days people like her knew their place.

The empty barrel insult, then, is a profound example of how society tries to silence women. One of Kelly's defenders was a radio host who called Wilson a "cheap sleazy Democrat whore." Calling female politicians names like these, of course, has nothing to do with alleged sexual behavior and everything to do with opposing powerful women. Perhaps this is related to Kelly's nostalgic reference to the time when women were sacred—and not meddling in politics.

By trying to discredit Wilson as a witness to the phone call, Kelly and his allies also refuse to honor her as a congressperson. The video of the building ceremony clearly shows that Kelly had lied and has no credibility in this matter. However, the truth can have less power when it is on the side of an African American woman than a White man in a general's uniform.

Besides attacking her credibility, Kelly also tried to strip Wilson of her insider status as a Washington politician. Kelly firmly categorized her as the Other when he used the word "sacred" regarding military matters. By listening in on the President's call, this civilian had allegedly violated a moral code and intruded into a restricted place (although she had been invited to listen to the call). This woman then had the nerve to call out the Commander-in-Chief instead of acknowledging her proper place.

Wilson, then, was anything but an empty barrel, but instead was a citizen who had spent years in community building before entering Congress. With this insult, Kelly had tried to dismiss every achievement and every speech of Wilson's as completely meaningless. Another aspect of the silencing of women is the invisibility of women's accomplishments, which Kelly tried to invoke. Nobody—especially Wilson—deserves this erasure of her years of hard work.

Although it was depressing to see Kelly's attempt to dismiss Wilson as a worthless object, the good news is that she had refused to back down. The public rejection of any efforts to silence her is heartening for anybody who respects the dignity of all persons. Kelly had claimed that Wilson was a liar and the Other—but his scorn had only amplified the power of this outstanding woman.

do not respect. Consider the reasons that you do not take this person seriously and the possibility that you had misjudged the person.

Notes

1. Dearden. L. (2014). Turkish President: "Equality between men and women is against nature." The Independent. Retrieved from www.independent.co.uk/news/world/europe/turkish-president-equality-between-men-and-women-is-against-nature-9879993.html
2. Quote cited on Goodreads site. Retrieved from www.goodreads.com/work/quotes/24987300-i-am-malala-the-girl-who-stood-up-for-education-and-was-shot-by-the-tal
3. Library of Congress website. Retrieved from www.loc.gov/item/2002708975/
4. Knowles, R. (2012). Georgiana Cavendish, Duchess of Devonshire (1757–1806). Regency History blog. Retrieved from www.regencyhistory.net/2012/10/georgiana-cavendish-duchess-of.html
5. Amanda Vickery's marvelous 2015 documentary *Suffragettes Forever! The Story of Women and Power* was produced by the BBC.
6. Edwin McMasters Stanton (1814–1869). (*n.d.*). Latin Library. Retrieved from www.thelatinlibrary.com/chron/civilwarnotes/stanton.html
7. For example, here is one link: www.isthatbaloney.com/these-17-photos-prove-hillary-clinton-is-a-tired-old-woman-who-should-never-be-president-006/
8. This article lists some of the attacks on Clinton before the 2016 election: O'Malley, N. (2014). 13 Reasons why Hillary Clinton shouldn't run for US president, according to conservatives. Sydney Morning Herald. Retrieved from www.smh.com.au/world/13-reasons-why-hillary-clinton-shouldnt-run-for-us-president-according-to-conservatives-20140620-zsfzu.html
9. D'Souza, D. (2016). *Hillary's America: The secret history of the Democratic Party.* Washington, DC: Regnery, p. 3

10. D'Souza, D. (2016). *Hillary's America: The secret history of the Democratic Party.* Washington, DC: Regnery, p. 26

11. D'Souza, D. (2016). *Hillary's America: The secret history of the Democratic Party.* Washington, DC: Regnery, p. 26

12. D'Souza, D. (2016). *Hillary's America: The secret history of the Democratic Party.* Washington, DC: Regnery, p. 12

13. Patterson, T. (2016). If Clinton loses, blame the email controversy and the media. LA Times. Retrieved from www.latimes.com/opinion/op-ed/la-oe-patterson-clinton-press-negative-coverage-20160921-snap-story.html

14. Filipovic, J. (2017). The men who cost Clinton the election. New York Times. Retrieved from www.nytimes.com/2017/12/01/opinion/matt-lauer-hillary-clinton.html?action=click&pgtype=Homepage&clickSource=story-heading&module=opinion-c-col-right-region&region=opinion-c-col-right-region&WT.nav=opinion-c-col-right-region&_r=0

15. Wilbur (2017). The Charlie Rose interview of Hillary Clinton chilled me to my bones. Daily Kos. Retrieved from www.dailykos.com/stories/2017/11/29/1719688/-The-Charlie-Rose-interview-of-Hillary-Clinton-chilled-me-to-my-bones

16. Traister, R. (2017). Our national narratives are still being shaped by lecherous, powerful men. New York Magazine. Retrieved from www.thecut.com/2017/10/halperin-wieseltier-weinstein-powerful-lecherous-men.html

17. Shane, S. (2017). The fake Americans Russia created to influence the election. New York Times. Retrieved from www.nytimes.com/2017/09/07/us/politics/russia-facebook-twitter-election.html

18. New Roy Moore accuser says he groped her when she was 16. (2017). Video retrieved from www.usatoday.com/videos/news/nation/2017/11/13/new-roy-moore-accuser-says-he-groped-her-when-she-16/107660550/

19. Timpf, K. (2017). If you refuse to condemn predators because of politics, you're disgusting. National Review. Retrieved from www.nationalreview.com/2017/11/roy-moore-defenders-disgusting/

20. This comment on Timpf's article is no longer available online. It was retrieved on November 10, 2017.

21. Gregoire, C. (2014). What sexual assault does to the brain. Huffington Post. Retrieved from www.huffingtonpost.com/2014/12/10/how-the-trauma-of-sexual-_n_6294546.html

22. Carlson, M. (2001). Smearing Anita Hill: A writer confesses. Time. Retrieved from http://content.time.com/time/nation/article/0,8599,167355,00.html

23. Nguyen, T. (2016). Anita Hill really was forced to put up with these incredibly sexist comments. Vanity Fair. Retrieved from www.vanityfair.com/news/2016/04/anita-hill-sexism

24. Lithwick, D. (2012). Dahlia Lithwick: The GOP's distrust of women. Madison. Retrieved from http://host.madison.com/ct/news/opinion/column/dahlia-lithwick-the-gop-s-distrust-of-women/article_a1194f12-a132-11e1-a00b-001a4bcf887a.html

25. Terry, C. (2017). Hot off the press: Women are humans, just like men (#ThisIsHowSexismEnds Series). Good Men Project. Retrieved from https://goodmenproject.com/featured-content/hot-off-the-press-women-are-humans-just-like-men-thisishowsexismends-series-jrmk/

26. Groskop, V. (2012). Why have vaginas—which were once worshipped—become taboo? The Independent. Retrieved from www.independent.co.uk/life-style/love-sex/men-women/why-have-vaginas-which-were-once-worshipped-become-taboo-8092761.html

27. Tarico, V. (2013). Twenty vile quotes against women by church leaders from St. Augustine to Pat Robertson. Valerie Tarico blog. Retrieved from https://valerietarico.com/2013/07/01/mysogynistquoteschurchfathers/

28. Fowler, J. (1999). Women in the Church study outline. The Christian in You. Retrieved from www.christinyou.net/pages/womeninchurch.html

29. Petersen, A. H. (2017). *Too fat, too slutty, too loud: The rise and reign of the unruly woman.* New York, NY: Plume Books, p. 231.

30. FLDS Beliefs 101—"Keep sweet." (*n.d.*). Retrieved from blog post: http://flds101.blogspot.com/2008/05/flds-101-keep-sweet.html

31. Kathy as told to Jan Brown. (2007). I grew up in a polygamist family: today's Christian Woman. Retrieved from www.
todayschristianwoman.com/articles/2007/may/i-grew-up-in-
polygamist-family.html

32. FLDS Beliefs 101—"Keep sweet." (*n.d.*). Retrieved from blog
post: http://flds101.blogspot.com/2008/05/flds-101-keep-
sweet.html

33. Kristiana Miller, a Quiverfull cult survivor, was interviewed
in the documentary *Growing Up Quiverfull—The Duggar's
Destructive Cult*. Retrieved from www.youtube.com/
watch?v=9WQy4LGUQRg

34. Karen, H. (2005). "Keep sweet." Blog. Retrieved from https://
bycommonconsent.com/2005/07/29/keep-sweet/

35. Peck, E. (2017). Women must be nice to gain influence at
work, study finds. Huffington Post. Retrieved from www.
huffingtonpost.com/entry/women-work-successful-liked_us_
59837533e4b041356ebeb350?section=us_women

36. Houston, P. (2016). Five crucial things the fifty-three-year-old
bitch knows that the thirty-nine-year-old bitch didn't (yet). In
Hanauer, C. (Ed.), *The bitch is back: Older, wiser, and "getting"
happier.* New York, NY: William Morrow, pp. 3–14.

37. Rucker, P. (2017). John Kelly refuses to apologize for false
attacks on Florida congresswoman. Washington Post. Retrieved
from www.washingtonpost.com/news/post-politics/wp/2017/
10/30/john-kelly-refuses-to-apologize-for-false-attacks-on-
florida-congresswoman/?utm_term=.b9153bfc562b

38. Marris, S. (2017). Dead soldier's mother: President Trump showed
"disrespect." SkyNews. Retrieved from https://news.sky.com/story/
trump-dead-soldier-knew-what-he-signed-up-for-11086199

39. Devega, C. (2017). "Empty barrel": The real meaning of John
Kelly's slurs against Frederica Wilson. Salon. Retrieved from
www.salon.com/2017/10/24/empty-barrel-the-real-meaning-
of-john-kellys-slurs-against-frederica-wilson/

4

INTERSECTIONALITY

INTRODUCTION

In 2016, one football player started to protest against racism by not standing when the national anthem was sung. Colin Kaepernick, concerned about the police violence committed against persons of color, first stood and then knelt in silent protest. When criticized a year later by an angry president, colleagues and others decided to also "Take a Knee." The dramatic scenes of hundreds of people kneeling in solidarity with Kaepernick (either for the Black Lives Matter movement or the right to free speech) have reinforced my belief in the interconnectedness between people. "We'd better not speak against misogyny if in the same breath we're not also speaking against transphobia and homophobia and racism and classism and poverty. This is one fight. It always has been"[1].

The word "intersectionality" is popular these days, but what does it even mean? Academics define it as the matrix of domination that includes oppression (e.g., race, gender). Kimberlé Crenshaw, the legal scholar who coined the term 30 years ago, describes how a 1976 lawsuit inspired her to look at how two identities (in this case, the race and gender of African American women) could intersect and amplify discrimination. General Motors did hire women, but only Whites. The company also hired African Americans, but only men. These African American women, then, were at the crossroads of oppression that the legal system refused to acknowledge—they lost their case[2].

Since then, Crenshaw and other scholars have expanded the parameters for intersectionality to include homophobia, transphobia, classism, ableism, and other forms of discrimination. Despite advances in social justice, though, society still overlooks many groups. She writes about police violence against African American women in this context: "Intersectionality alone cannot bring invisible bodies into view. Mere words won't change the way that some people—the less-visible members of political constituencies—must continue to wait for leaders, decision-makers and others to see their struggles"[3].

This book's definition of intersectionality focuses on how different aspects of a person can be dismissed or demonized. You may have been erased by someone saying, "Oh, you're just saying that because you're a woman/Latina/Midwesterner/etc." Millennials are dismissed for being spoiled brats, while Baby Boomers are dismissed for being spoiled old-timers. Besides refusing to listen to your voice, people may demonize you for your religious preference or other attributes. Fortunately, intersectionality promotes true democracy because it "undercuts the notion that by talking about a black experience, or a latino experience, or a trans experience, or a queer experience, or a disabled experience, we are somehow being anti-democratic"[4]. Speaking out on behalf of yourself and others, besides actually listening to the stories of others, is necessary for a civic society.

Intersectionality can be a divisive concept even within the progressive community. For example, a lesbian pride parade recently refused to let a Jewish woman march with the Star of David because of Israel's conflict with the Palestinians. A Jewish activist wrote that groups "have fractured again and again over ever-narrower definitions of the true cause of oppression. Similarly, the 'my oppression is greater than your oppression' game doesn't benefit anyone or anything but the status quo. In this historical moment, we do not have the luxury of splintering in pursuit of ideological purity"[5]. This point about comparing historical traumas deserves consideration. For instance, what is the point of asking whether the trans-Atlantic slave trade was worse than the genocidal slaughter of Native Americans? Both human-made catastrophes were horrific and merit our full recognition of their impact on current politics.

The term "oppression" can provoke concerns about whether we are competing against each other in the Oppression Olympics instead of working together. The term "hierarchy of oppression" refers to the belief that one group's pain is greater than the pain of other groups. This topic reminds me of how I interact with the others in the heated pool, most of whom have severe arthritis or other health problems. The conversation usually starts this way:

> "Really? You only had two joint replacements? Well, I've had three."
>
> "I had four!" chimes in somebody else.
>
> "I also had cancer once," says the person with only two replacements.
>
> "What stage? If it was only Stage One or Two, it can't be that bad."

"I had 13 surgeries in 10 years!" cries out a triumphant voice.

"But one of them was only an arthroscopy. Come on, does that one really count as a real surgery?"

Underneath this banter, of course, is the harsh reality of excruciating pain and frustrating disabilities. Obviously, pain is pain and suffering is universal. Quantifying pain is an exercise in futility—how can we really measure it? Common sense dictates that we would not consider a paper cut to be as severe as an amputation. Most people, though, hold stories of suffering that may not be obvious. Racism is an obvious oppression—as a White woman, I have not experienced that pain. However, many people have endured other types of oppression that would enable them to find common ground with diverse groups.

Another controversial aspect of intersectionality is the term "privilege," which can evoke frustration among White males and others who feel denigrated. Some may feel that these concepts can set up walls between the "privileged" and "oppressed" as if a person could not be both. Although the term "intersectionality" represents a tool for social analysis for some, others see it as a heavy club to beat them into admitting their privilege. Hopefully, we can reclaim the term as a positive way to initiate an in-depth dialogue.

Once when I was asked to lead a group discussion about intersectionality, I looked at the White males around the table. They appeared to expect yet another lecture on their privilege. Instead, I asked them when they had ever been dismissed or discriminated against. The stories poured out: mental illness, rejections based on not being manly enough, and antagonistic responses toward their atheism.

Our discussion then flowed smoothly toward the topics of police violence and other racial injustices. Although the "intersectionality" concept seems to impose an "us versus them" concept, it is wrong to assume that White males (or anybody else) have nothing but privilege while others have only oppression in their lives.

One woman who participated in the 2017 Women's March stated it well: "I am a black woman in this country, [a] cis-gender woman. I have a disability. I am an American citizen. All of those identities have given me either historic struggle and lack of access, and some of those identities have given me privilege"[6]. This quote describes my own life experience. The word "privilege" applies to me because I am White and did not grow up poor, while my graduate degrees are another advantage. However, I had grown up in a troubled family and have struggled with health problems for decades. Like many others, then, I can feel both blessed and cursed at the same time. No matter one's ethnicity or country of origin, for example, trauma can have a profound impact on one's well-being.

TRAUMA BACKGROUND

Adverse Childhood Experience

Although trauma is listed as one of the aspects of intersectionality, researchers have paid little attention to this critical topic. The public also seems unaware of how profoundly a trauma background can affect a person's life. Just the other day, I read a Facebook post criticizing a man for stating that he did not feel privileged because he had had a rough life. I responded that intersectionality is not just about race/gender/class, but a wide range of issues.

Intersectionality applies to the long-term effects of child abuse, which can affect even the next generation. One study discusses how some abuse survivors still have trouble trusting others, while expecting yet another hurtful experience. As a result, the survivors' children can also be affected by their traumatic upbringings years later[7].

The term Adverse Childhood Experience (ACE) refers to any kind of trauma, such as the death of a parent. According to a recent article by pediatricians, a child may have a toxic stress response that could harm their health if they do not get the proper help[8]. ACEs can affect a person's job performance, whether through absenteeism or poor concentration—thus causing financial problems[9]. Another key term is polyvictimization, which refers to the multiple traumas that a child could face: nonphysical violence, sexual abuse, child abuse, and witnessing violence against parents[10].

Besides these academic studies, another way to find out about ACE is by open discussion with others. Unfortunately, ACEs are quite prevalent; in the Anda study, "More than 1 in 4 grew up with substance abuse and two-thirds had at least one ACE! More than 1 in 10 had 5 or more ACEs!"[11]. After my own discussions with some friends who also had troubled childhoods, I compiled a brief list of how we were affected.

- Feeling ugly. This may seem like a trivial matter, but it is a relentless self-torture. No matter the clothes or make-up or Botox, the feeling of looking hideous can be persistent. I usually reacted to my body dysmorphia by not even trying to look attractive. My friends and

I know on the intellectual level that we are not really ugly, but our distorted perceptions can be bone-deep. Once when I was in Poland for a class trip, my African American roommate had to deal with overt racism. She burst out, "I feel like I'm a prisoner in my own skin!" Whether caused by child mistreatment or racist attacks, the feeling of being unsafe in our own bodies is unsettling.

- Feeling like a misfit. Despite my good intentions, I can still be a social klutz at times. It took me nine years of school before I finally found acceptance by my peers. This sense of being an outsider has continued through my adult years, which is frustrating because I tried so hard to conform. Disclosing to people about my childhood is tricky. Many people associate child abuse victims with drug addiction or being hopelessly disturbed, while a few even suggested to me that I should never be a parent because I was doomed to be an abuser myself.

- Believing in one's sense of mission. Whether through art or activism, my friends and I have a drive to achieve something great because we feel special. Growing up in an unsafe setting can create a keen sensitivity to others that may even seem psychic. This survival skill, of course, helped us to sense when a parent was going to explode. Besides this "gift" is the need to prove that our lives have meaning. This may be akin to race pride, when minority populations may feel motivated to triumph over the power of racism.

One type of ACE is sexual trauma, which can lead to ongoing traumas as adults. In a recent study of homeless women in

DC who were living without children, three-fourths of them reported violence that often started in childhood. One woman "lost her virginity when she was 13. Her friend's four brothers took turns raping her, after her friend helped tie her down. . . . 'I never got over what happened. From that day on, I grew up in age but in my mind I stayed 13 years old.'" She is now in her 60s, having fought drug addiction most of her life[12].

Besides homelessness, then, those who survive an ACE may also struggle with substance abuse. The high correlation between substance abuse and ACE (e.g., 80% for opioid addiction) indicates that trauma can have a devastating effect on persons. Opioid addiction is also related to physical pain because "studies have shown that individuals who have experienced childhood trauma are more likely to report chronic pain symptoms that interfere with daily activities and are more likely to be prescribed multiple prescription medications making them more likely to seek opioids for pain relief in adulthood"[13].

Unfortunately, women are increasingly at risk for substance abuse for reasons other than ACE. "Women using an addictive substance often bridge the transition from initial use to dependence more quickly" than men because of their body size, fat levels, hormonal swings, and other physiologic differences[14]. Alcohol and street drugs, then, can magnify the impact of traumas—and increase the risk for being victimized even more.

Trauma as Adults

Besides surviving trauma as children, many women also experience trauma as adults. The link between substance abuse and incarceration is indisputable, especially with the mandatory sentencing policies promoted by the War on Drugs[15]. Because of the War on Drugs, the female prison population shot up 744% from 1985 to 2015. A Republican congressperson, Kimberly Poore Moser, writes that 80% of incarcerated women have substance abuse problems[16].

As noted before, substance abuse and trauma history are usually related. In some studies of incarcerated women, up to 90% of incarcerated women have experienced some form of violence. In the study titled, "The Sexual Abuse Pipeline to Prison: The Girls' Story," the Human Rights Project for Girls discloses how girls who were abused end up trapped in the juvenile justice system. "This report exposes the ways in which we criminalize girls—especially girls of color—who have been sexually and physically abused"[17].

Women in prison, then, are retraumatized by their incarceration. *Howling Women*, a newsletter created by a group of "incarcerated survivors of violence and severe trauma," includes poetry that reflects the common experience of trauma survivors. "We're nothing but numbers, living in your hell"[18]. As sexual abuse survivors, these women must overcome their trauma histories. This poet remembers when she was a cathedral, "and now she feels like an inside-out purse"[19].

Domestic violence (also called Intimate Partner Violence) is another, different type of prison for thousands of women. Besides the emotional impact of the trauma, physical harm can also result from this type of oppression. Annie Davis, a clinical social worker who works in the field, once survived domestic violence herself as a young woman. She considers herself not only a survivor but also somebody who has transcended to a rich new life. In her testimony to the Ohio State Senate on a mental health parity bill (which passed in 2008), she describes her experiences with posttraumatic stress disorder (PTSD):

> My journey through healing began over twenty years ago when I was taken into a Ohio Domestic Violence Shelter. . . . I learned that the mysterious symptoms I have been experiencing were those of PTSD: hives, difficulty talking, hyperventilation, inability to think clearly, loss of visions, and problems with event recall. . . .
>
> Unfortunately, I had also developed TMJ (Temporomandibular Joint Dysfunction) which resulted from gritting my teeth in anxiety. Over the years, I had difficulty with my jaw because it would click or pop when I talked. The TMJ got so bad that it became painful to open my mouth to talk or eat. Because TMJ was not a covered condition under the insurance policy, we had to pay over $50,000 to cover the bills. We had no choice to take on this financial burden so I could perform the basic functions of life. [20]

RACISM AND TRAUMA

The Angry Black Woman Stereotype

Consider the life of an African American female who plays by the rules. As a young student, she complies with the strict dress code—even the hairstyle requirements that violate her ethnic identity. She watches her fellow students of color get suspended for "talking back" at a rate far higher than for White students[21]. Nobody had ever taught her the hidden history of African American women, including the NASA mathematicians recently featured in the movie *Hidden Figures*. Then she excels in her college studies, pretending to ignore those who tell her that she only got into that school because of "affirmative action." She knows how good she is, dammit.

Through the years, she finds herself softening her voice and smiling more often than she would like. The "Angry Black woman" stereotype hovers over her as a sinister reminder of how easily she could be dismissed. "Oh, you're just saying that because you're a woman" or "Oh, you're just saying that because you're Black" can be heard in her workplace. Every morning, she has to figure out how to dress attractively but still avoid the "video ho" image. Heaven forbid if she should look too sexy.

Dating can also pose problems. White men might say, "I have a thing for Black girls" as if she were the latest craft beer[22]. On Tinder, women of color must deal with comments such as "I'd love to have sex with a black girl. I've never been with one before. You in?" In fact, one writer reported that "Out of the hundreds of conversations I've had on the app, about half of them have involved a man tokenizing me for my ethnicity"[23].

Besides dating, speaking up at work (or keeping quiet) poses its own dilemmas for a Black woman. "In addition to the ABW (Angry Black Woman) syndrome, I believe that women of color who speak up have to work harder than our white female counterparts to prove our intelligence." One attorney noted that Black women "often find themselves confronted with the unfortunate dilemma of whether to illuminate their voices at all"[24].

Unfortunately, this stereotype can also have deadly consequences for Black women. Although most media coverage focuses on the male victims of police violence, women of color are also at high risk[25]. Officers who have been socialized to accept the Angry Black Woman stereotype, for instance, may overreact by seeing a Black woman as a threat instead of a citizen who needs protection.

> This gendered process of dehumanization drives police violence against unarmed women and girls who simply question police actions, express frustration with their treatment by police, or engage in a dispute with a white person. In these interactions, criminalizing narratives eliminate the possibility that a Black woman, Indigenous woman, or woman of color can be entitled to protection, demand to be treated with dignity, stand up for a family member, or just be angry or have a bad day. Instead, controlling narratives developed in service of colonialism and white supremacy transform women of color into a caricature, an implicit threat justifying violent responses . . . white supremacy demands such complete control of Black women and women of color that it takes very little to perceive us as out of control—particularly in combination with gendered perceptions that women are always out of control. Consequently, the minute a Black woman or woman of color questions or doesn't obey commands, police respond as if they have been physically threatened. [26]

The #SayHerName campaign is one attempt to publicize this injustice. Despite the discussion about the police violence against Black men, society still overlooks the beatings and rapes of Black women by police. One study of officers who were arrested for sex-related crimes, for example, notes that more than half had committed the crimes while on duty and one-fourth of the victims were minors. Unfortunately, the lack of comprehensive data about the female victims of police violence adds to the invisibility caused by sparse media coverage. One example is that women of color are just as disproportionately affected by the stop-and-frisk searches as men of color [27] (Box 4.1).

BOX 4.1

"AN ADVOCATE BY ACCIDENT"

Deona Hooper, the founder of the Social Work Helper website, is a tech-savvy activist who has confronted both racism and sexism head-on[44]. Life events had affected her on a personal and spiritual level that motivated her to fight social injustice. My interview with her includes these highlights:

- Self-advocacy can be the catalyst for social advocacy. In Hooper's case, she had to face not only racism but also medical problems as an uninsured person. (North Carolina had rejected the Medicaid expansion under the Affordable Care Act.) With a preexisting condition that no insurance company would cover, she had to wait two years for cancer surgery. She also had to fight to get proper care for her parents. For example, doctors are less likely to prescribe pain medications to persons of color.
- "Being Black prepared me for this job." Racism has played a major role in her development as an activist. As a social worker, she had to deal with clients who refused to work with her. Even as a professional, then, she could not avoid people who tried to diminish her. "I'm always Black before I'm a woman." Her parents, though, had taught her how to "navigate the same issues with grace." She can still find it hard to avoid being dismissed as an Angry Black Woman.

- "I identified my passion" was how she described her own drive to set up her own technology company with the Social Worker Helper site. Although she has encountered resistance about her support for controversial issues such as Black Lives Matter, she has not backed down. Also, she has had trouble finding business investors because she is a Black woman in the male-dominated field of technology. "This is just another roadblock."

- "Don't let people steal your joy." She is justly proud of accomplishments. Other advice she would give to other activists is to be strategic about picking your battles: "Some barriers you fight through and some you just go another way." Although people can drain you, it is critical to find a counterbalance in today's political climate. In her case, she now has the power to reach out to others around the world. Her joy, then, is to "uplift people's voices."

Native American Women

Another overlooked population facing crisis levels of violence is Native American women. "Native women are murdered at ten times the national average, and 84 percent of Native women have experienced violence in their lifetime. In 2016, North Dakota had 125 reported cases of missing Native women . . . but numbers are likely much higher as cases are often under reported and data isn't officially collected"[28]. Caroline LaPorte, an Native Affairs advocate, notes that the lack of data about this violence is part of the problem. "The result is that Native women die without names and their tribal nations grieve without answers"[29].

In 2017, Senator Heidi Heitkamp sponsored a bill called Savanna's Act in honor of a murder victim who was eight months pregnant. Requiring the federal government to work with the tribal governments, this bill would also set up protocols for handling homicide cases. If passed, it would help parents such as Limberhand, who fought for justice for her murdered daughter. When she first reported Hanna to be missing, the police told her that she was probably out partying. " 'We were watching her baby. She was breastfeeding him and always contacted us every 4–5 hours.' " Neither the federal or tribal officials were helpful, so she "soon saw that she and her family were on their own"[30].

Native American women must also confront a rape epidemic because they are twice as likely to be sexually assaulted as other women[31]. Traditionally, the White colonizers had regarded these women as part of the land grab. Another historical dimension to the sexual violence against Native American women is forced prostitution. A century before the term "human trafficking" was coined, the Dakota tribes had to either sell their daughters for food or watch them starve to death. The women were so desperate for food that they "collected what little corn they could at the fort, often sifting through horse manure in order to find enough grain to make soup"[32]. Today, Native girls are still being sold for prostitution.

One activist, Lisa Heth, has set up the Pathfinder Shelter on the Crow Creek reservation—the same place where her Dakota ancestors had sold their daughters. By providing comprehensive services to trafficking survivors, Heth is helping her community to overcome the historical trauma. "Our ancestors did what they had to do to keep their children alive. I see now why I was so driven to create this place. The ancestors were crying out for healing. At last, we've heard them"[33].

Latinas/Latinx

Historical trauma also affects the Latinas/Latinx population[34]. As one major component of the agricultural workforce, Latinas face a high risk for sexual assault. Mala Munoz, who works in a crisis center in Los Angeles, writes about the historical legacy of colonial violence against women, a violence that was justified by the *Conquistadores* as part of their conquest. In today's society, "The survivors we work with come from many walks of life — from undocumented mothers to Chicana high school students, undocuqueer Latinxs, to indigenous child sexual abuse survivors and Central American survivors of migratory assault. It seems there is no Latinx experience completely free from sexual violence"[35].

Latina farm laborers, especially, must survive hardships that the average consumer may not know about. One activist, Suguet Lopez, goes out into the fields to talk to women when they are away from their husbands and bosses. "Despite facing gender violence at home, many of these women tell me about going to work and facing assault there too. Pesticide exposure affects their reproductive health, and they don't make enough money to afford childcare. So I look at the intersection of all these issues . . . "[36]. Lopez has raised awareness on pesticide use because the workers "suffer from headaches, vertigo, cataracts and fungi that eat away their fingernails.

They face greater risks of cancer and neurological damage, and live in fear of another exposure or medical problem"[37]. Often the workers have no protective gloves or clothing to shield them from the toxic effects of more than one billion pounds of pesticides and herbicides sprayed each year in the United States.

Central American females (mostly younger than 18 years) who migrate through Mexico to the United States must face an 80% risk of sexual assault. The assumption that the women will probably be raped has prompted them to take contraceptives before the trip to avoid pregnancy. Criminal gangs, corrupt officials, and other migrants consider these females to be fair game. Sometimes the females end up as prostitutes in Mexico, either from coercion or lack of money. One woman who was planning to migrate to the United States said, "I've heard many horrible things. I've heard a story about a Honduran girl, who was raped along the way . . . they just left her there. . . . She went back to Honduras pregnant. I've heard that they'll trap [women] . . . that they do awful things to them. They force them to sell sex." However, she was still determined to make the trek because she believed that God would protect her by sending guardian angels[38].

Researchers admit that not enough studies have focused on Latinas and sexual assault, especially as related to child sexual abuse. One study notes that "a significant proportion of these women experienced lifetime sexual victimization. Interestingly, an overwhelming number of sexually victimized women experienced more than one type of sexual victimization or other forms of interpersonal violence. . . ." Advocacy efforts, then, should focus on gender violence as part of the larger picture of Latinas' lives[39].

Wage theft and sexual harassment also harm the lives of these farm laborers. As the Southern Poverty Law Center states, "They're the backbone of our food supply. Their hands sliced the chicken breast we had for lunch. Their sweat brought the fresh tomato to our plates. Their backs bent to pick the lettuce in our salads. They are America's undocumented workers. Every single day, virtually all of us rely on their labor" because at least 60% of the farmworkers are undocumented[40].

Immigration status has become the latest weapon against undocumented workers, especially the women who do not have the resources to apply for citizenship. During the Trump administration, hundreds of pregnant women have been detained without proper medical care. One woman who had a miscarriage stated that "It's difficult [because] the food there isn't good. They don't treat you well. You can't sleep well, you can't rest. Nothing, nothing there is good. They didn't take care of me or my baby like they should have"[41].

CONCLUSION

This chapter examined only a few aspects of intersectionality, with the dominant theme of trauma history. However, one cannot discuss trauma without noting that persons can find resilience within themselves and with supportive people. The social problems related to intersectionality can seem overwhelming if we do not also appreciate the gifts of diverse groups.

Indeed, intersectionality can bring us hope if we can achieve solidarity with other social justice causes. When asked what gave him hope right now, Cedric Lawson, a civil rights activist, stated that it was "Seeing people come together in smaller communities to affect big change that ripples across the country. Whether that be Black women voters in Virginia or Alabama, or trans communities standing up and being visible . . . seeing the courage of ordinary people every day—that's what gives me hope"[42].

ACTION STEPS

- Are you living in a comfort zone where most of the people in your social circle look like you? Break out of it! First, think about how we need cultural humility— the acknowledgement that we may know so little about another culture. Then if you are cis, reach out to the trans community. If you are able-bodied, consider how you could learn more about the disabled community . . . you get the point.
- If you belong to any social justice group, brainstorm about the next steps about building bridges with related causes. One way would be to listen to others' voices, such as this writer: "As an unapologetically black, queer, and cash poor femme, I accept that I can only speak definitively on my own experiences. . . . There exists a space between the oft chanted chorus 'silence is violence!' and the realization that when we advocate for other people we usually have no idea what we're talking about"[43].

Notes

1. Capretto, L. (2017). Glennon Doyle Melton: White feminism must be intersectional, or else it is nothing. Huffington Post.

Retrieved from www.huffingtonpost.com/entry/glennon-doyle-melton-white-feminism_us_58e7f97fe4b05413bfe30f5a

2. Crenshaw, K. (2015). Why intersectionality can't wait. Washington Post. Retrieved from www.washingtonpost.com/news/in-theory/wp/2015/09/24/why-intersectionality-cant-wait/?utm_term=.1ad83172331e

3. Crenshaw, K., Ritchie, A. J., Anspach, R., Gilmer, R., & Harris, L. (2016). *Say her name: Resisting police brutality against black women.* New York, NY: Center for Intersectionality and Social Policy Studies

4. Darer, M. (2016). The recent spate of anti-"identity politics" hand-wringing is proof that we need intersectionality more than ever. Huffington Post. Retrieved from www.huffingtonpost.com/entry/the-recent-spate-of-anti-identity-politics-hand-wringing_us_5851ea52e4b0865ab9d4e910

5. Rosenbaum, J. (2017). Doing better at intersectionality. Huffington Post. Retrieved from www.huffingtonpost.com/entry/doing-better-at-intersectionality_us_5953fc66e4b0f078efd986e5

6. Gebreyes, R. (2017). This woman just nailed the importance of intersectionality at the Women's March. Huffington Post. Retrieved from www.huffingtonpost.com/entry/intersectionality-womens-march-on-washington_us_5883e2bce4b096b4a23248bb

7. Menger Leeman, J. M. (2018). Living our parents' trauma: Effects of child abuse and neglect on the next generation. (Doctoral thesis, Australian Catholic University.) Retrieved from https://doi.org/10.4226/66/5a9dbe053362a

8. Oh, D. L., Jerman, P., Marques, S. S., Koita, K., Ipsen, A., Purewal, S., & Bucci, M. (2018). Systematic review of pediatric health outcomes associated with Adverse Childhood Experiences (ACEs). *BMC pediatrics, 18*(1), 83.

9. Anda, R. (2006). The health and social impact of growing up with alcohol abuse and related adverse childhood experiences: The human and economic costs of the status quo. In *National Association for Children of Alcoholics Forum* (Vol. 19).

10. Mossige, S., & Huang, L. (2017). Poly-victimization in a Norwegian adolescent population: Prevalence, social and psychological profile, and detrimental effects. *PloS One, 12*(12), e0189637.
11. Anda, R. (2006). The health and social impact of growing up with alcohol abuse and related adverse childhood experiences: the human and economic costs of the status quo. In *National Association for Children of Alcoholics Forum* (Vol. 19), p. 2.
12. Chandler, M. A. (2018). For homeless women, violence is a pervasive part of their past and present, report shows. Washington Post. Retrieved from www.washingtonpost. com/local/social-issues/for-homeless-women-violence-is-a-pervasive-part-of-their-past-and-present-report-shows/2018/02/19/b928d74c-10e6-11e8-9065-e55346f6de81_story. html?utm_term=.bf1ecafb6d77
13. Blanch, A. (2017). Policy brief on ACES and opioid addiction. Campaign for Trauma-Informed Policy and Practice. Retrieved from http://ctipp.org/News-And-Resources/ArticleID/13/Policy-Brief-on-ACEs-and-Opioid-Addiction
14. Huelsenbeck, R. (2017). Women and addiction: A critical health issue. San Diego Union Tribune. Retrieved from www. sandiegouniontribune.com/pomerado-news/opinion/editorial/guest-column/sd-guest-women-addiction-20170608-story.html
15. Amnesty International. (*n.d.*). Women in prison: A fact sheet. Prison Policy website. Retrieved from www.prisonpolicy.org/scans/women_prison.pdf
16. Moser, K. P. (2017). Substance abuse driving explosion of women in prison. USA Today, Cincinnati edition. Retrieved from www.cincinnati.com/story/opinion/contributors/2017/07/17/substance-abuse-driving-explosion-women-prison/483977001/
17. Human Rights Project for Girls, Georgetown Center on Poverty and Inequality, & MS Foundation for Women. (*n.d.*). The sexual abuse to prison pipeline: The girls' story. Rights for girls. Retrieved from http://rights4girls.org/wp-content/

uploads/r4g/2015/02/2015_COP_sexual-abuse_layout_
web-1.pdf

18. Jenni Lyn B.'s poem, "Madness and Oppression," cited in
Howling Women. Retrieved from https://incarceratedworkers.
org/sites/default/files/resource_file/la_vista_fall_2016_news-
letter_official.pdf

19. Dominique Christiana's poem, "The Howling Woman," cited in
Howling Women. Retrieved from https://incarceratedworkers.
org/sites/default/files/resource_file/la_vista_fall_2016_
newsletter_official.pdf

20. Cited in Ukockis, G. (2016). *Women's issues for a new generation: A social work perspective.* New York, NY: Oxford
University Press, p. 145.

21. National Women's Law Center. (*n.d.*). Let her learn: A toolkit
to stop school push out for girls of color. National Women's
Law Center website. Retrieved from https://nwlc.org/re-
sources/let-her-learn-a-toolkit-to-stop-school-push-out-for-
girls-of-color/

22. Mensah, E. (2014). Say what? 9 Annoying things white men
say on dates with black women. Madame Noire. http://
madamenoire.com/451724/9-annoying-things-white-men-
say-on-dates-with-black-women/8/

23. Brinkhurst-Cuff, C. (2015). Women of color get no love on Tinder.
Vice. Retrieved from www.vice.com/en_us/article/qbx8qp/
this-is-what-its-like-to-be-a-woman-of-color-on-tinder-514

24. Tulshyan, R. (2015). Speaking up as a woman of color
at work. Forbes. Retrieved from www.forbes.com/sites/
ruchikatulshyan/2015/02/10/speaking-up-as-a-woman-of-
color-at-work/#26588f322ea3

25. Despite the lack of a database about this topic, enough stories
have emerged to indicate a trend. Source: African American
Policy Forum. (2015). *Say her name: Resisting police brutality against Black women.* Center for Intersectionality and
Policy Studies. Retrieved from https://timedotcom.files.
wordpress.com/2015/07/b28d4-aapf_smn_brief_full_singles-
compressed.pdf

26. Crenshaw, K., Ritchie, A. J., Anspach, R., Gilmer, R., & Harris,
L. (2016). *Say her name: Resisting police brutality against black*

women. New York, NY: Center for Intersectionality and Social Policy Studies, pp. 236–237.

27. Crenshaw, K. (2015). Why intersectionality can't wait. Washington Post. Retrieved from www.washingtonpost.com/news/in-theory/wp/2015/09/24/why-intersectionality-cant-wait/?utm_term=.1ad83172331e

28. Heitkamp, H. (2017). Heitkamp introduces Savanna's Act to help address crisis of missing and murdered Native women. Press release on Senate website. Retrieved from www.heitkamp.senate.gov/public/index.cfm/press-releases?ID=1096ABC3-20B4-4DFA-8C84-EE58514314B5

29. Guha, A. (2017). Will Congress do something about missing, murdered native women? Rewire. Retrieved from https://rewire.news/article/2017/10/10/will-congress-something-missing-murdered-native-women/

30. Pember, M. A. (2017). "We all know someone": Tribal community, advocates seek to honor missing and murdered Native American women. Rewire. Retrieved from https://rewire.news/article/2017/03/21/know-someone-tribal-community-advocates-seek-honor-missing-murdered-native-american-women/

31. Savanna's Act. (2017). Fact sheet on Senate website. Retrieved from www.heitkamp.senate.gov/public/_cache/files/83eccfc2-baf5-4047-92b3-f0bcc4edd787/10-5-savanna-s-act---one-pager.pdf

32. Pember, M. A. (2017). Can this South Dakota shelter heal the centuries-long trauma of Native women? The Guardian. Retrieved from www.theguardian.com/us-news/2017/sep/02/south-dakota-sex-trafficking-victims-native-women-crow-creek

33. Pember, M. A. (2017). Can this South Dakota shelter heal the centuries-long trauma of Native women? The Guardian. Retrieved from www.theguardian.com/us-news/2017/sep/02/south-dakota-sex-trafficking-victims-native-women-crow-creek

34. Latinas/Latinx: As this heading indicates, the question of what to call this population is unresolved. The term "Hispanic" usually refers to those who come from a Spanish-speaking nation,

while the term "Latino/a" focuses on the geographic origin. Now the term "Latinx" attempts to degender the "Latino/a" distinction. For purposes of this section, the term "Latinas" will be used because gender violence still affects this group of women.

35. Munoz, M. (2017). 10 Reasons why colonialism strengthened rape culture in Latinx communities. Everyday Feminism. Retrieved from http://everydayfeminism.com/2017/07/colonialism-latinx-rape-culture/

36. Guidi, R. (2017). The women confronting California's farm conditions. Retrieved from Buzzflash website: www.hcn.org/articles/letter-from-california-agriculture-the-women-confronting-californias-farm-conditions?utm_source=wcn1&utm_medium=email

37. Lopez, S. (2015). Farmworkers need better safety protection now. Sacramento Bee. Retrieved from www.sacbee.com/opinion/op-ed/soapbox/article17042996.html

38. Bonello, D., & McIntyre, E. S. (2014). Is rape the price to pay for migrant women chasing the American Dream? Splinter News. Retrieved from http://splinternews.com/is-rape-the-price-to-pay-for-migrant-women-chasing-the-1793842446

39. Cuevas, C. A., & Sabina, C. (2010). Final report: Sexual Assault Among Latinas (SALAS) Study. Retrieved from www.ncjrs.gov/pdffiles1/nij/grants/230445.pdf

40. Southern Poverty Law Center. (2010). Injustice on our plates. SPLC website. Retrieved from /www.splcenter.org/20101107/injustice-our-plates

41. Pianas, R. (2017). Two women say they lost pregnancies in immigrant detention since July. Huffington Post. Retrieved from www.huffingtonpost.com/entry/immigrant-etention-pregnancy_us_59cbaee4e4b05063fe0e211b?ncid=inblnkush pmg00000009

42. Perez, M. Z. (2018). Queer and trans activists of color speak out on the future of activism. Colorlines. Retrieved

from www.colorlines.com/content/queer-and-trans-activists-color-speak-out-future-activism

43. Befriending Becky: On the imperative of intersectional solidarity. Huffington Post. Retrieved from www.huffingtonpost.com/entry/befriending-becky-on-the-imperative-of-intersectional_us_58a339efe4b080bf74f04114?utm_source=everydayfeminism.com&utm_medium=referral&utm_campaign=pubexchange_article

44. Phone interview with Deona Hooper on October 18, 2017.

WHEN MASCULINITY

BECOMES TOXIC

INTRODUCTION

Teddy Roosevelt, a man who was determined to be as manly as possible, was proud of his son playing football as a Harvard freshman. He proclaimed in 1903 that "I believe in rough games and in rough, manly sports. I do not feel any particular sympathy for the person who gets battered about a good deal so long as it is not fatal." However, the football fields in that decade were "killing fields" as dozens of prep school and college players died from head injuries, broken necks, and internal injuries[1]. As this picture (Illustration 5.1) of Dartmouth players in 1901 indicates, helmets and other protective equipment were not used.

Then Roosevelt's son himself incurred a severe injury to his eye, which prompted the president to reconsider his position. He convened the school leaders to order changes to the game rules so that the players would not pile on each other in a dangerous melee. However, he also urged these men to avoid emasculating the sport or make it "too ladylike"[2].

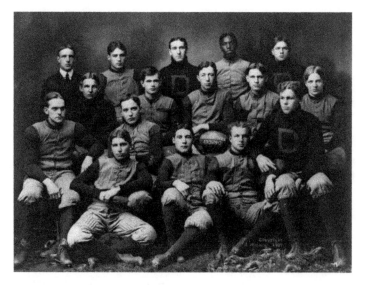

ILLUSTRATION 5.1 Dartmouth football team in 1901. Source: Library of Congress.

Today's controversy over the prevalence of repetitive head trauma (CTE—chronic traumatic encephalopathy) among football players mirrors the early history of this sport. In a recent study, 110 out of 111 brains of former NFL players showed signs of CTE. This condition causes dementia, cognitive difficulties, behavior and/or mood disorders, and other symptoms related to concussions. Although not every football player will get CTE, and new precautions have made the sport safer to play, concussions remain a troubling reality for many players[3].

Any discussion of toxic masculinity, then, is incomplete without considering its harmful impact on the males themselves. The term "toxic masculinity" became popular in the media in the mid-2010s, especially after several mass killings.

In the context of this chapter, "toxic masculinity" is defined as behaviors and attitudes of hypermasculinity that stress virility over cooperation and violence over compassion. Toxic masculinity can be toxic to women, other men, society, and the men's own health[4].

A Dartmouth professor has even taught a class linking toxic masculinity to the Orlando tragedy of 2016[5]. Connecting "gun phallocracy" with homophobia, End-Beng Lim uses the mass shooting as a symbol of toxic masculinity. The *Dartmouth Review* mocked the class because "The biggest takeaway for any student taking such a course would presumably be that masculinity, guns, and the Republican Party are waging a systematic war against queer people and Muslims . . . "[6].

The concept of toxic masculinity, then, has generated controversy that extends beyond gender issues. First, what really is "masculinity"? A recent Facebook post showed pictures of men covering their mouths with their hands to show an emotional reaction. The heading read: "Progressive males are not men; they move and gesticulate like women. The 'hand-over-mouth gesture is one example. Physically repulsive." This comment is describing "masculinity" with these criteria:

- Not being like women (i.e., "don't be a girly girl");
- Not showing too much emotion;
- Not being politically progressive; and
- Not displaying any mannerisms that could possibly be seen as gay.

Certain phrases come to mind: be a man, grow some balls, and man up. Another definition of masculinity appears in the

Combos' "American Manliest Cities" annual study that used "manly criteria like the number of home improvement stores, steak houses, pickup trucks and motorcycles per capita"[7]. A new criterion was added this year: "manly occupations (fire fighters, police officers, construction workers and EMT personnel)." Real men, then, drive motorcycles and run into burning houses to save babies. Since Combos is one of the corporate sponsors of NASCAR (National Association for Stock Car Auto Racing), it is not surprising that this product has chosen "manly men" as their niche market. Eating habits, then, are one indication of masculinity. Feirstein's 1982 satirical book, *Real Men Don't Eat Quiche: A Guidebook to All that Is Truly Masculine*, provides more proof that men should have carnivorous and voracious appetites.

These definitions of masculinity correspond with the Conformity to Masculine Norms Inventory[8]. The researchers provide 11 criteria for defining "masculinity:" desire to win, emotional control, risk-taking, violence, dominance, playboy behavior, self-reliance, primacy of work, power over women, disdain for homosexuals, and pursuit of status. Which of these criteria could be considered toxic? According to a recent meta-analysis of 78 different studies[9], a man is more likely to have negative mental health—and is less likely to seek help—if he stresses these norms. Not all norms are harmful, of course. The most harmful norms were self-reliance, playboy behavior, and power over women. Because playboy behavior and power over women are obviously sexist, the researchers conclude that "The robust association between conformity to these two norms and negative mental health-related outcomes underscores the idea that sexism is not merely a social injustice, but may also have a detrimental effect on the mental health of those who embrace such attitudes"[10].

This quote typifies a desire to win that has become toxic because the men's behavior is detrimental to themselves and others. Obsessed with winning in the stock market, the men are following a pecking order based on money. In this context, every man is a possible rival. Corruption in the stock market parallels cheating in sports games (e.g., steroid use) because winning is everything. Noncompetitive males, of course, deviate from this norm and are not seen as masculine (Box 5.1).

Masculine Norm Two: Emotional Control

When I was a child, I was told that Jackie Kennedy did not cry at her husband's funeral. This self-restraint was to be admired and imitated. To prevent being called hysterical or irrational, many women try to avoid emotional scenes at work or even at home. Men, of course, face even greater social pressure to show stern, unyielding faces. Gary Cooper in *High Noon*, for example, is the stoic hero who does the right thing without making a fuss.

Emotional control can be an important trait for thoughtful leaders who should avoid making rash decisions and for patient parents who should restrain from yelling at their kids. When working in a job that involves dealing with the public or other difficult situations, keeping one's cool is essential to remain employed.

Too much emotional control, though, can be destructive for both the person and those around them. Parents and other adults may enforce a strict behavior code on young boys about crying and other traits seen as effeminate. This can result in the inability to express any feelings, especially negative ones. One writer describes how the command to "be a

BOX 5.1

ON THE PORCH (CONVERSATION WITH TWO YOUNG MEN)

"We aren't the guys to throw the first punch."

I was sitting on the porch with two neighbors, both young men ("Bob" and "Chad") who were "chill" enough to talk to me about masculinity. Although I have plenty of male friends, they are not in their 20s or raised in this new era. (This conversation was not a research project, so my neighbors may not represent their cohort.)

Both men said that they respected women because they had been raised by single mothers. When I asked them if their fathers had been negative role models, Bob responded instantly: "Hell, yes." (Actually, he used a stronger word.) Bob had learned how to be a man from a neighbor who had a woodshop. Chad said that football coaches and friends' fathers had shaped his own masculinity. "It is imperative to have a father figure."

What did they learn from their father figures? These men "followed through. They took a stand." They rejected passive-aggressive behavior to be simply direct. Years later, Chad sat a fraternity brother down and said that he was going to teach him how to be a man. Chad mentored him to stand up for himself and not avoid conflict. If somebody said "F- you," for instance, he should reply "F- you, too." This was the only way to gain the respect of others in the frat house and on campus. Now the young man was doing well in a highly competitive office because he knows how to take a stand.

Besides earning respect, Bob and Chad discussed how violence was one aspect of their masculinity. Chad defined "justifiable violence" as self-defense and defending others. For example, somebody tried to instigate a bar fight with his friend. Another time, a guy grabbed the breasts of Chad's friend. After Chad had confronted him, the guy came back with a broken beer bottle to his face. Chad taunted him: "Do it, pussy." Fortunately, the guy backed down. "It went from defending a friend to wanting to beat the shit out of him."

Bob, a Marine veteran who had served in Iraq and Afghanistan, told the story of a subordinate who mouthed off and directly disobeyed orders. "When somebody gets out of line, it gets f-ed up." In this setting, obedience was essential to a unit's safety because somebody could even get killed without the proper discipline. "We have to trust him." So Bob took the guy behind a building to "break him into a submissive puppy." This resulted in the entire unit respecting Bob's authority more.

Handling defiance as a leader, of course, can also mean verbal aggression. At his last job as an assistant manager, Chad had to deal with an employee who was fighting with him just for the sake of it. Getting yelled at by Chad made him shape up.

Were these incidents related to the "alpha male" theme? Both men had strong opinions about this topic: "Guys who think about being alpha males too much aren't really alpha." They used the example of the Republican Party representing toxic masculinity because the politicians tried too hard to be "alpha." Bob said, "I'm not alpha, I just don't care about hierarchy." He had already proved to himself that he was a man through his military background and other life experiences.

"True alphas are not toxic. They have true strength and take care of everyone." Chad cited the example of one of his cats, who helped to socialize a feral cat and cared for a dying cat. "He can be an asshole, but he's a true alpha."

In this context, Chad's life goal is to be the "world's best husband and father one day." Right now he is in a committed relationship and helping out with his disabled mother. Working hard for his future family would be one indication of his masculinity. He related this ambition to a desire to win—"I want to win this." He noted that he felt some cultural pressure to have a successful career, "to club the deer and haul it back to the cave." However, he later said that he would not mind being a stay-at-home dad if his future wife made more money than him.

Risk-taking is another aspect of masculinity. Bob decided to join the Marine infantry instead of the other military options because he had told himself "don't be a pansy, join the Marines." For Chad, contact sports (especially football) and risky driving epitomized risk-taking in his life. He stated that "guys are more likely to get into stupid shit like fights." They both complained

about men trying to start bar fights with them because of Chad's size and Bob's Marine background.
Usually those trying to prove their manhood were
drunk. Alcohol, then, definitely increased the chances
for doing "dumb things." Chad said that "women
have fewer opportunities to do stupid stuff" at college
parties because the guys would have prevented them
from hurting themselves.

Protectiveness toward women also appeared in
their comments when asked about toxic masculinity as
related to dominance over women. "I would lose it" if
a close female friend got involved with an abuser. Bob
told of the time he beat up his future brother-in-law for
hitting his sister; they never talked about the incident
again. In discussing playboy behavior, they said that if a
guy screwed over a female friend, "it's not going to end
well." They accepted the hookup culture as "okay if the
girl is receptive." As long as the man is honest about his
intentions (i.e., no desire for a relationship), then it was
not toxic. However, both men thought that the hookup
culture was more harmful to women than men.

Besides playboy behavior, some males tried to
prove their manliness by antigay comments or even
attacks. Neither Bob nor Chad considered homophobia to be socially acceptable or common in college
now. Even in the Marines, it was deemed unacceptable
to be antigay.

If antigay sentiments may have decreased in the
new generation, the cultural pressure for a male's emotional control appears to be still strong. I had to ask Bob

and Chad, when was it okay for them to cry? They said that crying about major events would be acceptable, but not over something as minor as a breakup. If a woman posted on Facebook about being upset, for instance, her friends would advise her to "have a good cry." It would be "weird" for somebody to post that recommendation to a male. Women are allowed to show emotions when they are sober, but not men. Chad told me about a frat brother who broke up with his girlfriend: "it was one bottle of Jack Daniels a night." He would repeatedly apologize while crying, "I shouldn't cry, I should stop."

As the conversation wound down, I listened to the cicadas and reflected on the timeless themes of masculinity that still appeared in these young men's lives. Their honest reactions against homophobia and mistreatment of women, though, reassured me that our society could be moving forward through this generation. Hopefully, this conversation summary will inspire readers to have similar discussions with people who are different from them in age and in other ways. Not only did I learn a lot, but I also feel more connected to my neighbors.

man" damaged him through the years: "Taking refuge in traditional masculinity is a coping mechanism that works only so much as it deadens a man and his emotions. In its most pure state, masculinity is a hardening shell meant to protect men from the disappointments and travails of life . . ."[12]. As a "real" man, his stepfather would cry behind locked doors, determined not to show his weakness to others. The book titles, *I Don't Want to Talk About It: Overcoming the Secret Legacy of Male Depression* [13] and *Angry Men, Passive Men*[14], reinforce the concept of emotional control becoming toxic.

Because of emotional control, a male may not be able to be open about his learning problems at school, social anxiety disorder, or other embarrassing conditions. Also, a male struggling with undiagnosed depression may erupt in anger or internalize his feelings. The two choices, a raging outburst or a sullen resentment, can be dangerous to those around him. Verbal abuse, physical violence, and scapegoating others may result from too much emotional control. As one Afropunk blogger states, "It's really sad that, when we talk about manly men, so many of us automatically picture this Ike Turner type of dude who beats a woman's ass in order to assert his maleness. . . . This yet another example of why we need to normalize conversations and behavioral issues. Many sufferers don't know that they have a problem"[15].

Lastly, one tragic result of this aspect of toxic masculinity is the risk for lost chances in life. Ishiguro's haunting story in *Remains of the Day* (1989) describes a butler with such rigid control over his feelings that he is unable to connect with another person. He loses his chance to become a full human instead of merely being a loyal butler. Men who have trouble expressing their feelings may also be unable to be a fully engaged father to their children.

Masculine Norm Three: Risk-Taking

As somebody who grew up in Colorado, I used to enjoy hiking and even rock climbing. The adrenaline rush combined with the high altitude to create quite a sensation. Unfortunately, rock climbing was not a good idea for somebody with damaged knee joints who could (and did) wipe out at any time. Risk-taking, then, is beneficial only in the right circumstances.

Physical risks may include extreme sports and other thrill-seeking activities. Also, reckless driving can be fun; young male drivers usually have higher auto insurance premiums because of this type of risk-taking. Slowing down may not seem manly in the context of toxic masculinity, but it is certainly safer. Action movies that feature car chases, then, provide a vicarious experience for some viewers.

Legal risks also may be exciting for some people, who may enjoy taking drugs or stealing cars just for the excitement. People may take financial risks either on the stock market or in a casino. In 18th-century England, a man who had gambling debts that he could not pay was expected to do the manly thing and shoot himself. Fortunately, now Gamblers Anonymous and other support groups help those who cannot control their compulsive risk-taking (Box 5.2).

Masculine Norm Four: Violence

In 2017, the Air Force set up new posters on Langley Air Force Base with this quote from a 1955 manual: "Men cannot live without faith except for brief moments of anarchy or despair. Faith leads to conviction—and convictions lead to actions. It is only a man of deep convictions, a man of deep faith, who will make the sacrifices needed to save his manhood. . . ." For some mysterious reason, many women objected to this poster[16].

This anecdote illustrates how deeply masculinity is enmeshed with violence. For many Americans, of course, the US military represents morally acceptable violence.

BOX 5.2

TESTOSTERONE POISONING: MEDIA MYTH OR SCIENTIFIC REALITY?

Although the discussion of the Masculinity Norms stressed socialization as one possible cause of toxic masculinity, biology may also play a role. Do hormones and chromosomes really make a man more likely to be aggressive?

Aggression itself is a complex topic. First, researchers have created two categories of aggression: appetitive (desire for violence) and reactive (response to a negative situation). Another way to categorize aggression is the delineation between physical and relational. Females, of course, show aggressive behavior, so some studies focused on both genders[42].

In their early years, children may show "neuropsychological deficits that lead to impulsivity, poor executive control, and verbal delays, all of which makes these children more different to parent"[43]. Parents may worsen the situation by using corporal punishment or other inadequate methods. Other factors are high-crime neighborhoods and violent media images (e.g., *Grand Theft Auto* video game).

Besides neuropsychologic deficits, other possible causes of aggression include:

- Genetic factors such as serotonergic, dopaminergic, and endocrine pathways[44];

- The XYY chromosome, which has been widely disputed[45]; and
- Testosterone. Although a direct link between testosterone and violence has been hard to verify[46], some studies suggest a complicated relationship between the hormone and neural mechanisms in certain situations such as competition[47].

This quick review of scientific studies posits the intriguing question: is male aggression inevitable? One study of high-risk young males can provide us with a sense of hope. Self-compassion can reduce the rate of aggression and other troubling behaviors in the youth. In addressing toxic masculinity, then, we can emphasize the healing power of self-compassion as described in this excerpt: "Self-compassion, therefore, involves being touched by and open to one's own suffering . . . nonjudgmental understanding of one's pain, inadequacies, and failures . . . [and] self-kindness, a sense of common humanity, and mindfulness"[48].

Toxic masculinity, then, does not have to be a chronic or terminal condition. Hypermasculine men do not have to live in a gym trying for a chiseled chest, nor do they have to find themselves unable to fully love or fully accept somebody's love. Self-compassion could lead to empathy, which is the common basis for morality (i.e., the Golden Rule). Gender equality promises liberation for everybody trapped by gender roles.

The warrior archetype is willing to sacrifice himself or kill the enemy to save his community. Like police officers and other front-line workers, these men represent protection. In the movie *The Blind Side*, an African American football player finds acceptance by the White community because he represents the protector for his adopted family.

However, not all men support the military's state-sanctioned violence. One conversation I had was with a man who had been a conscientious objector (CO) during the Vietnam War brought up some striking points about toxic masculinity. During the interviews he had to undergo to achieve his CO status, the officials told him:

- "Show that you're a man."
- "You aren't a man if you object to war."
- "Do you have a girlfriend? What would you do if she were attacked? Why aren't you defending your country when it's under attack?"

This last statement parallels the famous question asked during the 1988 presidential debate when Michael Dukakis faced criticism for not supporting the death penalty. "Governor, if Kitty Dukakis were raped and murdered, would you favor an irrevocable death penalty for the killer?"[17]. A manly man, then, should be tough on crime on both the personal and political levels.

Besides the concept of protecting others, self-defense is sometimes regarded as morally justifiable violence. Often young males must face down their bullies with violence or else face censure from their peers, parents, and others. This social pressure may transform bullying victims into bullies themselves who perpetuate the violence to prove their masculinity. Bullies may receive social rewards for their be-havior[18], thus learning that violence is an effective way to control others. Fraternity hazings are another example of toxic masculinity.

Control through violence is also key to understanding men's violence against women. Violent men may demand fear-based respect from not only their wives but also their children, believing that intimidation is superior to nurturing. Also, rapists use violence, coercion, or other means in their distorted view of masculinity. This mentality appears in mass shooters such as Elliot Rodgers, who considered violence as a way to assert himself as a man—"If I can't have you girls, I will destroy you"[19].

Even animals are not safe from toxic masculinity. Dog fights, for example, involve men seeking status as "real" men through their dogs. One "dogman" states, "I expect the same thing out of my dog as I expect out of myself. A dog is only as good as his master." Because these dogs are honored only if they are willing to fight to the death, this determination symbolizes the dogman's own masculinity. A less aggressive dog, then, humiliates the owner and must be killed after the fight. "A true dogman will put a dog that quits (a cur) to sleep, instead of letting someone else have him (even as a pet)"[20].

Masculine Norm Five: Dominance

In a functional situation, leadership can be an essential com-ponent. Obviously, most organizations need structure as much as an orchestra needs a conductor. However, domi-nance can become toxic when it becomes embedded within a relationship or work setting. A man claiming power at all times might start feeling superior toward less assertive men (derided as "beta males" in the manosphere) and more assertive women or persons of color.

Dominance, though, may also entail proving one's manhood among other men. One male friend described the locker room atmosphere as an "unrelenting indoctrination" to be as masculine as possible. He stated that gang showers and other forced closeness were "intense psychological pressure" to avoid being victimized. In this setting, smaller or less muscular males were at risk for being picked on. Peer pressure, then, compelled some males to prove their machismo by beating up other guys. This comment struck a chord with me because I had been verbally bullied in school. I still cringe at the memories of how I would try to deflect the attacks onto a classmate, thus perpetuating the bullying culture.

Vin Diesel, pictured in Illustration 5.2, typifies the dominant male in his movies. During a 2016 interview with

ILLUSTRATION 5.2 Vin Diesel. Source: Shutterstock.

a Brazilian journalist, he kept on interrupting her to say things such as "God, you're so beautiful. . . . My God, she's so beautiful, man. Am I right or wrong? Look at her. How am I supposed to do this interview? Look at this woman. She's so beautiful. Talk to me, baby!" He repeatedly asked her out during the interview. His celebrity status apparently forced her to laugh it off instead of directly rejecting him[21].

The quest to become "alpha males" (i.e., the leaders of the pack who get their choice of females) is one trait of toxic masculinity. In the workplace, a dominant male might sexually harass his female employees and show disdain for those who demand respect as equals. The football culture exemplifies the "alpha male" concept, from the deified memory of Coach Woody Hayes of Ohio State who was an abusive and violent man [22] to the reports of rapes by football players and other athletes[23]. Physical intimidation, of course, is related to dominance as men "bulk up" in the gym and ask each other "how much they bench."

Besides athletics, dominance by males appears in the concepts of mansplaining (less well-informed men explaining things to better informed women), manologues (men pontificating about subjects they know little about), and manterrupting (men's propensity to interrupt women). Refusing to listen to others is an indicator of a dominant male because conversations become scenes of competition instead of communication.

One compelling example of dominance is the johns' preference for young girls they can order around like servants. By paying a pimp or brothel proprietor, a john can show off his hypermasculinity because "a man has his needs" and he has every right to fulfill them no matter the cost. The sex trade, then, remains a vital component of the playboy behavior norm as described next.

Masculine Norm Six: Playboy Behavior

Playboy behavior may range from harmless flirting to sexual addiction. Males learn quickly from the media and their peers that they not only should be heterosexual but also should have sex at an early age with several partners. Deviation from this norm can result in ridicule of sexually inexperienced men (e.g., the movie *The Forty-Year-Old Virgin*) and men who are faithful to their girlfriends/wives. Manly men should want sex all the time, no matter the consequences.

This social expectation of virility is related to "locker room talk," which became a controversial topic during the 2016 presidential campaign. After the tape of Trump boasting about "grabbing them by the pussy" became public and he dismissed it as mere locker talk, I had to ask my male friends whether men really talk about women like that in private. One man mentioned that somebody might brag about women thinking he was hot, but it would be humiliating to admit that he had to force an encounter. Several professional athletes also expressed their outrage about Trump's statement being considered locker room talk. Kendall Marshall, for example, tweeted: "PSA: sexual advances without consent is NOT locker room talk"[24]. Another article titled "Here's What Really Happens in Men's Locker Rooms" states that "it's rare to hear any conversation in a men's locker room and even rarer to hear interesting ones. I heard a guy proudly proclaim to his friends, 'I cheated on my wife!' once. I took their non-responsiveness as embarrassment for him"[25].

One male friend told me that young males may talk about women's body parts but that marriage usually means it is "time to shape up." Although it may be the norm for men to objectify women when they are immature, then, older men may be less likely to condone this behavior. At what age does a stud who "checks out" women become simply a dirty old man who leers at women?

The toxic aspects of playboy behavior also include an addiction to pornography that can escalate into predatory and even violent actions. (Technically, the term "compulsive use of pornography" is more accurate but is less widely used.) Pornography addiction has emerged as a major issue for many men and their partners. The article "Quiz: Are You Addicted to Porn?" in the *Men's Fitness* magazine includes this question: "Have you found that you need more and more porn, or that you have to visit increasingly hardcore sites to get the same buzz?"[26]. This question correlates with a therapist's comment in a medical article about porn addiction: "Most of the addicts will say, well, here's the stuff I would never look at, it's so disgusting I would never look at it, whatever that is—sex with kids, sex with animals, sex involving feces. At some point they often cross over"[27].

Crossing over may also involve behaviors related to sex addiction, such as voyeurism and exhibitionism. Sex addiction is one cause of destructive actions such as sexual assault and paying for sex. Mental health experts who do not agree with the term "sex addiction" may prefer to use the term "hypersexualized"[28], but the result is the same: troubled persons whose craving for the endorphin release hurts themselves and others.

Masculine Norm Seven: Self-Reliance

Any mature person must have a degree of self-reliance to achieve their autonomy. When self-reliance is part of a healthy growth experience, a person takes responsibility for their life decisions: school, work, and finances. This independence may later transform into interdependence—learning how to help others and how to ask for help.

The masculine norm of self-reliance, though, rejects the concept of interdependence. Real men do not ask for help. Related to the norm of emotional control, the self-reliant man is like a cowboy who spends weeks by himself on the range. He shoots rattlers and wolves; he bandages his own wounds without wincing.

As a result, loneliness can result from too much self-reliance. Men usually have fewer friends than women, and often their partners are their major emotional support[29]. Divorce and widowhood can increase the risk for early death unless a man learns to seek social connections.

Masculine Norm Eight: Primacy of Work

For some adults, making work their primary focus can be a beneficial decision. Entrepreneurs, professionals, and doctors may need to concentrate on their careers over other priorities. However, other aspects of life (e.g., family and health) also deserve consideration.

Besides the healthy desire to accomplish a career goal, many men may feel the need to provide for their families. Financial security, as symbolized by a house in the suburbs or a college savings account, provides satisfaction for the male provider because it is proof of his masculinity.

The primacy of work, though, can become a toxic trait if it develops into a man who loses his identity in his job. A father may become too busy to see his kids. Harry Chapin's haunting song "Cat's in the Cradle" includes these lyrics about endless broken promises after his son repeatedly asks: "When you comin' home dad?"[30]. The term "workaholic" has become a popular concept that became the title of a comedy show, but the effects of overwork can cause long-lasting damage[31].

After a man who is too invested in his career is laid off or retires, he may become a hollow shell. For example, Faludi (1999) describes how she visited a man who had been laid off from a well-paying job and later lost his wife. "That he was no longer able to do so (pay for the house) was a matter of vast, unspeakable shame. 'There is no way you can feel like a man. You can't. It's the fact that I'm not capable of supporting my family. . . . I. Feel. I. Have. Been. Castrated' "[32].

Masculine Norm Nine: Power over Women

This norm, exemplified by the "Father knows best" ideal, may connote a benevolent patriarchy. Chivalry is one aspect of this dominance, such as paying for a date's dinner. The social reward of being an "alpha male" is the assurance of not being "pussy whipped."

However, "power over women" also connotes an implicit threat to women who do not obey the dominant male. Dominance over women is related to the sex trade, putdowns of women at work (including sexual harassment), and the "boys will be boys" excuse. One man told me of how his boss ordered an attractive young female employee to flirt with a maintenance man so that he would help them. Strip clubs also emphasize a female's appearance and a man's right to judge her, usually on a 1–10 scale.

Masculine Norm Ten: Disdain for Homosexuals

The history of homophobia is a long and disturbing one, and it is tragic that even today the LGBT+ community feels threatened by violence. Many social scientists have linked masculinity with homophobia, including Kimmel (2004). The subtitle of his article, "Fear, Shame, and Silence in the Construction of Gender Identity" indicates the painful dynamic of men trying to prove their manhood by attacking a "less manly" male. "Masculinity must be proved, and no sooner is it proved that it is again questioned and must be proved again—constant, relentless, unachievable . . ."[33].

Proving one's manhood among other men, then, emerges as one cause of homophobia. Kimmel's point corresponds with a discussion I had with some male friends. One disclosed that he had been beaten up a lot in school because everyone considered him gay. Across the table, another man shared that he had been a jerk in high school and was one of those guys who picked on others. He said he "felt bad about it now." This was a painful moment because even after all the years had passed, the impact of school-aged homophobia can still affect us. The pressure to "man up" may be subtler for grown men than for young boys, but it can still have the power to wound.

The term "homohysteria" refers to the fear of males being called homosexual[34]. In a broader sense, though, the young people's use of the words "fag" and "gay" involves complex layers of meaning. In the book, *Dude, You're a Fag*, Pascoe

(2011) describes a high school culture in which the word "fag" does not necessarily mean homosexual but incompetent and thus unmanly. "[He] emphasized that this insult (faggot) literally reduced a boy to nothing. 'To call someone gay or fag is like the lowest thing you can call someone. Because that's like saying you're nothing' " [35]. Boys use jokes and other methods to monitor themselves and their peers' behavior to avoid the ultimate insult.

Obviously, the impact of homophobia can be crushing—the rate of suicide among LGBT+ youth is twice the national average[36]. Fortunately, thousands of schools around the world have promoted Gay-Straight Alliances to counteract homophobic bullying. One study of California schools indicates that Gay-Straight Alliances have reduced the feelings of hopelessness among LGBT+ youth, thus reducing the rate of suicide attempts[37].

Another promising sign appears in the shift in social attitudes. The widespread acceptance of same-sex marriage, the positive portrayals of LGBT+ characters on TV shows such as *Modern Family*, and the open discussion of once-taboo topics such as transgender persons have promoted a higher level of tolerance. For instance, a recent British study of an average high school discusses how using "gay" slurs is now seen as immature and frowned on. The older students usually tell the newcomer that "it is not on" and "it's just not acceptable any more" to use such terms in their school[38].

Masculine Norm Eleven: Pursuit of Status

Like the desire to win, the pursuit of status can have a positive side. Some climb up the corporate ladder or academic hierarchy to achieve personal success. Others join country clubs or use money as a benchmark of success. One reason that I made so many sacrifices for my PhD was that I wanted status in the community—I wanted to be taken more seriously than somebody with "only" a Master's degree.

Belittling others in a political campaign or in the workplace, though, is one toxic version of this trait. Ruthlessness and cruelty can also result if the pursuit of status intensifies, especially if a person starts believing in their own superiority. In the TV series *House of Cards*, the protagonist feels slighted by the new president so he seeks his revenge. Failure, then, can become the catalyst for self-harm or harm to others.

ACTION STEPS

Toxic masculinity does not have to be a chronic or terminal condition. Hypermasculine men do not have to live in a gym trying for a chiseled chest, nor do they have to find themselves unable to fully love or fully accept somebody's love. Gender equality promises liberation for everybody trapped by gender roles. Below are some suggestions for promoting healthy masculinity.

- Let little boys (and all males) cry. In 2017, the social media shared the story of a mother who comforted her son during a ball game. Jamie Primak Sullivan's eight-year-old son had been hit in the face with a ball. She raced to him on the field and "wrapped her arms around Max and he sobbed into her shoulder at the pain. A stranger quickly interrupted this moment between mother and son when he approached and said,

'You need to stop babying that kid.'" Later the mother posted on Facebook: "This notion that boys can never hurt, that they can never feel, is so damaging to them long term. The belief that any signs or gestures of affection will somehow decrease their manhood—this pressure to always 'man up' follows them into adulthood where they struggle to fully experience the broad scope of love and affection. The only emotion they healthily learn to express is happiness and then we wonder why they are always chasing it. They're taught that sadness is weakness, that talking about their fears or short comings makes them less than. They don't mourn properly. The struggle to grieve. They're afraid to cry. It all spills into the way they husband and father and I hate it. Love is a verb. It is something you do. It is not the same as babying, coddling or spoiling. It is something my son deserves. I will always love him when he is hurting and my prayer for him is that he is always open to receiving love so he can love in return and keep that cycle going"[39].

- Encourage self-compassion for young males. One study of high-risk young males can provide us with a sense of hope[40]. Self-compassion can reduce the rate of aggression and other troubling behaviors in the youth. In addressing toxic masculinity, then, we can emphasize the healing power of self-compassion as described in this excerpt: "Self-compassion, therefore, involves being touched by and open to one's own suffering . . . nonjudgmental understanding of one's pain, inadequacies, and failures . . . [and] self-kindness, a sense of common humanity, and mindfulness"[41].

Notes

1. Klein, C. (2012). How Teddy Roosevelt saved football. History Channel website. Retrieved from www.history.com/news/how-teddy-roosevelt-saved-football
2. Klein, C. (2012). How Teddy Roosevelt saved football. History Channel website. Retrieved from www.history.com/news/how-teddy-roosevelt-saved-football
3. Sifferlin, A. (2017). Degenerative brain disease found in 87 percent of former football players: Study. Tim. Retrieved from http://time.com/4871597/degenerative-brain-disease-cte-football/
4. One example of research is in this article: Raghavan, S. (2017). 6 Ways in which toxic masculinity destroys men's health. The Health Site. Retrieved from www.thehealthsite.com/diseases-conditions/cancer/ways-in-which-toxic-masculinity-destroys-mens-health-k1117/
5. Syllabus is available on https://bullybloggers.wordpress.com/2016/06/24/the-orlando-syllabus/
6. Farkas, S. (2016). #Orlando syllabus: Blame it on phallogocentrism. *The Dartmouth Review*. Retrieved from www.dartreview.com/orlando-syllabus-blame-it-on-phallogocentrism
7. Article retrieved from www.bestplaces.net/docs/studies/americas_manliest_cities.aspx
8. Mahalik, J. R., Locke, B. D., Ludlow, L. H., Diemer, M. A., Scott, R. P., Gottfried, M., & Freitas, G. (2003). Development of the Conformity to Masculine Norms Inventory. *Psychology of Men & Masculinity*, 4, 3–25. http://dx.doi.org/10.1037/1524-9220.4.1.3
9. Wong, Y. J., Ho, M.-H. R., Wang, S.-Y., & Miller, I. S. K. (2016, November 21). Meta-analyses of the relationship between conformity to masculine norms and mental health-related outcomes. *Journal of Counseling Psychology*. Advance online publication. http://dx.doi.org/10.1037/cou0000176
10. Wong, Y. J., Ho, M.-H. R., Wang, S.-Y., & Miller, I. S. K. (2016, November 21). Meta-analyses of the relationship between conformity to masculine norms and mental health-related outcomes. *Journal of Counseling Psychology*. Advance online publication. http://dx.doi.org/10.1037/cou0000176

11. Quote retrieved from the Independent Movie Base website: www.imdb.com/title/tt0993846/quotes
12. Sexton, .Y. (2016). Donald Trump's toxic masculinity. Article retrieved from New York Times website: www.nytimes.com/2016/10/13/opinion/donald-trumps-toxic-masculinity.html
13. Real, T. (1998). *I don't want to talk about it: Overcoming the secret legacy of male depression.* New York, NY: Scribner.
14. Allen, M. (1994). *Angry men, passive men: Understanding the roots of men's anger and how to overcome it.* New York, NY: Ballentine Books.
15. Lynette, N. (*n.d.*). Men have the right to be vulnerable: Toxic masculinity hurts everyone involved. Article retrieved from www.afropunk.com/profiles/blogs/men-have-the-right-to-be-vulnerable-toxic-masculinity-hurts.
16. Starnes, T. (2017). Faith-based posters removed from Langley Air Force Base display after feminist uproar. Fox News. Retrieved from www.foxnews.com/opinion/2017/02/28/faith-based-posters-removed-from-langley-air-force-base-display-after-feminist-uproar.html
17. McNulty, T. (1988). "Outrageous" debate question Angers Kitty Dukakis. Article retrieved from Chicago Tribune website: http://articles.chicagotribune.com/1988-10-15/news/8802070550_1_kitty-dukakis-mrs-dukakis-death-penalty
18. Why is bullying difficult to change? (2009). Education. Retrieved from www.education.com/reference/article/bullying-difficult-to-change/
19. Quote from his manifesto before he shot up a sorority house, cited in Raphael, D. (2016). Talking toxic masculinity. Article retrieved from www.dukechronicle/article/2016/10/talking-toxic-masculinity
20. Evans, R., Gauthier, D. K., & Forsyth, C. (1988). Dogfighting: Symbolic expression and validation of masculinity. *Sex Roles, 39,* 11–12, 825–838.
21. Brucculieri, J. (2016). Vin Diesel can't stop hitting on Brazilian journalist during cringeworthy interview. Retrieved from fwww.huffingtonpost.com/entry/vin-diesel-awkward-interview_us_585c22dae4b0d9a594579198

22. Bennett, B. (2013). Woody Hayes' last game coaching. Article retrieved from ESPN website: www.espn.com/college-football/bowls13/story/_/id/10215217/the-punch-ended-woody-hayes-career
23. For example, see the article: New Baylor lawsuit alleges 52 rapes by football players in 4 years, "Show 'em a good time culture." Retrieved from www.dallasnews.com.
24. Blau, M. (2016). Not "locker room" talk: Athletes push back against Trump's remark. Article retrieved from CNN website: www.cnn.com/2016/10/10/politics/locker-room-talk-athletes-respond-trnd/index.htm
25. Juzwiak, R. (2017). Here's what really happens in men's locker rooms. Retrieved from Jezebel website: http://jezebel.com/heres-what-really-happens-in-mens-locker-rooms-1793089713
26. Retrieved from www.mensfitness.com/women/sex-tips/quiz-are-you-addicted-to-porn
27. Article retrieved from www.webmd.com/men/features/is-pornography-addictive#1.
28. Lin, D. (2016). Sex addiction: Myth or reality. *European Psychiatry, 33*, S740–S741
29. Bingham, J. (2015). 2.5 Million men "have no close friends." The Telegraph. Retrieved from www.telegraph.co.uk/men/active/mens-health/11996473/2.5-million-men-have-no-close-friends.html
30. Lyrics retrieved from www.lyricsdepot.com
31. Killinger, B. (2013). The workaholic breakdown: The loss of health. Psychology Today. Retrieved from www.psychologytoday.com/us/blog/the-workaholics/201304/the-workaholic-breakdown-the-loss-health
32. Faludi, S. (1999). *Stiffed: The betrayal of the American man.* New York, NY: Harper Collins, p. 65.
33. Kimmel, M. S. (2004). Masculinity as homophobia: Fear, shame, and silence in the construction of gender identity. *Race, class, and gender in the United States: An integrated study*, p. 83.
34. McCormack, M., & Anderson, E. (2014). The influence of declining homophobia on men's gender in the United States: An

argument for the study of homohysteria. *Sex Roles, 71*(3-4), 109–120.

35. Pascoe, C. J. (2011). *Dude, you're a fag*. Berkeley: University of California Press, p. 55.
36. Centers for Disease Control and Prevention. (*n.d.*). Lesbian, gay, bisexual, and transgender health. Article retrieved from www.cdc.gov/lgbthealth/youth.htm
37. Davis, B., Stafford, M. B. R., & Pullig, C. (2014). How Gay-Straight Alliance groups mitigate the relationship between gay-bias victimization and adolescent suicide attempts. *Journal of the American Academy of Child & Adolescent Psychiatry, 53*(12), 1271–1278.
38. McCormack, M., & Anderson, E. (2010). "It's just not acceptable any more": The erosion of homophobia and the softening of masculinity at an English sixth form. *Sociology, 44*(5), 843–859.
39. Facebook quote retrieved from www.facebook.com/jaimeprimaksullivan/posts/1435398609826319
40. Neff, K. D. (2016). Self-compassion. *Mindfulness in Positive Psychology: The Science of Meditation and Wellbeing*, 37–50.
41. Barry, C. T., Loflin, D. C., & Doucette, H. (2015). Adolescent self-compassion: Associations with narcissism, self-esteem, aggression, and internalizing symptoms in at-risk males. *Personality and Individual Differences, 77*, 118–123
42. Lansford, J. E. (2016). Development of aggression in males and females. In Bushman, B. J., ed., *Aggression and violence: A social psychological perspective*. New York, NY: Rutledge, p. 61.
43. Weierstall, R., & Elbert, T. (2011). The Appetitive Aggression Scale: Development of an instrument for the assessment of human's attraction to violence. *European Journal of Psychotraumatology, 2*, 6345.
44. Waltes, R., Chiocchetti, A. G., & Freitag, C. M. (2016). The neurobiological basis of human aggression: A review on genetic and epigenetic mechanisms. *American Journal of Medical Genetics, 171B*, 650–675.
45. Raine, A. (2013). *The anatomy of violence: The biological roots of crime*. New York, NY: Vintage Trade.

46. Book, A. S., Starzyk, K. B., & Quinsey, V. L. (2001). The relationship between testosterone and aggression: A meta-analysis. *Aggression and Violent Behavior, 6*(6), 579–599.
47. Carré, J. M., & Olmstead, N. A. (2015). Social neuroendocrinology of human aggression: Examining the role of competition-induced testosterone dynamics. *Neuroscience, 286*, 171–186.
48. Barry, C. T., Loflin, D. C., & Doucette, H. (2015). Adolescent self-compassion: Associations with narcissism, self-esteem, aggression, and internalizing symptoms in at-risk males. *Personality and Individual Differences, 77*, 118–123.

6

WHEN A CULTURE IS

EMBEDDED WITH RAPE

INTRODUCTION

This chapter is not about rape, but instead is about how our culture condones and even encourages rape. As a writer, I took some time deciding on this title because the term "rape culture" can evoke reactions about rape that overshadow the actual topic. Rape/sexual assault is such a horrific crime that we may say to ourselves, "Only a monster could do such a thing." We may even picture a slobbering subhuman hiding behind a dark bush. Beyond the individual pathology of an attacker, though, is the social context. For example, an article about sex robots describes the new generation of sex dolls that are computerized to interact with humans. They enable the owners (mainly males who purchase female dolls) to regard "women as toys, women as objects for men to play with. By making these robots as realistic as possible—from self-warming models to those that speak and suck, from some with a pulse to others that flirt with their owners—their creators are selling far more than an inanimate sex aid"[1]. That was not creepy enough, though. Child sex robots are for sale, as are "Frigid Farrah" dolls that do not want to have sex so that men can simulate a rape.

The core of rape culture, then, is the dehumanization of females. If they are even visible, they are merely objects deserving of harsh treatment. A parallel would be the hate speech against Muslims, which dehumanizes and even demonizes the Other. Although not everyone who hears "every Muslim is a terrorist" will attack a Muslim, this connection between a hate-filled culture and a hate crime cannot be denied.

What is a culture? This definition is helpful: "The entire way of life of a group of people (including both material and symbolic elements) that acts as a lens through which one views the world and is passed from one generation to the next"[2]. Any culture, then, acts as a lens for our worldview. Gamers, vegans, Harry Potter fans, corporations, and churches all have their own distinct cultures. I can choose to avoid gamer culture by ignoring technology, and I can eat a hamburger in rejection of vegan culture. However, I simply cannot ignore rape culture because it is so pervasive.

"Rape culture" can be defined as "a society or environment whose prevailing social attitudes have the effect of normalizing or trivializing sexual assault and abuse"[3]. The first time I heard the term "rape culture," it was applied to street harassment, and that made no sense to me. I had been harassed countless times through the years, but I did not see any connection to the horrifying trauma of rape. Obviously, a guy who whistles or even shouts an obscene word to a female passerby is not necessarily a rapist. Now I realize that he is participating in rape culture by affirming its values of objectifying women and humiliating them because he can.

What created the lens for my own worldview regarding rape? As a child, I was socialized to regard rape as just a cultural behavior that sometimes should not be judged. The lesson I absorbed from the story of Abraham impregnating his servant/slave girl was that she had no say in the matter. Whatever her wishes, she had to submit her body to Abraham and God. In another story from the Holy Book, Moses told his men to rape the captive Midianite virgins (Numbers 31:15–54). The *Iliad* also encourages rape in its portrayal of Briseis, the war captive who is fought over by Achilles and Agamemnon. Though a "culture" deserves respect in most cases, we need to include critical thinking in our cultural relativism. The first step, of course, is to analyze our own culture that promotes rape in art, male dominance, and slut-shaming.

RAPE IN ART

This sculpture by Giambologna, the *Kidnapping of the Sabine Women*, exemplifies some key aspects of rape culture (Illustration 6.1). According to the Roman historian Livy, the ancient Romans needed wives, so they looked toward the neighboring Sabines. However, the Sabines would not allow the mingling of tribes because they feared the dominance of the Romans. Livy writes of the festival held by the Romans and attended by the Sabines. Livy insists that the women were allowed the choice to marry the Romans, but of course we will never know what really happened[4].

What we do know is that artists have been inspired for centuries by the *Rape of the Sabine Women* (a term more commonly used for this legend than "Kidnapping"). The

ILLUSTRATION 6.1 *The Rape of the Sabine Women* by Giambologna.
Source: Shutterstock.

sculpture shows a dominant male holding a woman who is protesting. And be sure to note the man underneath the abductor's feet; the scene is about conquest with a dash of titillation. Artists and writers have consistently honored the "heroism" of the Romans who seized what they needed for their tribe. This manly Roman displays strong muscles as he holds his captive and kicks down the loser.

According to the legend, the Sabine women later interceded in a battle between the Romans and Sabines. The women had accepted their fate. This incident corresponds with the cultural ideal that women may resist having sex at first, though they actually want it. To offer a contemporary example, Robin Thicke's controversial song "Blurred Lines" addresses a "good girl" when he sings, "you know you want it"[5]. An older example of this ideal is the famous scene from *Gone with the Wind* when Rhett Butler picks up Scarlett and carries her upstairs to rape her. On the staircase that night she had beaten him with her fists as he grabbed her, but in bed the next morning she is smiling with sweet content.

Another cultural ideal is the man's right to abduct/rape any female he chooses. Allegedly, a man has carnal desires (as represented by the sculpture's praise of male virility) that he cannot control. "A man has his needs" is one justification for rape. Sex and power become as hopelessly entangled as the bodies of the three people depicted in Giambologna's sculpture. The modern concept of "consent" as the dividing line between regular sex and criminal behavior has no place in this scenario. Instead, the artist seems to regard the abduction as a natural and even beneficial event.

Society is still struggling to define "rape" and "rape culture." It can mean brute force, psychological pressure, and/or reluctant submission. We have developed the concept of consent and then advanced from the "no means no" motto to "yes means yes." Many prefer the "yes means yes" motto because just saying "well, okay" should not be enough.

Another artistic depiction of rape, Degas' painting of *The Rape of the Sabines*, shows rape in a social/cultural context[6]. The scene is one of ugly disorder, with Roman soldiers manhandling the female victims in the public square. This turbulent scene shows the chaos inherent in any sexual assault. There is nothing sexy about sexual assault in this picture, which contrasts to the Giambologna sculpture's depiction of a lusty man and a pretty woman. The attack on the

Sabines is an attack on order itself. An official building in the background is darkened, while the Roman commander stands above the crowd.

In discussing rape culture, then, the word "rapacious" comes to mind. According to the *Oxford English Dictionary*, the words "rape" and "rapacious" come from the Latin word "rapere," which means to "seize"—originally, seizing property. The definition of "rapacious" is "aggressive greedy or grasping" with the synonyms of "voracious" and "predatory"[7]. In 2016, a leaked audiotape featured a celebrity claiming that he had the right to harass women because of his status, even to the point that he could "grab them by the pussy"[8]. The words "grab" and "rapacious" are interconnected. In Degas' painting, the Roman commander's red robe signifies his dominance as he presides over the rapes. Obviously, this arrogant man is claiming the right to seize any property or female. Compare him to a modern man in a business suit (a symbol of power like the red robe) who claims the right to grab women.

The painting also shows that nobody is restraining the use of power by the Romans. The Sabine men cannot protect their women. In today's America, sexual assault victims are often afraid to come forward because they could be called liars and sluts. Well-meaning police officers and prosecutors sometimes fail to protect the victims because of the vicious backlash.

Who is the victim here? A modern person would automatically reply that it is the women because they are going to be raped. However, the original definition of rape derived from the idea of property theft. Susan Brownmiller's classic book, *Against Our Will: Men, Women and Rape*, describes how women were the property of their husbands or fathers.

If a rapacious man stole a female (or her chastity), then the true victim was the husband or father. This would be similar to the outrage felt by a car owner who just got their car stolen. The Bible and other ancient documents record how the male victims should be financially compensated by the rapist[9].

Rape culture, then, is inherently a male-centered ideology. Females (both girls and women) are secondary or even tertiary concerns in the property dispute. Men dominate this painting because they are both the perpetrators and victims.

Unfortunately, modern artists continue to portray rape as a desirable action. *Last Tango in Paris* told the story a soul-dead man who had rough sex with a young woman to recover from his sadness. Marlon Brando was praised for his performance. Both he and the director were nominated for Oscars.

Recent news coverage reveals that the movie actually included an on-screen rape scene (forced anal sex with butter) that the actress had never agreed to or even expected[10]. Only the actor and director knew what was going to happen. The actress, Maria Schneider, had said she felt "raped" by this surprise attack, but few listened to her. This unknown 19-year-old actress had no power to protest her violation. She went through emotional problems because of this movie.

Years later, the director's frank admission of this rape has received publicity. Even though I never saw the movie and never will, I feel sick about this rape. Like *Deep Throat*, the movie shows a woman being brutalized on screen, and people are clapping. The narrative should instead relate the story of a young woman stumbling into a destructive relationship with a man who rapes her. She deserves respect for having survived this ordeal, and the men who participated in the rape deserve to be forever shamed for this unpunished crime.

Forty years after the *Last Tango in Paris* movie, rape has emerged as an entertainment staple in the popular shows and movies about victimized women. In *Rosemary's Baby*, the heroine is raped by the devil after being drugged by Satanists. Television shows continue the trend of presenting stories about women being raped, tortured, beaten, imprisoned, humiliated, and/or murdered[11]. Once a taboo topic, rape has become an essential feature of so many plots that it seems impossible to imagine our popular culture without this theme.

MALE DOMINANCE

Medieval Myths and Male Fantasy

In medieval Europe, a feudal lord allegedly had the right to deflower a peasant bride on her wedding night. The "right of the first night" (also called the *droit de cuissage*) did not really exist as a historical reality, but the myth lives on (4). Another disproven "fact" about the Middle Ages is the chastity belt. Lords allegedly locked up their wives' lower parts in an iron girdle that had only one key, thus creating a logistical nightmare for the wives' sanitation. The lords supposedly left for years to fight in the Crusades or other wars, content in the knowledge that their wives would have to be faithful[12].

Why do these myths persist? Alain Boureau, the historian who debunks the "first night" myth, writes that "The sexual content of the *droit de cuissage* has obviously done much to keep it in memory. The custom fascinates for its total otherness; it feeds the fantasy of an institutional, even juridicial, consent to violence"[13]. Also, modern people prefer to feel superior to primitive medieval folk. These myths continue to resonate on an unconscious level, an indication that rape culture still affects us.

First, the feudal lords represent arbitrary and absolute power. Like the Roman overseeing the rape of the Sabines, they symbolize hierarchical dominance. Today, some billionaires and other alpha males claim this power as if it were desirable instead of destructive. Another aspect of their control is evident in the beauty pageants and modeling industry, which resemble the fantasy of a lord deciding on which bride to "honor" with his attention. Some would consider this manifestation of power to be harmless because the female winners are rewarded, but others would call it benevolent sexism.

A second point is the fetishization of women's private parts, either their virginal purity or marital chastity. The disturbing idea of a feudal lord instead of the lower-born husband being the one to deflower a virgin reinforces the concept of a woman's sexuality as a commodity. The lord would not want her on the second night because her social value would already be diminished as "used goods." This theme continues today in the abstinence-only sex education classes, which sometimes compare a nonvirgin girl to a used piece of chewing gum[14].

Married women who were not "faithful" (including rape victims) also suffered from this form of male dominance. In the 1990s, the Bosnian ethnic cleansing (i.e., genocide) included the strategy of mass rapes because wives were often rejected later by their traditional-minded husbands.

One key aspect of the mythical chastity belt, then, is the psychological damage done to women and girls who did not (or could not) conform to the sexual mores of their community. Today's purity culture movement continues to belittle females who do not "save" themselves for marriage, thus stigmatizing them[15]. This movement wants to revive the "good old days" before the sexual revolution, when teens were taught that only "cheap" girls do not put the brakes on a boyfriend's sexual urges. One decades-old manual states that "The 'fast' girl who kissed and petted would be 'shopworn and shoddy with a low value sign on her before she ever wakes up to the fact that life gave her an extra measure of good thing'"[16]. In fact, once a newlywed couple discussed how she had refused to have premarital sex with him. He told her that if she had consented, he "would never have married her"[17].

Dianna E. Anderson, a Christian activist, describes the impact of making a purity pledge at the age of 14 in front of her church congregation. "We've been told a lie that our worth lies in what we do (or don't do) with our genitals. According to the proponents of Christian purity, we are 'damaged goods.' We are afraid to own our physicality. We do not know our own bodies and therefore, we do not truly know ourselves. We are afraid to express ourselves sexually. We do not have language to talk about the nuances of existing as a sexual being"[18].

Power of Language

The power of language is indeed remarkable, especially because it can define or even deny a social problem. Some men have decided to define "rape culture" on their own terms, as illustrated by a poster that appeared on the bulletin boards of an Ohio university that was hosting a sexual assault workshop. "Rape culture (noun)—When a woman sleeps with a guy and later regrets it. But since she doesn't want to have a bad reputation she blames it on the idea that society is at fault and that all men are animals. Typically found in female individuals who have 'Daddy Issues.' Common excuse by women who are floozies but don't want bad reputations. Synonyms include: Excuses, lies, and falsifying information. Example: Oh my god! I slept with Bill and I'm regretting it this morning! I know! I'll simply blame it on society rather than recognize my own poor choices." A former student of mine photographed it and wrote in black ink over it: "This is why women DON'T report. Stop victim blaming. #Stoprapeculture"[19].

These words would probably trouble anyone who supports rape victims, besides traumatizing some rape victims who saw this post. What particularly saddens me is that the person who posted this page is most likely young—these are not the words of an elderly man who grew up in another era. Whoever posted this note may have thought it humorous or really did consider it to be a political statement. Whether sarcastic or angry, these words are a weapon to hurt others. The one who wrote them did not care about any possible harm. To quote one lawmaker in another context, "Suck it up, buttercup."

Indeed, that is one aspect of rape culture—the complete disregard for the feelings of another person. Mocking a person's reaction as oversensitive or "politically correct" is a way to erase a person's dignity. On the spectrum of violence, denying a person's right to their feelings is a milder version of denying a person's right to their own bodily integrity. Obviously, the person who posted this sheet would be shocked to be placed on the same spectrum as a rapist (Box 6.1).

The power of language is also related to the dismissal of rape claims as attempts to hurt a man's reputation, misunderstandings between two drunk people, or "morning after" regrets. Examples of this mentality abound:

- An official of the Department of Education said jokingly that 90% of rape accusations on campus "fall into the category of 'We were both drunk.'" She later apologized for that statement, but the harm was still done[20].
- Todd Akins' notorious quote about "legitimate rape" not leading to pregnancies[21].
- Ant-abortion laws that distinguish between "forcible rapes" (i.e., "real" rapes) and other types of assaults that do not really count as rape, such as statutory rape of a minor[22].

SLUT-SHAMING

Related to the power of language is the power to shame females as "sluts" and other garbage. The connection between rape culture and slut-shaming is simple: If she's a slut, then it really wasn't rape. "A slut or ho is not only someone to be judged; she is also someone to be disbelieved. She has no credibility. As a result, when she's gang-raped, her friends are more likely to snap photos of her assault than to snap away the rapists"[23].

BOX 6.1

WHY THE BROCK TURNER CASE MATTERS

On a January evening in 2015, a college freshman attended a party. After being rejected twice by one young woman, he noticed that her sister was "alone and inebriated." He took the victim to a dimly lit, isolated area and sexually assaulted her behind a dumpster. Before the attack, he took a picture of her bare chest and posted a comment about her "tits." The prosecutor wrote, "This behavior is not typical assaultive behavior that you find on campus, but it is more akin to a predator who is searching for prey"[36].

Two men passing by noticed something strange—it looked like a man was having sex with an unconscious woman on the ground near a dumpster. They tackled the assailant and called the police. Newspaper headlines called the accused (and now convicted) rapist titles such as the "Former Stanford swimming star"[37], as if being an athlete AND a Stanford student outweighed the darkness of his crime. As many expected, he received a light sentence and served only a few months[38].

How could such a wholesome-looking youth be a rapist? Turner looked like a college freshman asking for an extension on his paper. Family and friends wrote letters to the court to defend him. It seemed inconceivable to his loved ones that Turner could do such a thing. It had to be a mistake, a drunken mistake caused by miscommunication.

According to two experts on sexual violence whom I had interviewed[39], cases like these demonstrate key insights about bystander intervention. As one expert said, "Rape is not like the weather—it's not inevitable." Indeed, rape is a choice made by an attacker. Rape is more than individual pathology, though, because society also plays a role. Yet the question is how we can be so antirape but still live in a culture in which rape is so common.

First, we sometimes use binary thinking about persons instead of viewing their behaviors as part of a spectrum. For example, we may judge a person as either a racist or a nonracist. This binary thinking would regard a rapist (or abuser or harasser) as nothing but an evil person instead of somebody who could be nice most of the time. If we think that "he can't be a rapist—he's my friend," then we might ignore the red flags of a possible attack. We simply do not want to acknowledge the complex truth about a multi-faceted person.

Also, we need to stop the monsterification of rapists/abusers/harassers. We may excuse someone's behavior by thinking, "They did not mean it that way." By breaking the binary thinking that could paralyze us if we see someone we know (and perhaps like) do something wrong, we can stop the monsterification. Because rape is such a horrific crime, we want to believe that only monsters could do such a thing. We may see creepy behavior in public but fail to call it out. For example, the average person can tell the difference

between flirting (i.e., a mutual exchange) and uncomfortable come-ons (e.g., the recipient is probably
withdrawing or cringing.)

It might be only natural to assume the best of
other people because it is painful to do otherwise.
Monsterification might help us cope with the idea
of gender-based violence, but it can prevent us from
realizing that most rapists look like nice guys who
might even be our friends.

Related to this justification for violence is the pervasive
belief that most females are up for grabs. If they wear any
type of clothing in public for any reason, then men allegedly
have the right to call them pretty, ugly, or slutty. Even the
French President's wife could not escape this humiliation
when the US President met her in 2017—"You're in such
good shape. She's in such good physical shape. Beautiful"[24].
The term "MILF" ("mother I'd like to fuck") is another example of slut shaming.

My definition of slut-shaming, then, stresses the wider
context of a woman being judged by others: A female (including preadolescent girls) must endure the body policing
by an audience of both females and males. *Is she showing too
much skin? Is her blouse too tight? Wow, she's got bedroom
eyes. Looks like she's been worked over by many men.*

Slut-shaming also focuses on behavior, such as
throwing oneself at men or flirting too much. *Is she swaying
her hips or licking her lips? Did she really go to that bar or
party? I heard she was a leg-opener. Why doesn't she respect
herself?*

While rape represents the most extreme violation of someone's bodily integrity, slut-shaming is also harmful because it assaults a person's sexual privacy. A rapist uses violence to control a person's body; rape culture uses shame to control a female's actions, words, and appearance.

Slut-Shaming Is Nothing New

In my college dorm, the staff held a survey of who was best dressed, worst dressed (yes, I was nominated for that honor), and other designations. One was for "the girl you'd like to take to Motel Six" and another for "the girl you'd like to take home to meet mom." Only later did I realize that these labels signified the age-old categories of Madonna (the Virgin Mary, not the famous singer) and Whore (the much-maligned Mary Magdalene).

The ancient Romans denigrated "sluts" and honored virgins and wives because sexual purity was part of their ideology. The value placed on the Vestal Virgins, for example, exemplified this stress on female modesty—these women would be buried alive if they were not chaste[25]. This custom reminds me of my reaction to the story of Julia, the slutty daughter of the Emperor Augustus. I was 15 when I first saw *I, Claudius*, a sensationalized version of Roman history. In one dramatic scene, a long line of men must face the Emperor as he asks them one by one if they had slept with his daughter. When he explodes, "Is there anybody here who has NOT slept with my daughter?" and the answer is silence, I had laughed. The punishment of Julia seemed just because she had dishonored her father. Years later, I wonder at my automatic acceptance of not only the double standard but also the tragic fate of a woman deemed a slut.

One intriguing variation of the slut theme appeared in the Middle Ages, when women accused of being witches were also accused of being promiscuous with both men and women. These witches wandered around the villages at night to seduce unwilling men because "All witchcraft comes from carnal lust, which is in women insatiable"[26]. Demonic possession and uncontrollable lust, then, posed grave dangers to the spiritual purity of a community.

The first time the word "slut" appeared in the English language, though, the word had little to do with sexual behavior and everything to do with being a low-class, dirty person[27]. Unfortunately, the impact of this insult can still be devastating. "The word 'slut' is the most destructive word you can say about a girl. You feel dirty and you want to go back under the radar"[28]. The word "bastard" (illegitimate child) parallels the word "slut" because both bastards and sluts are outcasts. In many cultures, bastards could not attend school, get a job, or get married. They were rarely allowed to be full members of society because their mothers were whores (or bitches, as in "son of a bitch").

Clothing

Clothing has usually been a marker for the Madonna/Whore division. Ancient cultures such as the Roman Empire proscribed clothing for the virtuous wife and the unvirtuous prostitute. The Vestal Virgins, of course, wore robes and veils as white as the gowns of today's brides[29].

In some traditional cultures, the veil often symbolized male protectorship. The implicit message was that a predatory male should look elsewhere or risk a family's wrath. The veil also indicated a higher social class than the average slut[30].

Today's dress code controversies in US schools echo this Madonna/Whore clothing theme. These codes convey the message to girls: How dare you have breasts and legs and arms? Two postings from the Internet (drawn from notes taped on school bathroom mirrors) illustrate my concerns. The first one reads: "When you interrupt a girl's school day to force her to change clothes, or send her home because her shorts are too short or her bra straps are visible, you are telling her that making sure boys have a 'distraction free' learning environment is more important than her education. Instead of shaming girls for their bodies, teach boys that girls are not sexual objects!!!"

The second note reads: "When you wear little to no clothing and dress provocatively because it's 'too hot out' or because you think it's 'attractive,' you are putting boys at a risk of having a distracting working environment and saying 'your clothing is more important than their education.' Instead of dressing like a thot, value the male education and dress conservatively."

According to *Urban Dictionary*, "thot" means "that hoe over there." This site defines "hoe" as a skank, loose woman, somebody who would have sex with anything with two legs, and a promiscuous slut. A "hoe for sho" is a female who is definitely a slut, while a "hoedified" female is too skanky to be touched. The online slang dictionary lists eight terms related to "hoe" that include "chicken hoe" as meaning a manipulative female.

The simple act of looking up the meaning of "thot," then, can descend into a rabbit hole of complex linguistic variations of the word "hoe." The word "slut" also has many variations, such as "slutacious whore nugget." Most are meant to be funny, but it's still disturbing that so many versions even exist. Scandinavians allegedly have more than 100 words for snow because the weather is omnipresent and inescapable. Can the same be said for the young people who are creating new terms for "sluts" and "hoes" in a culture dominated by the shaming of females?

Dress codes may also reinforce the mentality of judging a female based only on her appearance. Media images and peer pressure urge girls to look sexier, while they face social punishment for trying to express themselves. These contradictory messages can be maddening because they are only part of the suppression of women. One former student of mine wrote to me that "It doesn't matter what women do; if they're trying to be independent, state their opinions, or lead, they're shamed. Just as a female boss is a 'bitch' only because she's trying to lead and delegate, when a man doing the same thing is considered 'good.' And more along the lines of slut-shaming—a woman can be covered head to toe, but then she denies a man and is called a slut."

Suicide

If you are a slut, maybe you are better off dead. That has been the lesson for many females through the ages. For centuries, Saint Agnes has symbolized martyrdom for the sake of her virginity. Legend tells of her tormentors stripping her naked but her long hair protecting her modesty to the end[31]. Female virtue is sometimes linked with avoiding any implications of improper behavior.

Sadly, slut-shaming is still destroying the lives of many females. In the 1990s, Leora Tanenbaum started her research on slut-bashing (defined as direct attacks) after she herself had been harassed at school for once making out with a boy. The pre-Internet book she wrote, *Slut!*, includes several stories of girls who survived the bullying from their classmates—especially other females. Fortunately for these girls, though, they did not have to face cyberbullying. Tannenbaum's updated book on slut-shaming, *I Am Not a Slut*, is even more depressing than her first one because of the extra dimension of the Internet. New variations of hurting women online keep evolving every day. For instance, revenge porn occurs when a female's nude pictures or videos are distributed online without her consent.

The fact that one single person would kill herself over slut-shaming is tragic enough. It is indeed troubling that so many young females would rather die than face the humiliation of being considered a dirty piece of garbage. "Words hurt. Words kill," said the mother of a 13-year-old who had killed herself because of slut-shaming[32]. Rape victims also get called sluts, which obviously adds to their trauma. Tannenbaum writes, "I ask Melinda which was worse: having been raped, or having been called a slut. She doesn't hesitate with her reply. 'Being called a slut was worse than both rapes"[33]. In this context, is using the word "slut" ever appropriate?

"Slut" as a Term of Female Empowerment

Can claiming the word "slut" as a term of female empowerment be the answer? For example, the SlutWalk marches in 2011 called for an end to victim-blaming[34]. Tanenbaum argues against it because the usage can backfire. She describes how even using it in a positive context places females in a sexual context:

> The sexual double standard creates physical and emotional danger for females. Only girls, not boys are mistreated for being allegedly "too" sexual within a heterosexual context. Yet many people, female and male alike, regard girls and women through a sexual lens. Whether females are sexually active or not, we are seen as beings with sexual potential. Just walking, speaking, and breathing put us at risk for being judged to be "too" sexual. [35]

Tanenbaum presents another argument against the usage because of the false distinction between "good" slut and "bad" slut. A girl may call herself a slut and proudly wear whatever she wants, but still condemn a classmate for sleeping around too much. Since ancient times, females have called each other sluts (whores, etc.) because it gives them power. Scapegoating another person is a form of protection for the females at risk for being judged themselves. This is similar to the dynamic of a boy calling another boy a "fag" to avoid being bullied himself.

When I asked this question to a group of women, one commented that "language is very treacherous." She pointed out that a group of females may consider themselves to be in the company of equals—but are they really? Perhaps a female being teased about being a slut by other females may feel that she really is being denigrated (Box 6.2).

ACTION STEPS

- For more information about bystander intervention, you could start with the Green Dot campaign. This program, which started in 2006 at the University

BOX 6.2

MALE COLLEGE STUDENTS

Although the message about consensual sex has appeared on college campuses for years, its power can fade in the minds of male college students. Vanessa Grigoriadis, a researcher who visited several campuses for her book, *Blurred Lines: Rethinking Sex, Power, and Consent on Campus* (2017), brings up three points about sexual politics on campus.

First, power dynamics are still evident despite the advances of feminism. "Guys buy the kegs. Guys have the drugs. Guys play the sports that students flock to see on weekends. Guys rent the frat houses, and don't think that when they have parties they're desperate to get a bunch of guys they don't know in. Some frats remind the brother manning the door to maintain a two-to-one ratio of girls to guys for the evening"[40]. Because the male students have more power in many social situations, they can insist on getting oral sex from a girlfriend even if it gives her no pleasure.

Pornography has also affected the sexual culture on campus, especially its stress on anal sex and other practices. A Harvard study of male seniors reported that about half of them regularly watched porn. The ethos of modern porn is that a man's pleasure is primary and a woman's pleasure should consist of pleasing him.

Power dynamics and pornography, then, may be the reason that college males sometimes struggle to discuss the term "consent." When asked by the writer to define it, they first joke about it before describing a "gray zone" in which she may not be sure. In one conversation, a male said that "the male system is like a water system. You open a valve, water's going to spread everywhere!"

When the writer stated that stopping the sex act was still an option, the conversation took a strange turn. "He shrugged and said something that was meant to be ironic, or at least jokey, though it didn't quite come off that way. 'Bitch, I'm going to slit your throat,' he said, then he pointed to the dirty floor. 'Lay down and spread your legs. I'm going to pour hot metal in your vagina'"[41].

This disturbing scene shows a shift in power dynamics that really bothers me. When the writer had approached the group of young men at a bar, she probably felt safe because she was a mature woman. This age difference, besides her professional status, should have been enough to deter any inappropriate behavior. The topic and setting seemed harmless enough. But by expressing his ugly thought about sexual violence, he tried to strip her of her power and reduce her to an object to hurt. Perhaps he felt she had overstepped her bounds by challenging him, thus motivating him to punish her.

He had silenced her. She left the bar immediately after this assertion of power.

Here was a young man who had grown up in a "postfeminist" society where there appeared to be no more need for feminism. Why didn't the message of women's equality prevent him from semi-threatening a woman? Obviously, his socialization had included misogyny as well as any pro-equality influences. He said these words in front of his friends and in a public place, which makes one wonder what he would do in private without an audience to judge him.

Rape culture, then, is pernicious because it is both dangerous and subtle. How many overt and latent messages did this young man absorb before he started acting out to prove his manhood? And how can we change these messages so that rape culture will become obsolete in our lifetime?

Kentucky, has been proved effective in preventing sexual violence. The main website is https://alteristic. org/. Several other websites describe the Green Dot programs at high schools, colleges, the US Air Force, and other venues.

- Because most rapists are male, rape is also a men's issue. Fortunately, programs such as Men Can Stop Rape (www.mencanstoprape.org/) and its Healthy Masculinity Training Institute are promising developments in fighting rape culture.

Notes

1. Bates, L. (2017). The trouble with sex robots. New York Times. Retrieved from www.nytimes.com/2017/07/17/opinion/sex-robots-consent.html
2. Ferris, K., & Stein, J. (2012). *The real world: An introduction to sociology*, 3rd ed. New York, NY: Norton, p. 73.

3. *Oxford English Dictionary*. Retrieved from https://en.oxforddictionaries.com/definition/rape_culture

4. The rape of the Sabine women. (2015). Ancient Origins website. Retrieved from www.ahttps://en.oxforddictionaries.com/definition/rapaciousncient-origins.net/news-history/rape-sabine-women-002636

5. Lyrics retrieved from www.azlyrics.com/lyrics/robinthicke/blurredlines.html

6. Picture is posted on the Ancient Origins website at www.ancient-origins.net/news-history/rape-sabine-women-002636

7. *Oxford English Dictionary*. Retrieved from https://en.oxforddictionaries.com/definition/rapacious

8. Transcript: Donald Trump's comments about women. (2016). New York Times. Retrieved from www.nytimes.com/2016/10/08/us/donald-trump-tape-transcript.html

9. Brownmiller, S. (1975). *Against our will: Men, women, and rape*. New York, NY: Simon & Schuster.

10. Izadi, E. (2016). Why the "Last Tango in Paris" rape scene is generating such an outcry now. Washington Post. Retrieved from www.washingtonpost.com/news/arts-and-entertainment/wp/2016/12/05/why-the-last-tango-in-paris-rape-scene-is-generating-such-an-outcry-now/?utm_term=.d5f8d77ab8c9

11. Dockterman, E. (2014). There's a reason there's so much rape on your favorite TV shows. Time. Retrieved from http://time.com/50328/theres-a-reason-theres-so-much-rape-on-your-favorite-tv-shows/

12. Boureau, A.(1998). The lord's first night: The myth of the droit de cuissage. Translated by L. G. Cochrane. Chicago, IL: University of Chicago Press.

13. Boureau, A.(1998). The lord's first night: The myth of the droit de cuissage. Translated by L. G. Cochrane. Chicago, IL: University of Chicago Press, p. 4.

14. Hess, A. (2013). Elizabeth Smart says pro-abstinence sex ed harms victims of rape. Slate. Retrieved from www.slate.com/blogs/xx_factor/2013/05/06/elizabeth_smart_abstinence_only_sex_education_hurts_victims_of_rape_and.html

15. Valenti, J. (2010). *The purity myth: How America's obsession with virginity is hurting young women.* Berkeley, CA: Seal Press.
16. Peril, L. (2002). *Pink think: Becoming a woman in many uneasy lessons.* New York, NY: W. W. Norton, p. 98.
17. Peril, L. (2002). *Pink think: Becoming a woman in many uneasy lessons.* New York, NY: W. W. Norton, p. 101.
18. Anderson, D. E. (2015). *Damaged goods: New perspectives on Christian purity.* Nashville, TN: Jericho Books, p. 6.
19. Retrieved from Facebook post by a former student. I prefer not to name the university because I believe that it could have happened on any campus.
20. Guild, B. (2017). Education official blames most campus sexual assaults on drunkenness. CBS News. Retrieved from www.cbsnews.com/news/education-dept-official-says-90-of-campus-sexual-assaults-fall-into-the-category-of-we-were-both-drunk/
21. Cohen, D. (2012). Earlier: Akin: "Legitimate rape" rarely leads to pregnancy. Politico. Retrieved from www.politico.com/story/2012/08/akin-legitimate-rape-victims-dont-get-pregnant-079864
22. Terkel, A. (2011). "Forcible rape" language remains in bill to restrict abortion funding. Huffington Post. Retrieved from www.huffingtonpost.com/2011/02/09/abortion-forcible-rape-language-hr-3_n_820846.html
23. Tanenbaum, L. (2000). *Slut: Growing up female with a bad reputation.* New York, NY: Harper Perennial, p. 41.
24. Wildman, S. (2017). Trump to French President Macron's wife: "You're in such good shape!" Vox. Retrieved from www.vox.com/world/2017/7/13/15965434/trump-ladies-man-brigitte-macron-you-look-beautiful
25. Burton, M. (2016). Love, sex and marriage in ancient Rome. Psychology Today. Retrieved from www.psychologytoday.com/us/blog/hide-and-seek/201206/love-sex-and-marriage-in-ancient-rome
26. Quote from the 1486 handbook for witch hunters called *Malleus Malificarum.* Retrieved from https://

bookmanpeedeel.wordpress.com/tag/raw-power-witchcraft-babalon-and-female-sexuality/

27. Tanenbaum, L. (2015). *I am not a slut: Slut-shaming in the age of the Internet.* New York, NY: Harper Perennial.

28. Tanenbaum, L. (2015). *I am not a slut: Slut-shaming in the age of the Internet.* New York, NY: Harper Perennial, p. 19.

29. For more information about the Vestal Virgins, this website is helpful: https://vestalvirgins.weebly.com/vestal-virgins.html

30. Amer, S. (2014). *What is veiling?* Chapel Hill, NC: University of NC Press.

31. Richert, S. (2017). Saint Agnes, virgin and martyr. Thought. Retrieved from www.thoughtco.com/saint-agnes-of-rome-542518

32. Helena. (2012). Slut-shaming, suicide and why at this point we all know better. X0Jane Magazine. Retrieved from www.xojane.com/issues/bullying-suicide-and-why-point-we-all-know-better

33. Tanenbaum, L. (2015). *I am not a slut: Slut-shaming in the age of the Internet.* New York, NY: Harper Perennial, p. 237.

34. Stampler, L. (2011). SlutWalks sweep the nation. Huffington Post. Retrieved from www.huffingtonpost.com/2011/04/20/slutwalk-united-states-city_n_851725.html

35. Tanenbaum, L. (2015). *I am not a slut: Slut-shaming in the age of the internet.* New York, NY: Harper Perennial, p. 8.

36. Sanchez, R. (2016). Stanford rape case: Inside the court documents. CNN. Retrieved from www.cnn.com/2016/06/10/us/stanford-rape-case-court-documents/index.html

37. Sprankle, J. (2016). 8 Brock Turner headlines that totally miss the point. Bustle. Retrieved from www.bustle.com/articles/165164-8-brock-turner-headlines-that-totally-miss-the-point.

38. Former Stanford swimming star gets 6 months in jail for sexual assault at frat party. (2016). KTV website. Retrieved from www.ktvu.com/news/former-stanford-swimming-star-gets-6-months-in-jail-for-sexual-assault-at-frat-party

39. In-person interview with Julia D'Agostino (social worker who used to work at the Ohio Alliance to End Sexual Violence) on October 15, 2017 and phone interview with Susan Wismer

(social worker at the Sexual Assault Response Network of Central Ohio) on November 5, 2017.

40. Grigoriadis, V. (2017). *Blurred lines: Rethinking sex, power, and consent on campus.* Boston, MA: Houghton Mifflin, pp. 45–46.

41. Grigoriadis, V. (2017). *Blurred lines: Rethinking sex, power, and consent on campus.* Boston, MA: Houghton Mifflin, pp. 56.

7

PANDORA'S JAR

The Messy Politics of Reproductive Health

INTRODUCTION

Being a woman can be messy. I remember the first time I heard about menstruation and thought, "Eew, gross." Decades later, I still have that reaction. Periods were a time of wearing dark pants, dreading the mortification of a blood-stain, and enduring the cramps and headaches and fatigue. What does this complaint have to do with reproductive politics? If a relatively enlightened woman like me can be bothered by a natural female function, how does the average American male react to it? In one awareness event, feminists tacked sanitary pads onto telephone poles with a message: "Imagine if men were as disgusted by rape as they are by periods"[1]. This disgust is probably related to ignorance, as typified by a man thinking that a woman can control her bleeding during menses[2].

If modern men can show disdain and even contempt for women having periods (e.g., Megyn Kelly accused of "bleeding from wherever" when questioning Trump), this is nothing new. Dr. Amanda Foreman's marvelous documentary, *The Ascent of Woman,* includes a segment on the Pandora myth. The correct translation for the word "box" opened by Pandora was the word "jar," which also meant a woman's genitals. Symbolically, Pandora's introduction of evil in the world came from her vagina. The messy outpourings from a woman's "jar" are the menstrual blood and childbirth fluids. The ancient Greeks, like the Hebrews with their Eve myth, regarded women as necessary evils. In both societies, women symbolized sinful impurities instead of rational morality. The last element that flew out of Pandora's jar, of course, was hope—that is, a new baby. For some misogynists, the only good thing about females is their ability to reproduce.

This insight about Pandora's jar is directly related to today's debates on reproductive politics. Policymakers (and many people) not only are ignorant about the female reproductive system but also are disgusted by it. For the past few years, many have been horrified by the state and federal legislators enacting laws that were based on nonscientific (and even antiscientific) grounds. For instance, scientific evidence indicates that fetuses do not have the neurologic capacity to feel pain, but states have passed "fetal pain" laws against abortion[3]. The Guttmacher Institute and other reputable organizations have listed the laws that were based on willful ignorance of the woman's body[4].

The emotions of reproductive politics affect millions of women. A gynecologic ultrasound, for example, is not an abstract term for many women because the insertion of the wand is always invasive and sometimes painful. Some states require this invasive and unnecessary procedure before an abortion, which could be considered rape because it is the insertion of a foreign object without the patient's consent.

Women seeking abortions already know that they are pregnant. They do not need the painful punishment of a wand being put in their vaginas, which supposedly is going to make them "see the light" and cancel the abortion. Doctors are being forced to violate the first precept of the Hippocratic oath: First, do no harm.

The Supreme Court 2014 ruling on the Hobby Lobby case is also disturbing; intrauterine devices (IUDs) have the potential to save many women from hysterectomies. Arguing on religious grounds that the IUD was an abortifacient because it prevented implantation of the fertilized egg (a scientifically false belief), the Hobby Lobby company's owner requested that the IUD should be exempt from the birth control mandate. The idea of an employer denying women access to this vital medical service (whether for contraception or other reasons) is appalling. By ruling on behalf of religious dogma, the Supreme Court ruled against women's health itself[5].

The emotions of reproductive politics are powerful for both those who support and those who oppose legal abortion. Even the names of each side are controversial—those who oppose keeping abortion legal and accessible call themselves "pro-life," while others call them "forced-birthers." The antilegal abortion advocates use emotional persuasion, including pictures of fetuses and "baby killer" terms. The prolegal abortion advocates are sometimes called "pro-choice" and "pro-abortion" (as if abortion were a desirable option pressed upon poor innocent girls by wild-haired feminazis). This side also uses emotional persuasion, usually in the form of testimonies of those who had abortions. The impact of these stories, though, does not appear as compelling as the "baby killer" designation.

However, the battle over emotional persuasion may have swung favorably to the side of the women's health advocates in 2017 through the TV show *The Handmaid's Tale*. I had read Margaret Atwood's novel when it came out during the Reagan era. Like many others, I had regarded the threat of a patriarchal tyranny to be as remote as a comet striking the earth. The fictional repression of women by reducing them to mere vessels of procreation was a chilling idea, but I was more worried about the nuclear arms race and the US support of death squads in El Salvador. Who could know that three decades later, the issue of women's health would be symbolized by the striking figures of red-cloaked women with white bonnets and submissive stances? Some "handmaids" are appearing all over the nation to protest anti-choice bills, as seen in this event in Olympia, Washington in 2017 (Illustration 7.1). The idea of *The Handmaid's Tale*

ILLUSTRATION 7.1 Pro-choice protest using *The Handmaids Tale* theme.
Source: Shutterstock.

becoming more fact than fiction is alarming to those who are making the connections between the tide of anti-women's health bills and ancient misogyny.

THE POLITICS OF PERIODS

Dominant culture has deemed that women are inherently disgusting because they have periods. Disgust has many dimensions, including the physical: Periods can cause smelly messes. They also symbolize an uncontrollable, almost wild component of being human because it is so hard to control the blood flow. Sometimes women even require hysterectomies to stop the bleeding. Menstrual blood may become associated with irrationality to the point of craziness—how could a bleeding woman be calm and competent? When church fathers and other misogynists wrote about the sinful nature of women, perhaps they were feeling moral disgust at the idea of secret and mysterious blood of periods.

Recently in the news, a woman matter-of-factly told a male coworker that she was having menstrual cramps when he asked her about the heating pad on her lap. This news upset him so much that he went to Human Resources to report her[6]. Another woman was fired for having her period come unexpectedly and stain the chair[7].

The politics of periods indicate that being disgusted by menstrual realities can harm women. The assumption that tampons/pads are optional luxuries instead of urgent necessities, for instance, has permeated many policy decisions that make access to supplies difficult and even impossible at times.

Access to Supplies

The movements against the tampon/pad taxes in several states have emerged as one way to advocate for menstrual equity. However, an estimated 100 million women have been stranded without tampons/pads because they cannot afford to pay for the actual products. This has affected low-income girls who have to skip school every month. One New York politician said, "Feminine hygiene products are as essential as toilet paper. . . . No young woman should face losing class time because she is too embarrassed to ask for, can't afford or simply can't access feminine hygiene products." The common-sense solution, then, was to provide free tampons/pads in school restrooms in the Bronx and Queens—the first in the nation to implement this reform in 2016. A civic leader said that this action "will curb preventable absences and help young women on their path to achievement"[8].

Inspired by this story and the tampon/pad tax protesters, US Representative Grace Meng proposed the Menstrual Equity for All Act of 2016. Besides addressing the problem of females not being able to afford tampons/pads, this bill would require that prisons and jails supply women with an adequate number of products. One facility "denied inmates access to menstrual hygiene products, a condition considered inhumane and degrading. Female inmates in Connecticut only get five pads per week to *split* with their bunkmate, which means they may have to use a single pad for multiple days. I cannot imagine how humiliating that must feel"[9]. The bill also would ensure that homeless shelters could use federal funds to pay for tampons/pads.

Because millions of women are trapped in low-wage jobs that do not pay enough for necessities, food stamps (now called SNAP) are often traded for tampons. One single mother "doesn't have enough money left at the end of each month to feed her daughters full meals.... Now, with no other source of income, Eva breaks the law, selling her food stamps to pay for the rent, phone bill, detergent and tampons"[10].

Menstrual Pain

One woman with endometriosis has been fighting the medical care system for 12 years. She "was blacking out, vomiting uncontrollably from pain, even with ovulation" and almost dropped out of high school because of painful periods. It took her seven years to get a proper diagnosis. "They all told me I was being dramatic, and the pain was in my head, even though I would go to the ER all the time." Now she has found out about the only solution to her problem, a specialized surgery not covered by her insurance company. So she continues to live in pain and work only part-time because of this medical problem[11].

Because men still dominate corporations and legislatures, we must educate them about menstrual pain. One Twitter user gained notoriety for posting, "As a guy, I think menstrual pain is a myth." Somebody responded, "As a girl I think getting hit in the balls pain is a bigger myth." Unfortunately, another male wrote, "Girls make too much [sic] excuses for menstruation as if it's some difficult experience"[12]. On the brighter side, one Japanese artist created a menstrual cramp machine complete with electrodes on the lower abdomen and of course a device that dripped blood. One participant ran to the men's room, writhing in pain. The song lyric, "It hurts, doesn't it? Well, it's gonna hurt even more," was quoted in this article[13].

Is menstrual leave one possible solution for women coping with monthly pain? Some Asian countries such as Japan have instituted a leave policy, but most women do not use it to avoid being harassed or judged as weak. They may be right. One 2002 study focused on the reactions of people who saw a woman drop a tampon from her purse, which included criticism of her likeability and competence. "Menstrual leave is a loaded term, one that may cause people who have never experienced severe cramps to make unfounded assumptions; namely, 'that women are going to get free time off for something that isn't really a problem.'" Instead of calling it "menstrual leave," some employers should offer gender-neutral terms such as "flexible leave"[14].

Whatever it is called, many are concerned that menstrual leave could still cause more gender discrimination in the workplace. One Indian feminist, Barkha Dutt, writes that period pain is not that bad for women. "'First-day period leave' may be dressed up as progressive, but it actually trivializes the feminist agenda for equal opportunity, especially in male-dominated professions. Worse, it reaffirms that there is a biological determinism to the lives of women, a construct that women of my generation have spent years challenging." She is also concerned about the backfire effect on most Indian women who still need the basics: clean toilets, water supply, and sanitary pads[15].

Dutt's points about the risks of menstrual leave policy are solid because women still struggle to be taken seriously in the workplace. Unfortunately, millions of women suffer from dysmenorrhea (painful cramps) that a few pain relievers cannot fix—they have to grit their teeth and endure painful symptoms while trying to do their jobs. Why does the acknowledgement of dysmenorrhea have to undermine women's fight for equality? Biologic determinism aside, women's bodies are different than men's. We can fight the stigma of periods without denying the reality of menstrual pain.

International Trends

India is not the only country where menstruating women must endure stigma. Since ancient times, menstruation huts in many traditional cultures sheltered the females who were exiled from their families during their period. This practice can be unsafe because the isolation makes the females vulnerable to violence. One recent news story about a 19-year-old Nepali girl highlighted another risk of menstruation huts. Living in a region that commonly used these huts, she and other women were "considered unclean during menstruation, [so they] are sequestered for the extent of their periods. . . . It's a ritual that Shahi had likely endured many times before, but on Thursday night, alone on the floor of her uncle's cowshed, the teenager was bitten by a poisonous snake." She died a few hours later[16].

Menstruation, then, can cause serious injury and even kill females in countries that do not respect the health needs created by a natural function. Women "on the rag" have also been stigmatized in the United States, but not to this extent. Fighting the stigma is one critical step in helping women achieve menstrual health around the world.

On the International Women's Day of 2014, one conference theme was "Every woman's right to water, sanitation, and hygiene." One United Nations official declared that this "stigma around menstruation and menstrual hygiene is a violation of several human rights, most importantly of the right to human dignity"[17]. The stigma is especially heavy for sex workers, for whom one Indian agency has provided help. A speaker on its behalf "stressed that there is no dignity without basic necessities—water, sanitation, and sanitary napkins. 'We are talking about the dignity of women. . . . Sex workers are just like everyone else'"[18].

Another United Nations initiative is the Menstrual Hygiene Movement, which notes that "Menstruation is supposed to be invisible and silent, and sometimes, menstruating women and girls are supposed to be invisible and silent too. . . . The time has come to promote—loudly and unashamedly—the role of good Menstrual Hygiene Management (MHM) as a trigger for better and stronger development of girls and women. . . ."[19].

Another hopeful sign is the work of individuals such as Arunachalam Muruganantham, who invented a sanitary pad machine that is helping thousands of Indian women. Fewer than 12% of these women can afford pads, especially in the rural villages. "He was shocked to learn that women don't just use old rags, but other unhygienic substances such as sand, sawdust, leaves and even ash. . . . Women who do use cloths are often too embarrassed to dry them in the sun, which means they don't get disinfected." This lack of sanitation caused 70% of reproductive health problems in Indian women, including maternal mortality. Unfortunately, the inventor could not find female volunteers to test his pads. He used a football bladder filled with goat's blood and walked around the village wearing pads, which made the village think him insane, perverted, and even possessed by evil spirits. His breakthrough invention of a machine that makes cheap pads, though, made his years of research worthwhile [20] (Box 7.1).

BOX 7.1

PLANNED PARENTHOOD: BABY KILLING MACHINE OR PROVIDER OF MEDICAL CARE?

According to anti–legal abortion groups (also called "antis") such as Students for Life, Planned Parenthood (PP) clinics do nothing but slaughter babies and sell their body parts. This kind of misinformation can have deadly consequences—one shooter killed three people and injured nine others in Colorado Springs in 2015. The shooter called himself a "warrior for the babies"[53].

Critics of PP claim that PP advertises birth control and health screenings but does not advertise that they also provide abortions[54]. However, one could look up PP's website (www.plannedparenthood.org) and click on the "Get Care" tab and then "View Our Services" to find the services listed in alphabetical order. The first two items are "Abortion Services" and "Abortion Referral." Because the public uproar about PP focuses on its abortion services, it might be difficult to find anyone who did not know that PP provided abortions.

The theme of abortion clinics victimizing vulnerable girls is also common in the anti movement, stressing that females cannot be trusted with their own medical decisions. However, the PP site states, "The decision to have an abortion is very personal, and only you can decide what's best for you. But we're here to help answer whatever questions you may have, and make sure you get the care you need." Preabortion counseling stresses the question, "Are you sure?" because no medical provider would perform an abortion on an unwilling patient[55].

Critics also charge that PP uses tax dollars to pay for abortion services because the clinics are unprofitable. First, PP is a nonprofit organization. Second, the Hyde Amendment bans federal money (i.e., Medicaid) for abortions except in the cases of rape, incest, and to save a patient's life. This Amendment has been implemented since 1976[56]. Some antis, of course, criticize any tax dollars going to PP because of its association with abortion.

Allegedly, PP allots 94% of its services to abortions. This contention by the Republican Party and others has been disputed by both Factcheck and Snopes, especially because some PP clinics provide prenatal care in addition to the long list of other services. PP states that only 3% of its services are abortions. The gaping distance between 3% and 94%, of course, leads to disagreement about how each unit of service is measured[57].

PP critics also argue that PP is not necessary for nonabortion services, stating that community health centers have enough resources to help former PP patients. A recent debacle in Indiana, though, proves that PP is vital to the health of thousands; the state government slashed funding to PP, thus forcing five clinics to close in rural areas that desperately needed the services. None of the five even provided abortions. An HIV outbreak became a public health nightmare because people had nowhere to go to get tested and treated.

A PP official noted that the fact that Scott County was "without a testing facility until a few weeks ago is a glaring example of the kind of public health crisis that results when prevention and testing are left unfunded." The governor had to issue emergency measures to fight an epidemic that could have been easily prevented. This crisis in Indiana is but one example of what happens when PP clinics are shut down[58].

Another allegation against PP regards the Margaret Sanger and eugenics controversy, which is a key point made by many who want to defund PP. Some of Sanger's beliefs were outdated and offensive, which gives ammunition to the PP opponents. The context of her beliefs is benign: "Enforced motherhood is the most complete denial of a woman's right to life and liberty"; and "No woman can call herself free who does not own and control her body. No woman can call herself free until she can choose consciously whether she will or will not be a mother"[59]. Having seen the abysmal poverty of the slums, Sanger supported birth control rights (not abortion) for women suffering from multiple pregnancies. She was unafraid to set up clinics for African Americans and other ethnic groups. In 1966, Martin Luther King praised her: "There is a striking kinship between our movement and Margaret Sanger's early efforts . . . (she) had to commit what was then called a crime in order to enrich humanity"[60].

The darker side of Sanger, though, includes statements about eugenics that are appalling today. In the 1920s, reformers who wanted to fix society thought that eugenics (promoting only the births of desirable people) was the answer. Businessmen, church leaders, and politicians considered eugenics to be the ideal social engineering. Sanger became a follower of that trend to gain more supporters and perhaps because she really did believe that the disabled (mentally and physically) were a drain on society. She wrote in 1921 that "the most urgent problem today is how to limit and discourage the over-fertility of the mentally and physically defective"[61].

Sanger had opened up a clinic in Harlem and the deep South to serve African Americans, which has prompted today's critics to accuse her of the racist urge to exterminate the race. These critics ignore the fact that she herself was Irish—an undesirable immigrant group in that era. PP issued a well-researched factsheet that does not try to minimize her involvement with eugenics. However, PP "finds these views objectionable and outmoded. Nevertheless, anti–family planning activists continue to attack Sanger . . . because she is an easier target than the unassailable reputation of (PP)." PP adds that Sanger was an "early 20th-century founder [who] was not a perfect model of early 21st-century values" and compares her to the slave-owning Thomas Jefferson writing the Declaration of Independence[62].

The most sensational accusation against PP, of course, regards the alleged selling of baby parts. In 2015, the Center for Medical Progress (the name of a front group to support the anti cause) made a heavily edited video that made this claim. Although PP has received reimbursement for the shipping of fetal tissue for scientific research, Factcheck and other organizations have verified that PP has not made a profit[63]. The *New York Times* Editorial Board stated that "The Center for Medical Progress video campaign is a dishonest attempt to make legal, voluntary and potentially lifesaving tissue donations appear nefarious and illegal. Lawmakers responding by promoting their own anti-choice agenda are rewarding deception and putting women's health and their constitutionally protected rights at risk"[64]. Despite the advocacy for truth-telling, though, the myth of "Planned Parenthood sells baby parts" persists on the Internet.

ABORTION STORIES

Story of One Doctor and One Staff Member

The term "abortionist" carries a heavy connotation of back-alley butchers. In the modern era, "abortion provider" evokes a lesser degree of antagonism, but some of these doctors actually face death threats in the United States. Dr. Willie Parker, author of *Life's Work: A Moral Argument for Choice* (2017), relates his story of being an obstetrician-gynecologist who once opposed abortion but later becoming an abortion provider in the Deep South. He left a comfortable life in Hawaii to return to his Southern roots when he realized the dire need for his services. Although he does not hire a body guard or wear a bulletproof vest, he does take several precautions against a protester who might turn violent. For instance, he refused to buy a house next to his brother's home because he was afraid that it might be firebombed (11 people, including four doctors, have been murdered by extremists). Staying in temporary residences has increased his sense of safety[21].

Every morning when he approaches a clinic, he has to walk by protesters screaming, "Murderer! Baby killer! Filthy Negro abortionist!"[22]. He notes that his patients must walk by protesters who treat the women like murderers or idiots. "By the time a woman finds herself in my waiting room she has already walked a long, introspective road"[23] and deserves respect for her decision. "They demean her humanity by presuming to know better than she does what her best interests are"[24].

Parker's matter-of-fact description of the abortion process contrasts sharply with the misinformation propagated by the "antis." His patients' well-being requires not only reproductive services but also basic medical care that is limited by lawmakers.

> Having walked past the antis' posters every day of my work life for more than a dozen years, I have begun to develop a new insight about what these images might unconsciously mean. I have begun to see these manipulations as a twenty-first-century version of pseudoscientific fables that served to protect men's exclusive rights to fetal ownership. In the earliest efforts to understand reproduction, people believed that women were merely earth—potting soil—contributing nothing at all to the development of a new living being. With their "seed," as it was known, men contributed everything, from physical appearance to intelligence. Residing in the head of every sperm was a fully formed human being in

miniature, a homunculus, which would be "planted" inside the woman. She was the man's property: she existed to bear children for him, and any interruption or violation of that role was regarded as stealing, a violation of property rights— the same as trespassing on a farmer's field and stealing his corn or his wheat. I believe these posters unconsciously rearticulate that ancient claim: fetuses are miniature people, belonging exclusively to the men in charge. The men, therefore, are within their rights to punish anyone—including pregnant women and abortion doctors, like me—whom they regard as thieves and poachers. [25]

Parker's point about male ownership extends beyond the individual father's role to the patriarchal structure's role. In this context, antis regard a woman's fertility as a commodity separate from her own autonomy. By declaring themselves to be "pro-life" while refusing a woman's need for health care, the antis are continuing the tradition of not trusting women with their own bodies.

Although Doctor Parker has been the target of the antis, anybody associated with Planned Parenthood and related services can be vilified. For instance, one woman who worked at the intake desk of Planned Parenthood was called an "accessory to murder" by online critics. Despite this abuse, Abber is grateful that she had the chance to work at an agency that offered a "zero judgment zone" for the clients. "[Those] who seek out sexual health services . . . don't benefit from being judged on a few intimate choices they've made in their lives—and especially not by me. People benefit from being able to talk about and learn from their experiences—and receive the medical treatment they need"[26].

Stories of Women Who Ended Their Pregnancies

Sometimes I think that using the phrase "end a pregnancy" instead of the provocative word "abortion" might help with this discussion. "Terminate a pregnancy" seems harsh because it implies a terminus/final point of no return. For many women, though, an abortion is only one part of their life journey as a mother or nonmother. Whatever abortion is called, we cannot deny the essence of a life-changing moment that may bring relief and pain.

One woman had an abortion at age 19 and felt mixed emotions about this decision that is both common and taboo. She wrote, "Yes, I felt relief and gratitude in great measure after my abortion, but my first thought after my procedure was a feeling of awe: Women are complex, fierce, powerful creatures, and I could not believe so many of the one in three women who experience abortion were bearing this alone"[27].

Another woman who got pregnant at age 19 had missed some doses of the birth control pill. Unfortunately, she had had to wait for payday to pick up them up—they cost $30. In a troubled relationship with a boyfriend who did not use condoms, she felt far from ready to be a parent. "At the time of my abortion, I was working hourly jobs that left me living paycheck to paycheck. . . . I was in no state to—financially or emotionally—care for another person"[28]. For her, access to abortion meant being able to achieve her aspirations because "Women who get abortions do so because we want a better life for our families and ourselves"[29].

The doctor and staff at the clinic impressed her: "Now, when I say my abortion was amazing, I'm not kidding." For years, she kept it a secret even from her liberal mother, and now she regrets her silence because she wants to fight the stigma. In fact, the title of one article is "Why I Will Never Stop Talking About My Abortion." She wishes that more people would realize that, when they are discussing abortion, they could be in the same room with women who have had one. "Abortion is such a political issue. But the thing is, when I had my abortion, I wasn't thinking about politics at all. All I was thinking was, 'I need an abortion and I need one now'"[30].

More and more women are speaking out, including the founders of the #Shoutyourabortion. One of the founders, Amelia Bonow, states that many people expect women who have had abortions to feel "some level of sadness, shame, or regret. But you know what? I have a good heart and having an abortion made me happy in a totally unqualified way. Why wouldn't I be happy that I was not forced to become a mother?"[31].

Stories of Regret

Antis often argue that women (and men) suffer from postabortion syndrome, an agonizing mental condition caused by guilt and sadness. The website HopeAfterAbortion.com, for example, includes resources for the "abortion victims of America" who feel distressed. One counselor, Sister Paula Vandegaer, describes the long-term effects of abortion regret. Karen, a 23-year-old who is successful in her career, "feels dead and dull inside." The abortion she had in college haunts her, making her feel ashamed of both the decision and her current emotional state. "Abortion is an extremely unnatural experience for a woman's body and her maternal instinct" because her body and mind were preparing for motherhood when the pregnancy was abruptly stopped[32]. The regrets may lead to destructive behaviors, including suicide. Sometimes postabortion syndrome may not appear for several years after the procedure.

Experts, including researchers of a longitudinal study who followed 667 women for three years, dispute that postabortion syndrome even exists. The results of this study on the decision rightness and emotional responses to abortion were compelling: 95% of the women stated that they had made the right decision. Other studies confirm the assertion that in most cases, women had few regrets about their abortions[33]. The "no regrets" movement includes testimonies, such as this one from a woman who was 18 years old when she got pregnant: "No way was I prepared to carry a baby for 9 months and take care of a newborn. No way"[34].

Who is right about women regretting abortions—the postabortion syndrome camp or the researchers who support the "no regrets" assertion? Enough evidence contradicts the claim that postabortion syndrome is a widespread problem, but one cannot generalize about the experiences of millions of women over decades. Every woman's story is too multilayered and complex for any simplistic statement.

IF ABORTION WERE CRIMINALIZED IN THE UNITED STATES

One does not need to read the eerily prophetic novel *The Handmaid's Tale* to consider how women's health care would be affected if abortion were criminalized in the United States. The current dilemma caused by Catholic hospitals provides a foreshadow for this troubling possibility.

In 2012, a woman in Ireland developed septicemia from her pregnancy and needed an abortion to save her life. The theocratic influence of the Catholic Church prohibited this procedure, and she died. Unfortunately for thousands of American women, this story is relevant to their own reproductive health because of a recent upsurge of Catholic-run hospitals caused by mergers. One in six hospitals is now Catholic, with the concentration in some states such as Wisconsin as high as 40%[35].

For example, some pregnancies are doomed to fail and could even threaten the life of the mother if they are not terminated. Therapeutic abortions, though, are usually prohibited in Catholic hospitals. One doctor described the impact of religious restrictions on her practice as: "You're in this limbo of knowing that the right thing to do is to induce her labor because she is going to get sick. . . . [I]t's not common but they can die, they can become septic and die from something that we could treat and prevent and never have them get ill"[36]. In one case, a woman had to endure 24 hours of labor, including a loss of blood so severe that she needed a transfusion, to deliver a nonviable fetus. The American College of Obstetrics and Gynecology determines the standard of care for such cases as either mifepristone (the "morning after" pill that can induce labor) or a dilation and extraction procedure. "[M]any Catholic hospitals across this country are withholding emergency care from patients who are in the midst of a miscarriage or experiencing other pregnancy complications"[37].

Catholic regulations do prohibit not only abortions but also a wide array of procedures that have nothing to do with healing but everything to do with ideology. The lawyers for Franciscan Health, for example, wrote that "Franciscan sincerely believes that providing insurance coverage for gender transition, sterilization, and abortion would constitute impermissible material cooperation with evil," and that "Like the Catholic Church it serves, Franciscan believes that a person's sex is ascertained biologically, and not by one's beliefs, desires, or feelings"[38]. As a result, the US Conference of Catholic Bishops has issued directives that interfere with the practice of modern—and humane—medicine. What could be more humane than offering a rape victim emergency contraception? Most Catholic hospitals, of course, would disagree with the assertion that rape victims should not be forced to go through a pregnancy.

Vulnerable communities such as rural towns and low-income neighborhoods often have no other options but Catholic hospital systems. This multibillion-dollar business no longer stresses charity but profit, including Medicaid and Medicare money. Government funding, however, provides no protection for those women who require the best care[39]. For instance, a patient undergoing cesarean delivery can often request a tubal ligation during the surgery. This common-sense request ensures that the woman does not have to be opened up twice, but most Catholic hospitals prohibit tubal ligations because sterilization is against their doctrine.

In one case, a woman fell and dislodged her intrauterine device (IUD) from her uterus. This caused both heavy bleeding and excruciating pain. She went to a Catholic hospital, where the doctor told her that her "hands were tied" because of the hospital policy against contraception. She was "turned away and told to find a different hospital that offered secular care. 'I walked away from the doctor's office feeling shocked and stigmatized. . . . Hospitals and doctors' offices should be places for healing and not judgment' "[40]. She had to wait two weeks before her insurance policy would cover her treatment at a secular hospital.

When I think about the pain that must have resulted by that dislodged IUD, I wonder how any doctor could violate the Hippocratic oath by denying her care. "First, do not harm"—in what way is refusing to treat a woman in serious pain not a harmful act?

The Personhood Amendment also offers a clear picture of what would happen if abortion were criminalized. Proposed in several states, such as Colorado and Mississippi, this initiative is the gold standard of antis because it is so thorough. It defines a fertilized egg as a legal person. Presidential candidate Mitt Romney supported it in 2012, despite his documented lack of knowledge that it could also lead to a law against all hormonal birth control. If passed, the Personhood Amendment would:

- Ban all abortions in all cases;
- Prohibit hormonal birth control, including IUDs, "morning after" pills, and even birth control pills; and
- Ban the disposal of embryos in a laboratory, which would be hugely detrimental to the in vitro fertility process.

One opponent is Mississippi fertility specialist Dr. Randall Hines, who said that "the amendment reflects 'biological ignorance.' Most fertilized eggs . . . do not implant in the uterus or develop further. 'Once you recognize that the majority of fertilized eggs don't become people, then you recognize how absurd this amendment is.'" Interestingly, several anti-abortion groups also opposed the amendment because it was too drastic[41].

Although the large-scale Personhood Amendment initiatives have quieted down by 2017, several states continue the small-scale efforts to reduce access to abortion services. A 2017 bill in Missouri, for example, would "impose tighter restrictions on abortion providers and allow real estate agents to refuse to sell or rent them land." Because SB5 directly challenged the St. Louis ordinance that also protected women from discrimination based on their reproductive decisions (i.e., birth control and/or abortion), some news outlets incorrectly reported that SB5 would allow this kind of discrimination. When *Newsweek* reported about this false alarm, it did raise the point that state law did not explicitly protect women from this type of discrimination[42].

Would women ever be punished for their reproductive decisions? During the 2016 US presidential campaign, Donald Trump stated that there had to be "some form of punishment" for the women who had an abortion—a taboo topic for most anti-choice activists[43]. The anti-choice side usually portrays the abortion provider as evil and the pregnant woman as a victim or weakling who did not know any better. When Trump followed the logic of the anti-choice argument that abortion was murder, then, he stirred up a debate. His future lawyer Jay Sekulow stated that "If we believe the child is a person . . . the personhood of the child, that should be protected under the Constitution, that someone that knowingly, willfully and voluntarily takes the life of that person could be—not should be, could be—held culpable under criminal laws of the various states"[44]. Another conservative speaker said that a woman who has an abortion is as guilty as someone who "hires a contractor to kill someone. Conservatives herald 'the rule of law' when discussing illegal immigration, but why do the rules suddenly change when we are talking about the killing of an unborn child?"[45].

How bad was it before the *Roe v. Wade* decision in 1973? An article in *Scientific American* describes the disproportionate impact that abortion laws had on marginalized women (e.g., women of color and low-income women) because rich White women could always find a doctor to help them. "As the pre-*Roe* era demonstrates, women will still seek the necessary means to end a pregnancy. Cutting off access to abortion care has a far greater impact on the options available and the type of care a woman receives than it does on whether or not she ends a pregnancy"[46].

Does criminalizing abortion affect the rate of abortions on the international level? The answer is no. One report from *The Lancet* notes that, after reviewing the abortion data from around the world, "We did not observe an association between the abortion rates for 2010–14 and the grounds under which abortion is legally allowed"[47].

In fact, criminalizing abortion actually increases the rate of abortions. The Guttmacher Institute reports that "Globally, 25% of pregnancies ended in abortion in 2010–2014." In this context, illegal-abortion countries have the rate of 37 abortions per 1000 women and legal-abortion countries have the rate of 34. Women in illegal-abortion countries are less likely to have access to birth control, thus making abortion more likely[48].

Although we do not know how many unsafe abortions are done worldwide, we do know that complications from unsafe abortions can be catastrophic not only for the woman but for society. In 2012, almost seven million women were treated for complications, and some estimate that many more do not get any treatment at all. "Treating medical complications from unsafe abortion places a considerable financial burden on public health care systems and on women and families in developing regions" because it requires hundreds of millions of dollars to provide care[49].

FINAL THOUGHTS

When Pandora opened up the jar to release the evils of the world, strife and hatred flew into the air. The abortion debate is one example of the bitterly fought battles between people committed to ideologies. Unfortunately, the anti positions once seen as too extreme for the mainstream have gained some credence. In 2018, for example, *The Atlantic* briefly hired Kevin Williamson despite his statements that women who had abortions should be punished as murderers. When asked by a reader whether women should get life without parole, he responded: "I have hanging more in mind"[50].

Hope was the last thing that flew out of Pandora's jar. One piece of good news is that a 2015 Gallup poll showed that 53% of Americans aged 18 to 34 years support abortion rights. Interestingly, 52% of the 35- to 55-year-old group are also pro-choice, and the 55 and older group experienced a sharp rise of support for pro-choice[51]. Life experience, then, could diminish the intense reactions against abortion.

Another hopeful sign appeared in Oregon in 2017, when a law that ensures abortion rights was passed. The Reproductive Health Equity Act will protect women no matter what happens on the federal level[52]. Such laws indicate that millions of Americans are waking up to the stark reality that women's lives are at stake—and that women must reclaim the power over our own bodies.

ACTION STEPS

- In addition to Planned Parenthood, several organizations have supported reproductive health. NARAL Pro-Choice America has a strong record of advocacy (www.prochoiceamerica.org).
- Helping low-income women to obtain abortions has become an urgent issue as abortion providers become scarcer. Travel expenses, for example, can be a significant barrier as more and more clinics shut down. One example of an abortion fund is Ohio's Women Have Options (www.womenhaveoptions.org).

Notes

1. Retrieved from www.reddit.com/r/TumblrAtRest/comments/2ylfc5/imagine_if_men_were_as_disgusted_with_rape_as/
2. Romm, C. (2015) There will be blood. The Atlantic. Retrieved from www.theatlantic.com/health/archive/2015/10/men-talk-about-periods/411931/
3. Cohen, I. G. (2012). The flawed basis behind fetal-pain abortion laws. Washington Post. Retrieved from www.washingtonpost.com/opinions/the-flawed-basis-behind-fetal-pain-abortion-laws/2012/08/01/gJQAS0w8PX_story.html?utm_term=.7472fbfa79bc
4. For example, read the public health perspective from George Washington University: https://publichealth.gwu.edu/WHI-medication-abortion. Also, the Guttmacher Institute monitors state abortion laws on this site: www.guttmacher.org/united-states/abortion/state-policies-abortion
5. Khazan, O. (2014). Here's why Hobby Lobby thinks IUDs are like abortions. The Atlantic. Retrieved from www.theatlantic.com/health/archive/2014/03/heres-why-hobby-lobby-thinks-iuds-are-like-abortions/284382/

6. Licata, E. (2017). World's most fragile dude reports coworker to HR for having period cramps. Mommyish. Retrieved from www.mommyish.com/dude-reports-coworker-hr-period/

7. May, A. (2017). Woman allegedly fired for period leaks suing former employer. USA Today. Retrieved from www.usatoday.com/story/news/nation-now/2017/08/23/woman-allegedly-fired-period-leaks-suing-former-employer/592947001/

8. Feeney, S. A. (2016). New York City to become first to provide free tampons and sanitary products to students. Am New York. Retrieved from www.amny.com/news/new-york-city-to-become-first-to-provide-free-tampons-and-sanitary-products-to-students-1.11573642

9. Meng, G. (2017). Our laws period-shame women—so I'm going to change them. Marie Claire. Retrieved from www.marieclaire.com/politics/features/a25464/congresswoman-grace-meng-menstrual-equity-bill/

10. Wessler, S. F. (2010). Timed out on welfare, many sell food stamps. The Investigative Fund. Retrieved from www.theinvestigativefund.org/investigations/immigrationandlabor/1252/timed_out_on_welfare,_many_sell_food_stamps/

11. Nittle, N. (2017). For those with endometriosis, lack of access to surgical option compounds the pain. Rewired website. Retrieved from https://rewire.news/article/2017/09/07/endometriosis-access-surgery/

12. Weiss, S. (2017). A man (yes, a man) just said "menstrual pain is a myth" and Twitter users are not having it. Glamour. Retrieved from https://www.glamour.com/story/man-said-menstrual-pain-is-a-myth-twitter-responds

13. Hornyak, T. (2010). Menstrual machine teaches men about, well. . . . CNET. Retrieved from www.cnet.com/news/menstruation-machine-teaches-men-about-well/

14. Lampen, C. (2017). Can "period leave" ever work? BBC website. Retrieved from www.bbc.com/capital/story/20170908-can-period-leave-ever-work

15. Dutt, B. (2017). I'm a feminist. Giving women a day off for their period is a stupid idea. Washington Post. Retrieved from www.washingtonpost.com/news/global-opinions/wp/2017/

08/03/im-a-feminist-but-giving-women-a-day-off-for-their-period-is-a-stupid-idea/?utm_term=.269d06602723

16. Pokharel, S. (2017). Nepali "menstruation hut" ritual claims life of teenage girl. CNN. Retrieved from www.cnn.com/2017/07/10/asia/nepal-menstruation-hut-deaths-outrage/index.html

17. United Nations Human Rights. (2014). Every woman's right to water, sanitation, and hygiene. UNHR website. Retrieved from www.ohchr.org/EN/NewsEvents/Pages/Everywomansrightto watersanitationandhygiene.aspx

18. United Nations Human Rights. (2014). Every woman's right to water, sanitation, and hygiene. UNHR website. Retrieved from www.ohchr.org/EN/NewsEvents/Pages/Everywomansrightto watersanitationandhygiene.aspx

19. Kaiser, S. (*n.d.*). Menstrual hygiene management. Sustainable Sanitation and Water Management website. Retrieved from www.sswm.info/content/menstrual-hygiene-management

20. Venema, V. (2014). The Indian sanitary pad revolutionary. BBC World Service. Retrieved from www.bbc.com/news/magazine-26260978

21. Parker, W. (2017). *Life's work: A moral argument for choice.* New York, NY: Atria Books.

22. Parker, W. (2017). *Life's work: A moral argument for choice.* New York, NY: Atria Books, p. 6.

23. Parker, W. (2017). *Life's work: A moral argument for choice.* New York, NY: Atria Books, p. 8.

24. Parker, W. (2017). *Life's work: A moral argument for choice.* New York, NY: Atria Books, p. 9.

25. Parker, W. (2017). *Life's work: A moral argument for choice.* New York, NY: Atria Books, p. 157.

26. Abber, C. (2015). What I learned working the front desk at Planned Parenthood. Women's Health. Retrieved from www.womenshealthmag.com/life/what-i-learned-working-at-planned-parenthood

27. Underwood, K. (2017). I had an abortion at age 19 and it changed my entire outlook on life. Women's Health. Retrieved from www.womenshealthmag.com/health/young-woman-abortion

28. Sherman, R. B. (2015). I've been thankful for my abortion every single day since I had it. Women's Health. Retrieved from www.womenshealthmag.com/life/abortion-access-aspirations
29. Sherman, R. B. (2015). I've been thankful for my abortion every single day since I had it. Women's Health. Retrieved from www.womenshealthmag.com/life/abortion-access-aspirations
30. Sherman, R.B. (2016). Why I will never stop talking about my abortion. Women's Health. Retrieved from www.womenshealthmag.com/life/uninterrupted-renee-bracey-sherman
31. Abber, C. (2015). No, you're not a bad person if you've had an abortion. Women's Health. Retrieved from www.womenshealthmag.com/life/shout-your-abortion-hb2
32. Vandegaer, Sister P. (*n.d.*). After the abortion. Hope After Abortion website. Retrieved from http://hopeafterabortion.com/?p=109
33. Bahadur, N. (2015). 95 Percent of women do not regret getting abortions. Huffington Post. Retrieved from www.huffingtonpost.com/entry/no-women-do-not-regret-getting-abortions_us_55a41166e4b0b8145f734040
34. I had an abortion. Experience project. Retrieved from www.experienceproject.com/stories/Had-An-Abortion/756722
35. Uttley, L, Reynertson, S., Kenny, L., & Melling, L. (2013). Miscarriage of medicine: The growth of Catholic hospitals and the threat to reproductive health care. American Civil Liberties Union website (MergerWatch Project also wrote this report.) Retrieved from www.aclu.org/sites/default/files/field_document/growth-of-catholic-hospitals-2013.pdf
36. Littlefield, A. (2017). Catholic rules forced this doctor to watch her patient sicken—now, she's speaking out. Rewire website. Retrieved from https://rewire.news/article/2017/09/07/catholic-rules-forced-doctor-watch-patient-sicken-now-shes-speaking/
37. Uttley, L, Reynertson, S., Kenny, L., & Melling, L. (2013). Miscarriage of medicine: The growth of Catholic hospitals and the threat to reproductive health care. American Civil Liberties Union website (MergerWatch Project also wrote this report.) Retrieved from www.aclu.org/sites/default/files/field_document/growth-of-catholic-hospitals-2013.pdf

38. Littlefield, A. (2017). Will a Catholic hospital merger gut health care in Gary, Indiana? Rewired website. Retrieved from https://rewire.news/article/2017/05/25/will-catholic-hospital-merger-gut-health-care-gary-indiana/

39. Uttley, L, Reynertson, S., Kenny, L., & Melling, L. (2013). Miscarriage of medicine: The growth of Catholic hospitals and the threat to reproductive health care. American Civil Liberties Union website (MergerWatch Project also wrote this report.) Retrieved from www.aclu.org/sites/default/files/field_document/growth-of-catholic-hospitals-2013.pdf

40. Uttley, L, Reynertson, S., Kenny, L., & Melling, L. (2013). Miscarriage of medicine: The growth of Catholic hospitals and the threat to reproductive health care. American Civil Liberties Union website (MergerWatch Project also wrote this report.) Retrieved from www.aclu.org/sites/default/files/field_document/growth-of-catholic-hospitals-2013.pdf

41. Eckholm, E. (2011). Push for "personhood" amendment represents new tack in abortion fight. New York Times. Retrieved from www.nytimes.com/2011/10/26/us/politics/personhood-amendments-would-ban-nearly-all-abortions.html

42. Newsweek Staff. (2017). Women on birth control could not be barred from working, according to new Missouri bill. Newsweek. Retrieved from www.newsweek.com/missouri-abortion-sb-5-crisis-pregnancy-centers-630165

43. Blue, M. (2016). Religious right legal leader: Of course states could punish women for abortion. Right Wing Watch. Retrieved from www.rightwingwatch.org/post/religious-right-legal-leader-of-course-states-could-punish-women-for-abortion/

44. Blue, M. (2016). Religious right legal leader: Of course states could punish women for abortion. Right Wing Watch. Retrieved from www.rightwingwatch.org/post/religious-right-legal-leader-of-course-states-could-punish-women-for-abortion/

45. Tashman, B. (2016). Right-wing pundit defends Trump's abortion "punishment" comments. Right Wing Watch. Retrieved from www.rightwingwatch.org/post/

right-wing-pundit-defends-trumps-abortion-punishment-comments/

46. Gold, R. B., & Donovan, M .K. (2017). Lessons from before abortion was legal. Scientific American. Retrieved from www.scientificamerican.com/article/lessons-from-before-abortion-was-legal/

47. Sedgh, G., Bearak, J., Singh, S., Bankole, A., Popinchalk, A., Ganatra, B., . . . Johnston, H. B. (2016). Abortion incidence between 1990 and 2014: Global, regional, and subregional levels and trends. *The Lancet, 388*(10041), 258–267.

48. Guttmacher Institute. (2018). Induced abortions worldwide. Guttmacher Institute website. Retrieved from www.guttmacher.org/fact-sheet/induced-abortion-worldwide

49. Guttmacher Institute. (2018). Induced abortions worldwide. Guttmacher Institute website. Retrieved from www.guttmacher.org/fact-sheet/induced-abortion-worldwide

50. Chamberlain, S. (2018). Liberal magazine *The Atlantic* drops writer who claimed abortions should be "treated like homicide." Fox News. Retrieved from www.msn.com/en-us/tv/news/liberal-magazine-the-atlantic-drops-writer-who-claimed-abortions-should-be-treated-like-homicide/ar-AAvwG8L

51. Saad, L. (2015). Americans choose "pro-choice" for first time in seven years. Gallup News. Retrieved from http://news.gallup.com/poll/183434/americans-choose-pro-choice-first-time-seven-years.aspx

52. Cauterucci, C. (2017) Oregon passes sweeping law enshrining abortion rights and funding for all. Slate. Retrieved from www.slate.com/blogs/xx_factor/2017/07/06/oregon_passes_sweeping_law_enshrining_abortion_rights_and_funding_for_all.html

53. Steffen, J. (2015). Planned Parenthood suspect: "I am guilty . . . a warrior for the babies." Denver Post. Retrieved from www.denverpost.com/2015/12/09/planned-parenthood-suspect-i-am-guilty-a-warrior-for-the-babies/

54. The Students for Life of America website includes the Planned Parenthood Project, which is an effort to close down all Planned Parenthood clinics. Retrieved from http://studentsforlife.org/plannedparenthood/

55. The Planned Parenthood website is www.plannedparenthood. org

56. The impact of the Hyde Amendment on low-income women is described in this article: Light, J. (2013). Five facts you should know about the Hyde Amendment. Bill Moyers website. Retrieved from billmoyers.com/content/ five-facts-you-should-know-about-the-hyde-amendment/

57. Lee, M. Y. H. (2015). For Planned Parenthood abortion stats, "3 percent" and "94 percent" are both misleading. Washington Post. Retrieved from www.washingtonpost.com/news/fact-checker/wp/2015/08/12/for-planned-parenthood-abortion-stats-3-percent-and-94-percent-are-both-misleading/?utm_ term=.46af7ca0ea0f

58. Bassett, L. (2015). Indiana shut down its rural Planned Parenthood clinics and got an HIV outbreak. Huffington Post. Retrieved from www.huffingtonpost.com/2015/03/31/ indiana-planned-parenthood_n_6977232.html

59. Ervin, B. (2013). No woman can call herself free. Huffington Post. Retrieved from www.huffingtonpost.com/valerie-ervin/ no-woman-can-call-herself_b_2965996.html

60. Latson, J. (2016). What Margaret Sanger really said about eugenics and race. Time Magazine. Retrieved from http://time. com/4081760/margaret-sanger-history-eugenics/

61. Latson, J. (2016). What Margaret Sanger really said about eugenics and race. Time Magazine. Retrieved from http://time. com/4081760/margaret-sanger-history-eugenics/

62. Planned Parenthood. (*n.d.*). Opposition claims about Margaret Sanger. Planned Parenthood factsheet. Retrieved from www. plannedparenthood.org/files/8013/9611/6937/Opposition_ Claims_About_Margaret_Sanger.pdf

63. Levitan, D. (2015). Unspinning the Planned Parenthood video. Factcheck. Retrieved from www.factcheck.org/2015/07/ unspinning-the-planned-parenthood-video/

64. New York Times Editorial Board. (2015). The campaign of deception against Planned Parenthood. New York Times. Retrieved from www.nytimes.com/2015/07/22/opinion/the-campaign-of-deception-against-planned-parenthood.html

8

REFLECTIONS

The Inner Work of Activism

WORKING ON OUR OWN BIASES

Self-Reflection for Thoughtful Activists

In the midst of the #MeToo movement and other remarkable feminist upsurges, it would seem absurd to talk about self-reflection and cultural competence as a component of activism. Who has time to sit down and contemplate when so much has occurred since Trump took office? Besides the fear of losing momentum, activists may feel that every rollback of women's rights requires urgent action. However, thoughtful activism requires a focus on the long-term future in addition to the immediate present. If activists are building a strong movement instead of a temporary taskforce, they must consider the inner work of activism as a foundation.

Thousands of articles and books have focused on cultural competence (defined as being able to respect and communicate with diverse persons), so it would be impossible to summarize the highlights in one chapter. However, activists must work on their own biases if they want to achieve intersectionality. Self-reflection is one way to start the process. Using myself as a case study, I can ask: What did I learn about diverse groups growing up, and how has this affected me today?

Remembering old jokes from your childhood can be one way to recapture how you were socialized. Humor can sometimes reveal ugly prejudices. Polack jokes were common in the 1970s, such as the one about a "dumb Polack" using white-out on a word processing screen. I also heard jokes about Mexicans (called "wetbacks" because they swam across the Rio Grande) and African Americans (who had it made because the government gave them everything). Women drivers still face ridicule. When I recently used the search term "women driver jokes" on the Internet, I found several, including the meme showing a huge multicar pileup with the heading: "Annual meeting of women drivers." Like dumb blonde jokes, some stereotypes never seem to die.

In the 1970s, the TV and movie industries had just discovered that not everybody could relate to the *Leave It to Beaver* setting. I was eight when *The Mary Tyler Moore Show* first aired, thus uplifting young girls like me. This happy, successful career woman who did not have to be married to "count" in society was a great role model for my cohort. I also saw Archie Bunker's racism being openly mocked on *All in the Family*, in addition to shows that featured African Americans as main characters. These advances toward diversity may seem pitiful and even quaint by today's standards, but they were a giant leap forward at the time. Even after reading critiques of dated shows such as *Good Times* (a positive representation of an African American family), I still think that they made me less racist.

Yes, I grew up in a racist setting, and I still need to work on myself. Like many other Whites, I am horrified by overt racism—such as the Charlottesville rally in 2017—but still struggle with the implications of White privilege. (*Note:* I stopped using the word "Caucasian" after I found out that the originator of that concept was a rabid racist.)[1].

When I started my social work career in my late 30s, I finally felt compelled to think about race and other diversity issues. That is one key trait of White privilege, of course, because racism rarely affected me on the personal level. Privilege was below my radar, like the automatic doors that swish open for me but slam shut for the unprivileged.

In addition to race/ethnicity is the wide range of differences between people: religion, age, social class, education level, disabilities, and the rest. We are living with a rapid rate of social change that appears to benefit some groups, such as the LGBT+ community. For instance, the new norm appears to be avoiding homophobic comments, such as the casual use of terms such as "fag."

The bad news, though, is that the new generation of White adults are not necessarily more motivated than their elders to fight racism. Young White adults are likely to show signs of color- blind racism, or "racism without racists." For example, they may explain housing segregation as the natural result of similar groups wanting to live together instead of discrimination[2].

Related to this research is a 2015 study that claims that millennials may support interracial marriage, but not much else. "Unfortunately, closer examination of the data suggests that millennials aren't racially tolerant, they're racially apathetic: They simply ignore structural racism rather than try to fix it"[3]. Because this study took place before the Black Lives

Matter movement became so strong, the issue of police violence against Blacks may have shifted some people's minds.

Although this chapter could have covered several types of bias, only three types were chosen to demonstrate the power of self-reflection for our advocacy. Before we start trying to fight social injustice, we need to look at our own possible contributions to the problem. First, beauty bias is a powerful weapon against women. Few of us want to be called ugly or be ignored because of our looks. Another weapon of oppression is ageism—the indifference or even hostility toward older persons. The last bias is transphobia or discomfort with trans persons, which would inhibit the alliance between feminists and trans rights advocates. Without recognition of our own biases, then, we may delay the advancement of human rights.

Beauty Bias

Since I was a child, I would rate a person's attractiveness based on the beauty standards imposed on my consciousness. As a teen struggling with acne, for example, I would look at clear-skinned females with unbearable envy. Almost always, I would compare myself unfavorably with others based on their looks. Research shows that my behavior followed the "What is beautiful is good" norm that saturates our society[4].

The social foundations of the beauty bias (also known as appearance discrimination) are so deeply embedded that it will take hard work to fight it on the collective level. Deborah Rhodes' excellent book, *The Beauty Bias: The Injustice of Appearance in Life and Law* (2010), is a good start for this discussion. Stating that 90% of American women consider their appearance to be "important to their self-image," she notes that attractive people get better grades, better jobs, and social approval. As a lawyer, she lists the reasons that appearance discrimination is wrong:

> "[It] offends principles of equal opportunity";
> "[It] reinforces group subordination";
> "[It] restricts self-expression and cultural identity"; and
> "[It] both reflects and reinforces class privilege." [5]

Indeed, it would be foolish to act as if our looks did not matter. "Beauty may be only skin deep, but that is deep enough to confer an unsettling array of advantages. Although most of us learn at early ages that physical attractiveness matters, few of us realize how much. Nor do we generally recognize the extent to which our biases conflict with meritocratic principles"[6].

We would like to believe that the playing field is fair, a belief that is the basis of meritocracy (i.e., a system that rewards ability and talent). However, women seen as prettier usually get more positive attention than the plainer ones. This is true for men, too, of course. Once I was at a conference at which the president of a small college spoke about achieving one's goals. He was a handsome man, which made me ponder during the speech how many doors had been opened for him for that reason. At question time, I raised my hand and asked him whether he had considered how privilege had played a role in his success. He seemed to expect the usual point about gender or race. Instead I asked, "Have you ever wondered what your life would be like if you had had a facial deformity?" He appeared startled but receptive to the idea that his looks may have been a factor in his career.

When a child feels ugly growing up, it can have long-lasting effects. Rhodes states that "In essence, individuals' unattractiveness in their early years can set off a chain of developmental difficulties that ultimately become self-reinforcing. Ridicule and marginalization often lessen self-confidence and social skills, which then translate into less satisfactory interpersonal and career experiences in later life"[7]. For some persons, the ugly duckling motif never goes away. This can be damaging to one's career and social life—or it can be a bridge to greater empathy with others. Identifying with the underdog is one way to cope with such insecurities.

Where do we even begin to fight the insidious aspects of the beauty bias within ourselves? "Appearance should be a source of pleasure, not shame. Individuals should be able to make decisions about whether to enhance their attractiveness without being judged either politically correct or professionally unacceptable"[8]. That first sentence resonates with as much power as this bumper sticker slogan: "Start a revolution: Love your body."

Working on our own self-image can help us confront our own beauty bias. Introspection is one way to befriend yourself. One way to stop denigrating oneself is to stop comparisons with others: To compare is to despair. There will always be somebody out there who is better looking, more articulate, and more competent than you. Instead of honoring your own uniqueness, then, you may fall into the trap of thinking things like, "I wish I were as pretty as her." This negative thinking reinforces the beauty bias both in ourselves and in society.

Once we start uprooting the beauty bias from our thinking, we can focus on uprooting it from our social interactions. Fat-shaming (also known as weight bias and weight discrimination) is a difficult problem because it is so prevalent. Even as a child, I knew about the thinness norm and acted on it because I had the advantage of being skinny. My scrawniness (now long gone!) became a source of power over the heavier girls. Now that I am on the other side of the equation, I know that people judge me as I had once judged others.

Judgement, then, is the key component to fat-shaming. People may look askance at an overweight person ordering fries at McDonalds—yes, it is called food-shaming. Sometimes a friend or relative may give someone a look that says: "Are you going to eat *that*?" Although fat acceptance and anti-dieting groups are fighting this type of judgement, the fat-shaming attitudes are slow to change. Moral disgust can spark anger toward a person perceived as lazy and gluttonous. Like a drug addict, an overweight person may evoke the "how can you do that to yourself?" response[9]. Contempt, an emotion based on moral superiority, is another way for a person to judge an overweight person[10]. If you feel disgust and contempt toward yourself for your eating and/or exercise habits, does that reflect on your interactions with people who are heavier than you?

Because society delights in shaming us, two other types of shame have emerged in our popular lingo. Body-shaming refers to the disapproval of all types of bodies: too skinny, too bare-chested, too short, too tall—the list goes on. Obviously, males have to deal with their own body issues if they have "dad bods" instead of "six-pack abs." Men who are not gym rats and women with flat chests will probably get fewer dates. Another consideration is facial features because mainstream society values a symmetric and oval face[11].

Slut-shaming based on clothing choices is certainly a related topic. Supposedly, a female who wears form-fitting or skin-baring clothes is "asking for it." Of course, women in sweats and other unsexy attire have always had to deal with harassment. Women should have the right to wear anything they damn well please without any negative consequences. If they want to wear a dress that emphasizes their curves or a low-cut blouse to show off "the girls," nobody should criticize or judge these women.

However, we do judge other women's clothes. When I see a celebrity wear a dress that shows off her side boob or a woman in the store wearing short shorts that reveal half of her butt, I think of the clothes as provocative. This opinion would never excuse any harassment, of course. Sexy clothes, though, do raise the issue of being taken seriously as a woman. Women politicians who always wear pantsuits, for example, may evoke exasperation from those who want to see a woman in a dress. Cleavage and skirt length can also cause remarks.

Besides slut-shaming, clothing choices can result in harsh criticism if somebody is poorly dressed. I used the term "poorly" deliberately because class issues (i.e., money) intersect with the beauty bias. Some women are too poor or busy to spend much time on their wardrobe. Others are indifferent dressers and barely notice what they put on in the morning. Makeup, plastic surgery, and other commodities in the beauty business can be an overwhelming aspect of trying to look young and pretty. Some women try hard to improve their appearance, but others spend less time and effort. Whatever decisions a woman makes about her hair or face or clothes, we should step back from judging them by the beauty standard.

Racism and colorism (discrimination based on the darkness of a person's skin) are other facets of the beauty bias. In the past, African Americans tried to straighten their hair and use skin whitener. It is sickening that skin whiteners are still being used, especially in Asia and Africa. I was only a child when the "Black is beautiful" movement occurred, but it left a lasting impression with me. Like confronting the classism of the beauty standard, valuing the beauty of diverse women is one way to promote intersectionality. Beauty bias also affects older women, which will be discussed in the next section.

IMPLICIT BIAS AND AGEISM

The term "implicit bias" has emerged as a new approach to fighting prejudice (i.e., prejudging others). Many people are now considering how their own unconscious reactions may have racist or other discriminatory overtones. Although implicit bias is pervasive, our brains are malleable and can erase the biases[12]. One way to evaluate your hidden biases is by taking the Implicit Association Tests developed by Harvard University[13].

Implicit biases, then, are blind spots in our mental landscape. In *Blindspot: Hidden Biases of Good People* (Banaji & Greenwald, 2013), the authors discuss how biases are caused by "social mindbugs" that sort people into two categories: trustworthy and untrustworthy[14]. In other words, is this person part of my social group?

Whenever I present on implicit bias and ageism to social work audiences, I expect them to claim that they are not ageist. We're social workers, so we can't have negative attitudes toward older adults! So I first ask them to ask the person next to them how old they are. Next, they have to say to that person: "Really? You look much older than that!"

This exercise evokes many reactions, especially dismay. Nobody wants to ask such a forbidden question, nor say such a rude thing. I ask the audience what the comment of looking older implied, and they respond with adjectives such as haggard and unwell. This automatic reflex to the idea of "old age" is so embedded in our culture that we do not recognize it as harmful. Try it on yourself with a mirror: How would you feel if you said to your reflection that you looked old today? However, you may not want to try the "You look much older" comment on somebody older than 25.

Although I know of no hate groups against older adults, implicit ageism is ubiquitous in our lives[15]. Age-defying cosmetics, plastic surgeries, hair dyeing, and other offers to drink at the Fountain of Youth are multibillion-dollar moneymakers. Women especially start facing age discrimination in their 20s; no matter how old he is, a male on the OkCupid website requests a female in her early 20s[16]. How did we learn to be so ageist?

Study this picture (Illustration 8.1) closely because two aspects of implicit bias apply here. First, visual mindbugs are "ingrained habits of thought that lead to errors in how we perceive, remember, reason, and make decisions." These lead to unconscious inferences, in which our eyes and brains make automatic judgments[17].

- This crone looks like the witch from Hansel and Gretel or Snow White—what do you remember about those fairy tales? She was evil (hence old people are bad) and she lived alone in the forest (hence old people should be rejected by the village).
- Describe her physical features in detail. How do they relate to other images of older women in Disney movies such as *Tangled* and *The Little Mermaid*?

ILLUSTRATION 8.1 Old witch stereotype. Source: Entofolio.

- Consider the contrast with this image of a young mother (Illustration 8.2) Describe why this woman epitomizes goodness instead of evil.

In addition, visual mindbugs are memory mindbugs, which can make incorrect connections[18]. False alarms can result, such as thinking that all Muslims are terrorists. How can we debug our memories so that we can recognize the beauty of old age?

ILLUSTRATION 8.2 Mother and child, *circa* 1913. Source: Library of Congress.

First, think about any negative experiences you may have had with an older person. Was there a mean grandparent or ornery neighbor who made you link old age with difficult personalities? Obviously, some mean kids turn into mean adults and then may end up being even meaner as they age—but many older adults are quite likeable. It is amazing how an unpleasant memory can have a heavier impact on one's mind than an innocuous one.

Besides previous encounters with a difficult older person, we may be influenced by the power of language. Consider these terms: over the hill, cranky old lady (the Hallmark cartoon of Maxine is my heroine!), old fart, and grumpy old man. You may even have used these terms for yourself with self-deprecating humor—"hey, I had another senior moment." In contrast to these terms are the stereotypes of older adults as sweet (grandma baking cookies) and/or wise (especially for Asians and other persons of color). If we approach an older adult (or ourselves) with this language and these stereotypes, we become blind to the real person.

Old age is also associated with a dreaded future. Fear, then, is one outstanding feature of ageism. Until we confront our own fears about aging, we may not overcome our implicit bias. Ask yourself which aspects of aging you dread or even fear. Possible topics include:

- Fear of mortality;
- Fear of being dismissed as a "sweet old lady" or "dear old grandpa";
- Fear of being invisible;
- Fear of not looking young anymore;
- Fear of grief;
- Fear of nursing homes;
- Fear of dependence;
- Fear of dementia; and
- Fear of physical disability.

Ageism, then, is a complex form of implicit bias that takes a lot of energy to tackle. One idea is that we could be kind to ourselves by telling the mirror that we are proud and beautiful at any age. Then we could extend our self-acceptance to accepting others as possible friends no matter their age. If you do not have a friend who is decades older than you, then it is time to make a new one (unless you are in your 90s, then you have a good excuse). Friends come in all shapes and sizes and ages—celebrate the diversity between age groups!

DISCOMFORT WITH TRANSGENDER PERSONS

Discomfort or phobia? The term "transphobia" may not be fully relevant in this book because I doubt that any of my readers has an irrational fear of trans persons. People who believe that trans persons are satanic are probably reading a book about the demonic possession of feminists instead of this book.

Although many of us well-meaning persons may not be irrationally afraid of those who cross the gender line, we may feel a sense of discomfort when meeting somebody who is trans, queer, intersex, gender fluid, or any other variation. (To simplify this section, I am using the word "transgender" as an inclusive term.) Instead of beating yourself up for not being able to keep up with the new norms or how many letters should be in the LGBTQIA + acronym, let us first consider the possibility of "social change fatigue."

If you haven't heard of the term "social change fatigue," it is because I made it up myself. A National Public Radio (NPR) news story about technology fatigue (i.e., weariness at having to learn yet another innovation) inspired me to think about how social change is happening so fast that some of us may be simply tired. A woman had mentioned to me how her husband was struggling with the conversations about gender: "When the Supreme Court approved same-sex marriage, he was okay with it. Then Caitlyn Jenner came out—he gets it now about transgender. But all this nonbinary and gender fluid stuff? It's so hard for him!"

This husband is not alone. Once when I presented to a Jungian group about this topic, a gay man came up to me and expressed his confusion about meeting a nonbinary person in a bar. "I thought I knew about all that stuff—I've been out since forever. But I must be behind the times!" Another time, I had presented at a TransOhio conference and a trans man told me that his young middle-schoolers were using gender terms that were new to him. If those in the forefront of fighting for equality feel that they cannot keep up with these gender issues, how can an average person like the woman's husband keep up? As Illustration 8.3 shows, gender identity can be a confusing topic.

This concept of social change fatigue, though, is *not* an excuse for us to shrug our shoulders and simply give up on adapting to the new gender norms. Some may claim that trans persons are just exploiting identity politics by claiming minority status. However, these critics are not justified in saying that society cannot handle these changes right now.

ILLUSTRATION 8.3 Gender sign. Source: Shutterstock.

Trans persons have existed in history for as long as cis persons[19]. Acknowledging that trans persons deserve as much respect and dignity as anybody else is critical for any progressive movement.

Instead, "social change fatigue" could be a partial explanation for why some well-meaning people may feel discouraged about understanding the once-hidden variations of gender. Where did they get their ideas about gender? How do they know what they know? Only by asking these questions can we construct a bridge between the current understanding and the new gender norms.

Hopefully, using myself as a case study will help us to understand transphobia. Cross-dressers were my first exposure to crossing the gender line because in those days, few saw any distinction between the cis men who wore female apparel and the trans women. Cross-dressers were called transvestites, as in the "Sweet Transvestite" of the *Rocky Horror Picture Show*. In the classic comedy movie *Some Like It Hot*, Tony Curtis and Jack Lemmon had to dress up as women to escape from the mob. The humor of men's freakish behavior also appeared in *M*A*S*H*, in which Corporal Klinger kept on dressing as a woman to get out of the army. Later, the show *Bosom Buddies* (the sitcom about men hiding in a sorority) and the movies *Tootsie* and *Mrs. Doubtfire* all reinforced one strong message for me: Men dressed up as women to get something, whether an acting job or time with their children. Other than the *Rocky Horror* example, these cross-dressers simply had an ulterior motive for crossing the gender line.

Today's debates about the "bathroom bills" (i.e., the prohibition of trans persons using the bathroom of their authentic gender) reflect the idea that the only reason a man would "claim" to be a woman would be to get something—in this case, the chance to attack females in public restrooms[20]. The people who support discrimination against trans persons probably watched enough episodes of *M*A*S*H* to make them experts on this issue. Was Corporal Klinger trans or cis? It would not matter to the transphobic people who show genuine fear at the idea of the Other. Anybody who does not look female enough is vulnerable to attack because of transphobia. Trans men (and any male) also face risks in the public sphere if perceived as not masculine enough. Although cis people face fewer threats than trans people, they share the same concerns about safety and nondiscrimination.

Unfortunately, the question of cross-dressing dominated the discussion about trans issues for those in my generation. If you ever meet somebody who says something transphobic, you may want to ask, "Where did you get your information about this while growing up?" Chances are that the media had exposed them to a pile of mishmash. (Forgive me for that pun, I could not help it!)

When I was a kid in 1975, I heard about Renee Richards having the first "sex change" operation (now called gender reassignment or gender affirmation). My initial reaction was, "How weird." As a cis person, though, I had the luxury of not being concerned about this topic for years. In high school, I did have a friend who was an androgynous-looking male. He also had a nongendered name. A teacher kept on calling him "she" until I went up to him to say, "I wish you would stop calling my friend a girl. It's really upsetting him." The teacher was flabbergasted because he had really thought that my friend had been a girl. This was my first experience with a person who could have been intersex, transgender, or gender fluid. Now that I know more about this topic, I know that I could have been a better ally.

Trans issues were weird to me as a child, and it took me years to develop enough knowledge and sensitivity to become a trans advocate. Hopefully, my story proves that positive change is possible. Gloria Steinem also went through a similar change of heart regarding trans women. In 1977, she had publicly attacked Renee Richards as "a frightening instance of what feminism could lead to" and "living proof that feminism isn't necessary." She asked, "If the shoe doesn't fit, must we change the foot?" She even praised the book *Transsexual Empire: The Making of the She-Male*[21] in 1983. Today, though, she is a strong advocate of trans rights[22]. Some of my readers may be trans-exclusionary radical feminists (TERFs) who believe that trans women are not "real" women. However, I posit that it is a human rights issue for people to claim their own gender (or nongender) identity (Box 8.1).

The Kirwan Center stresses that our brains are malleable and that we can unlearn our implicit biases[23]. As discussed in the previous section on ageism, visual mindbugs can cause automatic assumptions about a person based on cues such as dress and speech. What are the visual mindbugs related to gender, especially nonbinary? Dress, body shape, posture (e.g., females usually sit with legs together, but males could be manspreading), and movements are some signs of gender. If we picture an androgynous person who shows no clear indication of either gender, this nonbinary image can be disorienting. Does the mind have a need to categorize people on first sight? Race/ethnicity could be a parallel to this question. Sometimes people ask an Asian American or another person of color, "Where are you from?" and then respond to the answer of "Florida" with "But where are you *really* from?" This offensive behavior may signify the need for their brains to categorize that person in a racial/ethnic category.

BOX **8.1**

TERMS AND ISSUES

Bathroom bills: attempts to prevent trans persons from using the public restrooms of their gender identity (not the one assigned at birth).

Misgendering: the refusal to use the preferred pronoun (he or she) of a transgender individual. For example, the lawyers fighting Gavin Grimm's attempts to use the men's room in his school call him "she." As one analyst states, "Broadly speaking, misgendering is a tactic used to reinforce the existing panic, fear, and disbelief around transgender identities"[26].

Intersex: According to the Intersex Society of North America, this term refers to "a variety of conditions in which a person is born with a reproductive or sexual anatomy that doesn't seem to fit the typical definitions of female or male. For example, a person might be born appearing to be female on the outside but having mostly male-typical anatomy on the inside"[27].

Transgender: the umbrella term for "people whose gender is different from their 'assigned' sex at birth— that written on their birth certificate. Gender can refer to one's own, internal sense of being a man or woman, or another type that doesn't fit either category. Gender can also be expressed externally"[28].

Transsexual: This term is sometimes used to refer to those who undergo medical treatments (e.g., hormones and surgery) to reassign one's gender.

However, this word was once used instead of "transgender," so it can be confusing if the context is not clear. It is recommended that you simply use the term "transgender" to avoid misunderstanding.

Cisgender: means "same gender" instead of "across gender." This term refers to those who identify with their birth-assigned genders.

Nonbinary: This term stresses the idea that gender is a spectrum, not two categories of male and female. Some persons do not identify with either gender.

Pronouns: To avoid accidental misgendering, you can ask people what is their preferred pronoun. You may want to introduce yourself with your pronoun to normalize it. A new trend is simply to use "they" or "their" for a single person—why should we still be using gendered pronouns? Another variation of pronouns is "ze/hir."

Surgery: part of the transition. Sex reassignment surgery (SRS) is also called gender affirmation surgery. These procedures are either top (e.g., removal of female breasts) or bottom (i.e., genital alterations). The term "sex change" is no longer used. This may be an obvious point, but never ask trans persons if they had this surgery because it is a gross invasion of privacy.

Trans man: a person who was assigned "female" at birth but identifies as male (FTM).

Trans woman: a person who was assigned "male" at birth but identifies as female (MTF).

Cross-dresser: usually refers to a heterosexual male who likes to wear women's clothes. Drag queens are usually gay males who dress up for fun and entertainment. When the media wants to distort the perception of trans persons, they might use the picture of a flamboyant drag queen instead of somebody wearing regular clothes.

Gender dysphoria (once called gender identity disorder): the clinical term for those who do not identify with their assigned gender. Listing this condition in the *Diagnostic and Statistical Manual of Mental Disorders* (DSM) makes some trans persons feel stigmatized, but "some transgender advocates believe the inclusion of Gender Dysphoria in the DSM is necessary in order to advocate for health insurance that covers the medically necessary treatment recommended for transgender people"[29].

Gender nonconforming: the term for persons who do not conform with gender norms. Not all gender-nonconforming persons are trans, and not all trans persons are gender nonconforming[30].

Genderqueer: those "who experience their gender identity and/or gender expression as falling outside the categories of man and woman"[31].

When I see a person who is not clearly male or female at first glance, I find myself looking again before I stop myself. Why do I have to categorize this person? A grad student in Sweden wrote about this reaction when describing an incident on campus. He wore a little eye makeup but otherwise presented as male. "Later in the evening, when my colleagues and I were leading an exercise, one of the young people asked me whether I was a he or a she. I responded that it didn't make much difference to me. After asking incredulously whether I was serious and being assured that I was, he told me in no uncertain terms, 'Get away from me!'"[24].

As more persons are presenting themselves as nonbinary, we may be able to overcome this need to categorize by gender. Whether we are cis, trans, nonbinary, or any other variation of gender, we are all valuable and deserve to be valued by others. "Nature loves variety but society hates it"[25].

Notes

1. Khan, R. (2011). Stop using the word "Caucasian" to mean white. Discover blog. Retrieved from http://blogs.discovermagazine. com/gnxp/2011/01/stop-using-the-word-caucasian-to-mean-white/#.WnJbAUxFyUk
2. Bonilla-Silva, E. (2017). *Racism without racists: Color-blind racism and the persistence of racial inequality in America.* Lanham, MD: Rowman & Littlefield.
3. McElwee, S. (2015). Millennials are more racist than you think. Politico. Retrieved from www.politico.com/magazine/story/2015/03/millenials-race-115909
4. Shahani-Denning, C. (2003). Physical attractiveness bias in hiring: What is beautiful is good. Hofstra University website. Retrieved from www.hofstra.edu/pdf/orsp_shahani-denning_spring03.pdf
5. Rhodes, D. L. (2010). *The beauty bias: The injustice of appearance in life and law.* New York, NY: Oxford University Press, p. 93.
6. Rhodes, D. L. (2010). *The beauty bias: The injustice of appearance in life and law.* New York, NY: Oxford University Press, p. 23.
7. Rhodes, D. L. (2010). *The beauty bias: The injustice of appearance in life and law.* New York, NY: Oxford University Press, p. 26.
8. Rhodes, D. L. (2010). *The beauty bias: The injustice of appearance in life and law.* New York, NY: Oxford University Press, p. 87.

9. Researchers have recently focused on moral disgust in our interactions. For example, see Russell, P. S., & Giner-Sorolla, R. (2013). Bodily moral disgust: What it is, how it is different from anger, and why it is an unreasoned emotion. *Psychological Bulletin, 139*(2), 328.

10. Contempt is another fascinating topic. For example, see Fischer, A. H., & Roseman, I. J. (2007). Beat them or ban them: The characteristics and social functions of anger and contempt. *Journal of Personality and Social Psychology, 93*(1), 103.

11. Rhodes, D. L. (2010). *The beauty bias: The injustice of appearance in life and law.* New York, NY: Oxford University Press, p. 24.

12. The Kirwan Institute for the Study of Race and Ethnicity has done excellent research on implicit bias. See kirwaninstitute.osu.edu/

13. See the Project Implicit website at https://implicit.harvard.edu/implicit/

14. Banaji, M. R., & Greenwald, A. G. (2013). *Blindspot: Hidden biases of good people.* New York, NY: Bantam Books, p. 16.

15. Levy, B. R., & Banaji, M. R. (2002). Implicit ageism. In T. D. Nelson (Ed.), *Ageism: Stereotyping and prejudice against older persons.* Cambridge, MA: MIT Press, pp. 49–75.

16. Rudder, C. (2015). Men's favorite ages are 20, 21, 22, and 23: A data dive by the co-founder of OKCupid. Jezebel. Retrieved from https://jezebel.com/mens-favorite-ages-are-20-21-22-and-23-a-data-dive-1731660984

17. Banaji, M. R., & Greenwald, A. G. (2013). *Blindspot: Hidden biases of good people.* New York, NY: Bantam Books, p. 4.

18. Banaji, M. R., & Greenwald, A. G. (2013). *Blindspot: Hidden biases of good people.* New York, NY: Bantam Books, p. 6.

19. See the website about trans persons in history: www.wevebeenaround.com/episodes/

20. Steinmetz, K. (2015). Everything you need to know about the debate over transgender people and bathrooms. Time. Retrieved from time.com/3974186/transgender-bathroom-debate/

21. Raymond, J. G. (1979). *Transsexual empire: The making of the she-male.* New York, NY: Teachers College Press.

22. Robyn. (2013). Gloria Steinem does a 180. Voices on the Square. Blog post retrieved from https://m.dailykos.com/stories/2013/10/04/1244223/-Gloria-Steinem-does-a-180

23. The Kirwan Institute for the Study of Race website: kirwaninstitute.osu.edu/

24. Juge, G. (2014). "Get away from me!": Implicit and explicit transphobia in Swedish-speaking men. Master's Thesis.

25. Cited in Juge, G. (2014). "Get away from me!": Implicit and explicit transphobia in Swedish-speaking men. Master's Thesis.

26. Finch, S. D. (2017). How conservatives' legal strategy to misgender trans plaintiffs could backfire. Rewire. Retrieved from https://rewire.news/article/2017/10/06/conservatives-legal-strategy-misgender-trans-plaintiffs-backfire/

27. See the website of the Intersex Society of North America for more information: www.isna.org/faq/what_is_intersex

28. A guide to transgender terms. (2015). BBC website. Retrieved from www.bbc.com/news/magazine-32979297

29. Jardin, X. (2015). How to talk about Caitlyn Jenner: A guide to speaking and writing about transgender people. Boing Boing (based on GLAAD—Gay and Lesbian Alliance Against Defamation.) Retrieved from https://boingboing.net/2015/06/01/how-to-talk-about-caitlyn-jenn.html

30. Jardin, X. (2015). How to talk about Caitlyn Jenner: A guide to speaking and writing about transgender people. Boing Boing (based on GLAAD—Gay and Lesbian Alliance Against Defamation.) Retrieved from https://boingboing.net/2015/06/01/how-to-talk-about-caitlyn-jenn.html

31. Jardin, X. (2015). How to talk about Caitlyn Jenner: A guide to speaking and writing about transgender people. Boing Boing (based on GLAAD—Gay and Lesbian Alliance Against Defamation.) Retrieved from https://boingboing.net/2015/06/01/how-to-talk-about-caitlyn-jenn.html

9

TAKING ACTION

The Outer Work of Activism

INTRODUCTION: THOUGHTFUL ACTIVISM

In 2017, the #MeToo campaign elicited thousands of descriptions of assaults and harassment. One of the memories that came to my mind was a minor incident that had occurred when I was a teenager waiting at a bus stop. Countless times before, I had been honked at and yelled at as cars passed by. So when I heard a car honk behind me and a male voice call out, "Hey, do you want a ride?" I responded in my usual way.

I turned around with my middle finger extended.

The man who I had flipped off was Father John, a priest from my church. I stammered out an apology, but he said he understood. Thankfully, I was not excommunicated for this encounter.

Of course, I was not acting as a thoughtful activist but as a ticked-off teenager who had just wanted to wait for the bus without being harassed. I had never considered my problem to be a social one that was embedded in the centuries-old traditions of punishing women for being in the public sphere by themselves. Certainly, I did not have the language or understand the context of street harassment.

As a teenager, I could be tactless. Once I was at a restaurant where the table next to me had two men hassling the waitress. She was trying to smile despite their sexual advances. I said quite loudly so that the whole restaurant could hear, "Don't you hate it when men bother women when they are just trying to work? Why can't they just leave her alone?" The men quickly paid their bills and left, while my poor sister gave me a mortified look. Yes, it felt good to call out those men.

This incident came to mind when I was reading about bystander intervention. As an adult, I had to rethink what I had done that day. I asked a restaurant server what she thought a customer should do if they see somebody at the next table harassing her. She told me that her primary concern would be the tip she would probably lose from those male customers. Asking for the manager might or might not work because it depended on the manager's view of whether the customer was always right versus defending the staff. I asked her whether it would be acceptable for me to call out the rude customers but also double-tip her to make sure that she did not get stiffed. She said that might work.

Thoughtful activism, then, requires more than an automatic reaction to a perceived problem. Planning one's actions by considering the possible consequences is essential. We do not want to make matters worse by acting self-righteously but thoughtlessly. Also, thoughtful activism means allying oneself with other movements and using political tools. Advocacy is hard work, but it can also be richly rewarding.

ALLIANCES WITH OTHER MOVEMENTS

Labor Movement

Although unions have not always supported female workers, women's rights and labor rights remain inseparable because the capitalist system can be as crushing as patriarchy. The 1888 strike by the Match Girls in London, for instance, struck a powerful blow against the match factory owners who paid starvation wages. The phosphorus used in match production was so toxic that workers developed "phossy jaw," in which part of their face was eaten away. Another compelling moment in labor history occurred at a parliamentary hearing when a female worker told the politicians about the effects of carrying wooden pallets on her head all day. She took off her bonnet to show a bald scalp, a shocking sight for Victorians who so highly valued women's hair[1].

Another example of empowered women appeared in the 1912 labor strike by workers in Lawrence, Massachusetts. About 20,000 workers (mostly women) faced hostile authorities in their quest for decent wages. The mortality rate for children younger than six years was 50% because the living conditions and food were so bad.

Few could believe that so many workers from so many ethnic backgrounds could unite for such a bold action—30 different languages were spoken during the organizing. Of course, critics called these workers "radical immigrants" in the ages-old attempt to label activists as the Other. Despite being desperately poor and often illiterate, women joined the movement for a better life.

The workers briefly won the battle for "bread and roses"—wages not just for bare survival, but for a dignified life. The lyrics of the "Bread and Roses" song (by James Oppenheim) show the power of this yearning for dignity:

> As we come marching, marching, in the beauty of
> the day
> A million darkened kitchens, a thousand mill lofts grey
> Are touched with all the radiance that sudden sun discloses
> For the people hear us singing, Bread and Roses, Bread
> and Roses. [2]

To ensure safety for their children during the violent days of the strike, many Lawrence strikers sent their children to nearby cities. Police even went to the train station to harass the parents and children. This exodus (pictured in Illustration 9.1) resulted in the Children's March (1912) in New York City, which publicized the plight of the working classes. Later, a congressional hearing even featured young speakers who had experienced child labor.

A current example of labor rights for a female-dominated occupation is the Unite Here union for hotel workers. Besides wages and benefits, one key issue is protecting the housekeepers from the guests who harass them. One former employee said, "We don't know if the predators are there" when the housekeepers enter the rooms. "They feel they have a right to the lady who cleans the room." According to the Equal Employment Commission, housekeepers are at high risk because of "language differences, 'significant power disparities' between employees and management, reliance on customer satisfaction, physical isolation, and alcohol consumption"[3].

ILLUSTRATION 9.1 Children of Lawrence strike, 1912. Source: Library of Congress.

As a result of Unite Here activism, all unionized hotels in New York City now have a panic button for the housekeepers. Hotels in Seattle provide their housekeeper with other devices for their protection. The renewed interest in the sexual harassment issue in 2017 has made the public aware of not only high-profile Hollywood cases but also the common dangers faced by women rendered vulnerable because of their race and economic status.

Waitresses are also subject to repeated sexual harassment not only by customers but also by the staff. Restaurant Opportunities Centers (ROC) United, a national movement that advocates for restaurant workers, has researched this issue and found that "90% of those who work for tips in restaurants report experiencing unwanted sexual comments or behaviors in the workplace." Racism also affects the wages of restaurant workers, with Whites earning almost $4 more per hour than non-Whites. Also, restaurants often placed Whites in better paying positions. Women earned 21.8% less than their male counterparts. As a result, women of color are most likely to work in the lowest paying jobs.

Fortunately, ROC United has not only researched these inequalities but also proposed three solutions:

- Helping restaurant employees to succeed not only through job training but also through advocacy efforts such as the One Fair Wage campaign to ensure living wages instead of subminimum wages;
- Working with restaurants to "Take the High Road" to profitability through fair labor practices; and
- Encouraging customers to wield consumer pressure on restaurants through the Diners United program. [4]

In a letter to Governor Cuomo (New York) dated December 19, 2017, Women in Leadership used the heading, "One Fair Wage: Time to End the Subminimum Tipped Wage and Prevent Sexual Harassment in New York's Restaurants." This letter stresses that relying on tips made female servers extremely vulnerable to sexual harassment not only from the customers but also from the staff and supervisors. This claim is supported by one lawsuit in which one woman claimed that because she would not perform oral sex on her supervisor, he assigned her other duties that kept her from waiting on tables and getting tips[5].

Feminism and labor activism, then, are natural allies. Fortunately, labor unions are on the rise because of more millennial participation[6]. No longer the domain of White men, 65.4% of workers covered by a union contract are women and/or people of color. In fact, Black workers are more likely than Whites or Hispanics to be represented by a union[7]. As more workers realize that their low pay and/or working conditions are part of a larger problem, feminists and labor unions can offer answers (Box 9.1).

Ecofeminism—Women Fighting for Environmental Survival

For centuries, writers have linked women with nature. Emily Dickinson's metaphor is typical of this connection: "Nature—the Gentlest Mother is,/Impatient of no Child—The feeblest—or the waywardest—/Her Admonition mild—"[8]. It seems unavoidable, then, to link ecological concerns (environmentalism) with feminism. Coined in 1974, the term "ecofeminism" combines the ecological crisis caused by human exploitation of nature and the social struggles caused by male exploitation of females[9]. "Women must see that there can be no liberation for them and no solution to the ecological crisis within a society whose fundamental model of relationships continues to be one of domination"[10].

Early pioneers of the environmentalist movement have saved countless lives, besides reducing the ravages of an out-of-control urge to exploit nature no matter the cost. Rachel Carson, regarded as the Godmother of Ecofeminism, first raised the alarm in 1962 about the dangers of pesticides. She had little status as a female scientist and as a biologist in the era of missile-building mania, but her book *Silent Spring* changed our consciousness about the world. The first chapter starts with a fable that includes these haunting lines:

BOX **9.1**

HOW TO BE A TRANS ALLY

Another group for possible collaboration is the trans rights movement. Some readers may not be familiar with the basics of acting as a trans ally, so I consulted a trans activist and also adapted some material from a *Campus Pride* article [34] for this section.

- Like cis persons, every trans person is unique, so try not to stereotype them. If you have met a trans person, you have met only one trans person and not the entire community.
- Never, ever disclose that somebody is trans unless you have that person's permission. Trans persons face so much discrimination and violence that they must be careful about when and where to disclose.
- Never, ever ask a trans person if they have had "the surgery." That question is both intrusive and offensive. Respect their privacy.
- Not every trans person will be considering surgery and/or hormones. "Realize and acknowledge that being transgender is a spectrum. . . . Everyone is on their own personal journey" [35].
- Try to avoid gendered language because assuming a person's gender can backfire. Instead, ask for a person's preferred pronouns. Some settings such as academia are now encouraging introductions with a comment on gender preference, which normalizes the checking in process of pronouns. "I

automatically feel safer when someone introduces themselves like that to me" (trans activist).

- Misgendering (referring to a person by the wrong gender) can be hurtful if intentional. Deliberately calling somebody by the wrong pronoun is a hostile action.
- If somebody you know has recently transitioned and you slip up by calling her a "him," for example, that would be just human error. However, such accidents could "out" a trans person and even endanger them.
- Dead naming is a variation of misgendering. Using the "old" name of somebody who has claimed a new name and identity can be distressing. For instance, many people still insist on calling Caitlyn Jenner "Bruce" despite the public declaration on a magazine cover: "Call Me Caitlyn." A *Healthline* article notes, "When you refer to a person who is transgender by their nonaffirmed name, it can feel invalidating. It can cause them to feel like you don't respect their identity, you don't support their transition, or that you don't wish to put forth the effort to make this necessary change"[36].
- If you are confronted about making a mistake, do not make it about you. Do not blow it up into a huge incident or require comfort from the trans person you had misgendered or deadnamed.
- Respect people's privacy regarding restroom use. Try not to "clock" or "read" someone in the restroom, even if you have no malicious intent.
- Be careful when you decide to advocate for a trans person—check in with them first. "Specifically, do

not pick battles on someone else's behalf. For example, your boss might be misgendering your coworker. If you confront that boss without talking to your coworker, you could make matters worse. Despite your kind and supportive intentions, your intervention could invite professional and personal backlash for the coworker. They may have been dealing with the boss in their own way. Most trans people carefully pick their battles to avoid greater consequences. So, in order to stand up for someone (I would say as a general practice, not just with trans people), touch base with them first and see how they would (or wouldn't) like you to proceed" (trans activist).

- Like other marginalized groups, trans persons may get angry sometimes. "Downplaying someone's anger is probably one of the worst things you can do as an ally. An example of this from the trans perspective is 'but think about how hard it is for [person getting your name/pronouns wrong]'. I PROMISE you that any trans person you talk to has spent years of their life agonizing about how other people may react to/feel about their transition, and doesn't need a reminder" (trans activist).

There was once a town in America where all life seemed to live in harmony with its surroundings. . . .

Then a strange blight crept over the area and everything began to change. Some evil spell had settled on the community; mysterious maladies swept the flocks of chickens; the cattle and sheep sickened and died. Everywhere was a shadow of death. The farmers spoke of much illness in their families. . . .

There was a strange stillness. The birds, for example—where had they gone? Many people spoke of them, puzzled and disturbed. The feeding stations in the backyards were deserted. The few birds seen anywhere were moribund; they trembled violently and could not fly. It was a spring without voices. On the morning that had once throbbed with the dawn chorus of robins, catbirds, doves, jays, wrens, and scores of other bird voices there was now no sound; only silence lay over the fields and woods and marsh. [11]

Only 18 months after the book's publication, Carson died. I consider it tragic that she did not live long enough to see the impact of her work, including the ban of the DDT pesticide and the worldwide recognition that we could be killing our planet. What I admire so much about her is not only her fierce defense of both human and nonhuman life but also her eloquent writing. Because her message was so well presented and her knowledge so in-depth, she succeeded as an environmental activist.

Other pioneers in ecofeminism include the Chipko women of the Himalayas in northern India—the original tree huggers. In 1974, these women were determined not to let deforestation continue to damage their lands. Flooding had become too common because of the relentless tree-cutting. The Hindi word "Chipko" means to cling, which is what these women did to the trees that had been marked to be cut down[12]. As a result, 10,000 square miles of forests were saved. Also, the women felt empowered to demand more share in the decision-making processes[13]. By the 1980s, several other Indian women's groups sustained the "Embrace the Tree" movement as the Gandhian method of nonviolent noncooperation protest achieved results[14].

Climate change, of course, has worsened the flooding risks in India and its region. Bangladesh is especially vulnerable to the rising sea levels. Next time you hear somebody sneer about the tree-huggers, then, tell them about the Chipko women and how they were clinging for their very lives.

As a movement for human survival, then, ecofeminism has developed into many forms. The water protectors in the Dakota Area Pipeline (DAPL) resistance movement are a striking example of how women continue their battle against environmental dangers. Called the "black snake" by the activists, the pipeline is a $3.7 billion project. The protests started in 2016 with prayer circles at the building sites, then expanded to camps in the Standing Rock area. One activist states that the pipeline "threatens to contaminate our primary source of drinking water and damage the bordering Indigenous burial grounds, historic villages and sundance sites that surround the area in all directions. . . . I have seen where their machines clawed through the earth that once held my relatives' villages"[15]. As the sign in Illustration 9.2 shows, these activists deserve the name "protectors" of the earth.

The filmmakers of *End of the Line,* a documentary about the women in these protests, stated that "the women of Standing Rock have been injured by water cannons, concussion grenades, rubber bullets, tear gas, mace, sound cannons, and unknown chemical agents. They have been sexually assaulted on the front line. Kept naked in their jail cells and denied legal representation. Locked in dog kennels. Permanently blinded"[16].

Spotted Eagle, a Lakota elder, had been an infant when the government had seized some family land in 1944 to build a reservoir. "This lifelong fight for water is something that

ILLUSTRATION 9.2 Standing Rock protest. Source: Shutterstock.

I was born into"[17]. Raised by her grandmother who taught her the Native culture, she established the Brave Heart Society for girls to relearn their culture.

In 2016, Spotted Eagle testified in front a congressional committee about how the Western European mindset does not even try to comprehend the Native cultures. "I'd like to begin by acknowledging that an entire realm of Native thought is marginalized, declared unknowable and consequently left out of every serious decision. The arrival of western Columbian philosophy on our shores brought ideas rooted in the concept of manifest destiny"[18]. Her discussion of the "bio-political" issues includes not only the corporate/political control over the lands that affects the Natives' water and food supplies but also carbon emissions and even human trafficking. Men in the labor camps were alleged to cause a sharp rise in the sex trade as Native girls were at high risk for trafficking.

In a statement to President Obama that she coauthored with other Native groups, Spotted Eagle expanded on the concept of bio-politics, in which "human life processes are managed under regimes of authority over knowledge, power and 'subjectivation.' In other words, our indigenous bodies, which are essentially a direct reflection of Mother Earth, have been and continue to be controlled by corporations and governments that operate for profit without regard for human life"[19].

Gracey Claymore, another Native representative who spoke before a congressional committee, was only in her teens when she joined the movement. She led a youth delegation to New York City in 2016 to confront presidential candidate Hillary Clinton about taking a stand on the DAPL issue.

The water protectors are protecting not only their own water source but also the water downstream. "Without water there is no life, and this is our main source. It's not just our issue. Everybody downriver of us is going to be affected, all the way down to the Gulf of Mexico. We're not just looking out for ourselves; we're looking out for all people"[20].

The Standing Rock movement, then, shows the power of solidarity: solidarity between different tribes, solidarity between Native and non-Native, solidarity between genders, and solidarity between generations. The bigger picture, as noted by Michelle Cook, stresses the power of community over oppression: "We are fighting the Dakota pipeline, but we're also fighting the whole system of violence. The whole system which has called us savages. Which has denied us our ability to be human—and we're responding to that by creating a community that has its own values. That respects its women"[21].

POLITICAL TOOLS

The Power of Writing

"So this is the little lady who started this great war." These are the famous words that Abraham Lincoln supposedly said to Harriet Beecher Stowe, author of *Uncle Tom's Cabin*[22]. This 1852 novel forced Americans to realize that they could no longer ignore the moral atrocity of slavery. As Illustration 9.3 shows, the human drama of this story was stirring and unforgettable.

When she resided in Cincinnati as a young woman in the 1830s, Stowe lived just across the Ohio River from the slave state of Kentucky. I have visited her Cincinnati house, where the Reverend Lyman Beecher presided over a family of women's rights activists. If only I could have listened to one of their lively discussions! Stowe visited Kentucky enough times to witness a slave auction and other aspects of slavery. Because the Ohio River was such a vital crossing point for the slaves running for their freedom, Stowe was in an ideal place to help the Underground Railroad.

Stowe married a fellow abolitionist and moved with him to Maine. A religious vision (and probably the death of an infant son) inspired her to write the emotionally powerful novel that affected so many readers[23]. What struck me about my visit to her Ohio home was the anecdote that she was raising seven children at the time she wrote the book. Money

ILLUSTRATION 9.3 *Uncle Tom's Cabin.* Source: Library of Congress.

was tight for this family. Allegedly, she sat at her kitchen table while home-schooling her older children, tending to the babies, preparing meals, *and* writing the book. Whenever I come up with excuses about being too busy to write, I picture Stowe at that table and marvel at her perseverance (Box 9.2).

More than 100 years later in 1963, Betty Freidan wrote *The Feminist Mystique.* This book, often credited with sparking the women's liberation movement (second wave of feminism), expresses the dilemma of women who felt trapped by social restrictions. In the early 1960s, Betty Friedan had conducted a survey of her former college classmates and

BOX **9.2**

TIPS FOR THE RELUCTANT WRITER

When you go to a gym, do you hop on the treadmill and go full speed? No, first you warm up! Writing uses muscles like physical exercise does—remember, the brain is a muscle, too. So most writers need a slow start before they go full speed. You will need pen and paper for this exercise, not a computer.

1. Draw a tree (this sounds stupid, but it can relax you).
2. Write down words and phrases about your topic.
3. For each word or phrase, write down three ideas under each one. (For example, under "social injustice" you can write "racism.")
4. For each idea, give a specific example. "Racism—acting surprised if a woman of color has professional credentials."
5. Now you have enough material to start writing a paragraph about one of the topics.
6. Give yourself permission to make spelling and grammar mistakes—you can always fix them later. This is only a rough draft. Let the words flow out of you. Write quickly and spontaneously.
7. Later, you can use this rough draft for further development. Or you can just throw it away. Either way, you warmed up your brain and exercised your writing skills—congratulations!

was motivated to write about their experiences. Despite the material comforts of their homes, these women still lacked fulfillment:

> The problem lay buried, unspoken, for many years in the minds of American women. It was a strange stirring, a sense of dissatisfaction, a yearning that women suffered in the middle of the twentieth century in the United States. Each suburban wife struggled with it alone. As she made the beds, shopped for groceries, matched slipcover material, ate peanut butter sandwiches with her children, chauffeured Cub Scouts and Brownies, lay beside her husband at night—she was afraid to ask even of herself the silent question—"Is this all?"
>
> For over fifteen years there was no word of this yearning in the millions of words written about women, for women, in all the columns, books and articles by experts telling women their role was to seek fulfillment as wives and mothers. . . . Experts told them how to catch a man and keep him, how to breastfeed children and handle their toilet training, how to cope with sibling rivalry and adolescent rebellion; how to buy a dishwasher. . . .
>
> The suburban housewife—she was the dream image of the young American women and the envy, it was said, of women all over the world. . . . "There's nothing wrong really," they kept telling themselves. "There isn't any problem." [24]

Although Friedan was speaking of middle-class White women in the early 1960s, the major point of her writing is still relevant. Women (and everyone else) should have choices about their careers and families regardless of social acceptance. Now that we are more aware of the other forms of oppression that include racism and ableism, we can adapt Friedan's message to our own activism. Few of us can tell ourselves that "There isn't any problem" anymore.

Like Friedan, Gloria Anzaldua had sparked a shift in thinking through her writing. As the author of *Borderlands/ La Frontera: The New Mestiza* (1987) and other works about living as a marginalized person, she describes the inner struggle of somebody who must claim her power.

Who gave us permission to perform the act of writing? Why does writing seem so unnatural for me? I'll do anything to postpone it—empty the trash, answer the telephone. The voice recurs in me: *Who am I, a poor Chicanita from the sticks, to think that I could write?* How dare I even considered becoming a writer as I stooped over the tomato fields bending, bending under the hot sun, hands broadened and calloused, not fit to hold the quill, numbed into an animal stupor by the heat.

How hard it is for us to *think* we can choose to become writers, much less *feel* and *believe* that we can. What have we to contribute, to give? Our own expectations condition us. Does not our class, our culture as well as the white man tell us writing is not for women such as us?

The white man speaks: *Perhaps if you scrape the dark off of your face. Maybe if you bleach your bones. Stop speaking in tongues, stop writing left-handed. Don't cultivate your colored skins nor tongues of fire if you want to make it in a right-handed world. . . .*

I say *mujer magica*, empty yourself. Shock yourself into new ways of perceiving the world, shock your readers into the same. Stop the chatter inside their heads.

Your skin must be sensitive enough for the lightest kiss and thick enough to ward off the sneers. If you are going to spit in the eye of the world, make sure your back is to the wind. Write of what most links us with life, the sensation of the body, the images seen by the eye, the expansion of the psyche in tranquility: moments of high intensity, in movements, sounds, thoughts. *Even though we go hungry we are not impoverished of experiences.* [25]

The Power of Oratory

At the Golden Globe Awards on January 7, 2018, Oprah Winfrey gave a rousing speech that included these lines: "[W]e all have lived, too many years in a culture broken by brutally powerful men. And for too long, women have not been heard or believed if they dared to speak their truth to the power of those men. But their time is up. Their time is up. Their time is up"[26]. This speech amplified the impact of the #MeToo movement in which thousands of alleged victims shared their stories of harassment and assault. Only time will tell whether Winfrey's "time's up" movement will be a one-day wonder or a long-lasting movement. Even if the speech does not change history, it illustrates the simple power of oratory that can still resound in this high-tech era.

When I watched her speech, I could not help but recall the famous speeches given by Sojourner Truth during the days of slavery. She spoke out about the double standard of White women (treated as pure, helpless creatures) and Black women (treated as property) in this 1851 speech, "Ain't I a Woman?" As Illustration 9.4 shows, she showed an inner strength.

> That man over there say women need to be helped into carriages and lifted over ditches—and ain't I a woman? I could work as much as a man and bear the lash as well—and ain't I a woman? I have borne five children and seen them almost all off into slavery and when I cried out with a woman's grief, none but Jesus hear—and ain't I a woman? [27]

I Sell the Shadow to Support the Substance.
SOJOURNER TRUTH.

ILLUSTRATION 9.4 Sojourner Truth. Source: Library of Congress.

Victoria Woodhull, the first woman to run for president, is another famous speaker in US history. Her remarkable life story includes stints as a child psychic, a 15-year-old bride to an alcoholic, a cigar girl at a raunchy San Francisco port, the first female stockbroker (with her sister), publisher, and proponent of free love[28]. When she ran for president in 1872, she was called both a lunatic and a prostitute. The Equal Rights Party may have died out, but not her legacy as the first woman to speak to a House committee in 1871.

Woodhull's speech for women's suffrage to the House Judiciary Committee was short but pointed. Illustration 9.5

ILLUSTRATION 9.5 Victoria Woodhull testifying before the Judiciary Committee of the House of Representatives in 1871. Source: Library of Congress.

captures the drama of this event. She argued that logically, the Fourteenth and Fifteenth Amendments already granted women the right to vote. Some of the committee members had to agree with her. Later she wrote, "I come before you to declare that my sex are entitled to the inalienable right to life, liberty, and the pursuit of happiness. By what right do you refuse to accept the vote of a citizen of the United States?"[29].

Eighty years later, Margaret Chase Smith emerged as a soft-spoken but well-respected politician from Maine. Having married a man who honored her political ambitions, she ran for his congressional seat after he died. Then in 1950, she became the first female senator. As Illustration 9.6 shows, she appeared as a respectable, soberly dressed woman with a pearl necklace. One biographer notes:

ILLUSTRATION 9.6 Margaret Chase Smith. Source: Library of Congress.

If leadership is problematic for women, one form remains appropriate, that of moral authority. It was a venue through which Smith strode through with self-conscious courage and pride. She seldom made important speeches or thrust herself out front on an issue, unless she felt justified by a higher moral imperative. When Smith acted as a moral speaker, she created a role for herself outside politics, above politics, a strategy to obtain power by criticizing power. Smith became well known for her propensity to chastise others for breaches of ethics or morality. In cartoons and commentary, she was often characterized as a purse-lipped schoolmarm, reducing her colleagues to little boys who had forgotten their manners. This gendered trope, this symbol of female authority, was one with which both she and her contemporaries were comfortable. [30]

The stern morality of this brand-new Republican senator appeared in her first speech to the Senate. Four years before the Senate finally condemned Joseph McCarthy for his anticommunist crusade that ruined the lives of several innocent citizens, Smith spoke firmly against his misdeeds. "I would like to speak briefly and simply about a serious national condition. It is a national feeling of fear and frustration that could result in national suicide and the end of everything that we Americans hold dear. It is a condition that comes from the lack of effective leadership . . ."[31].

The history of speeches by women, then, is the history of social change. It may take courage to speak out for justice, but it must be done. Women have remained quiet for far too long (Box 9.3).

BOX 9.3

TIPS FOR THE RELUCTANT SPEAKER

1. You may have heard of the advice to picture your audience as in their underwear. Better yet, picture them as naked. Even better—picture them as naked mole rats, those disgusting, squirmy creatures with protruding teeth that can bite through anything. So if an audience member dares to criticize you, just think: "Well, at least I'm not a naked mole rat like you."

2. Fear of public speaking can be linked to fear of social rejection and its consequences. Embrace this fear of rejection. Ask yourself, "What is the worst

thing that could happen if my speech flops?" You could lose your credibility and job and friends and family and home and everything you value. On the brighter side, though, you are not a naked mole rat.

3. Have faith in your material. You must be an intelligent person—you're reading this book, right? You must have keen insights that will stun the audience—or not. Maybe your ideas are drab and boring. If you put your audience to sleep, that would not be a tragedy. Most Americans are sleep-deprived anyway.

4. Let your message resonate in yourself and the audience. Unless somebody forced them at gunpoint to listen to your speech, the audience wants to hear your message. Don't be afraid to speak for at least two hours. The audience wants proof that they are as hardy as any nineteenth-century crowd listening to their politicians.

5. Avoid humor at all costs. As evident in these tips, trying to be funny just does not work. Always remember that making jokes about naked mole rats to an audience of pointy-teethed mammals with purplish, wrinkly skin is a bad idea.

The Power of Political Advocacy

Working within the system, of course, has many disadvantages. However, successful movements require both insiders and outsiders—the pragmatists and the dreamers. Political advocacy, which requires both patience and compromise, is one way to work inside the system. Senator Kirsten Gillibrand (New York) has been an inspirational leader for many. In her book, *Off the Sidelines: Raise Your Voice, Change the World* (2014), she offers this advice on advocacy:

> Please believe me: Your story matters. Keep telling it until it falls on the right ears. Once, a veteran who lost a limb in Vietnam told me, "When I strap on my leg, I strap on my patriotism. Why isn't the VA supporting me?" Those two sentences moved my office to work until we got him $60,000 in benefits and back pay. This story also opened my eyes to the backlog of veterans' claims caused by the chronic underfunding of the Veterans Administration.
>
> I also hear stories form mayors, church leaders, activists, philanthropists, and community leaders about all kinds of suffering we must address. "Our food bank sees more families and more children than ever before, but less food is coming in, because of the tough economy. Could you help?" Or, "My church runs an after-school program for at-risk youth, and we're running out of funding. Can you get us federal money to stay open?" When people raise their voices, they give leaders opportunities to truly help and serve. [32]

Having taught advocacy classes and attended a few Social Work Advocacy Days at the Ohio State Capitol, I heartily agree with Gillibrand's assertion that stories matter. However, facts and figures also matter. An effective persuasion technique is to tell a compelling story about the issue and then present the data.

For example, I once worked with a state representative on a bill to promote tenants' rights during the foreclosure crisis of 2008. As a renter, I had moved into a duplex without being told that the house had been under foreclosure for seven months already. The landlord deliberately withheld such critical information from me and my duplex neighbors. One week after a knee replacement, I hobbled to the door when a sheriff's deputy appeared with an orange eviction notice. It turned out that a high percentage of those being evicted from houses during that crisis were renters, not owners. I did not have 30 days to vacate—only three. Too disabled to even consider getting into a car much less start packing, I frantically called around to get help. Not until a local news team filmed a story about my dilemma (complete with me with a walker struggling to walk) did I get an extension for the moving date.

The strategy for the testimony on House Bill Nine, the bill that would have required property owners to disclose pesky details such as foreclosure status, stressed both emotional stories and housing data. For the committee hearing, I testified about how the landlord did nothing illegal by not warning me about the impending foreclosure. Then a mother testified about how she got evicted twice because of crooked landlords who had failed to warn her about their unpaid mortgages. After the stories came the data from housing experts who emphasized the widespread nature of this problem in Ohio. Unfortunately, the Ohio Senate failed to pass this bill, so renters can still be victimized by dishonest landlords.

This experience taught me that anytime I think that "there oughtta be a law!" I should think about advocacy. First, I look up any groups that may have started a similar effort. I ask about how it worked out for the group and also about why a law has not been proposed or passed. What are the possible barriers?

Advocacy, then, is a group project (Box 9.4). Another consideration is which level of government would best apply to the advocacy efforts. For example, I support Planned Parenthood. Should I focus on the federal funding or on

BOX **9.4**

THE ROLE OF SOCIAL MEDIA

Would the Black Lives Matter (BLM) movement have started without that famous Facebook post? After the killer of Trayvon Martin was found not guilty of murder in 2013, Alixia Garza posted a "Love note to Black people." This post included these famous words: "Black people, I love you. Our lives matter." Her friend Patrisse Cullors shared her post, besides adding the hashtag #BlackLivesMatter. A third woman, Opal Tometi, "reached out to them to create a digital platform to keep the conversation and the movement going." Police brutality is not the only issue, since poverty and other injustices are also threats to Black lives[37]. As one BLM activist stated, "Many of the front-runners of the Black Lives Matter movement have been women and young people. . . . We are the generation that does not tolerate intolerance, and we are not afraid to speak out against the 'uncomfortable' topics"[38].

Stating that social media can be an influential instrument for advocacy, then, is like stating that water is wet. Another striking example of its influence is in the #MeToo movement, which was started by Tarana Burke in 2006. She had been working with young girls and was meeting 12-year-olds "dating" men in their 20s. The idea that this Internet forum, which started in Alabama for mostly girls of color, grew to a worldwide phenomenon is indeed astonishing. In 2006, the platform used was MySpace (an early rival to Facebook) and the term "viral" simply meant flu bugs. Then the Harvey Weinstein scandal broke out in 2017, a scandal about a man getting away with harassment and assault for decades. Millions of women (and men) posted their stories about abuse as they demanded justice. At least 85 countries had their own versions of the #MeToo campaign, including the French version called "Expose Your Pig"[39]. Only a few months later, the impact of #MeToo was so strong that *Time Magazine* named the movement "Person of the Year." As Burke reflected on recent events, she said, "it's hopeful that the world is changing to a place where we can have open discussions about sexual violence and how it affects people millions and millions of people around the world"[40].

the state restrictions on the clinics? Other causes definitely apply to only one level of government. Calling the mayor's office about a Supreme Court nominee makes no sense—and calling your US senator about garbage pickup is also a waste of time.

When approaching a legislator, do your homework on this individual. (Obviously, you already did your homework on the issue itself!) Do not assume that a party affiliation would determine all of their positions. I categorize legislators into three categories:

- Allies. Some legislators may already support your stance. For example, once the social workers were lobbying to stop the conversion therapy industry ("pray away the gay") from doing further harm to LGBT+ youth. We met with a staff member of a legislator who was already sponsoring a bill against conversion therapy. Our discussion focused on how best we could work together to get the bill passed. Obviously, we did not spend time trying to persuade somebody about our position when they were already on our side.

- Neutral or swing vote legislators. This group is the highest priority because you could actually affect their votes on your issue. A gentle method might work best. For example, I would say, "I am a social worker and I'm concerned about the conversion therapy industry. Because social workers provide so many mental health services, we have some expertise on this issue. Do you have any questions about conversion therapy or why we oppose it?" Instead of saying, "Hey, vote the right way or else!" offer information to open up a dialogue. The legislator might be genuinely confused about the issue or may have been misinformed. As politicians, legislators have probably had enough people yell at them through the years. So even though they may duck the issue or say that they are voting against your cause, you still want a relationship with them. (Not a romantic relationship, but a political one. Your life as an advocate is complicated enough, right?)

- Hardliners against your cause. Strategically, I would put only a token effort into the advocacy but not hope for miracles. Diehard homophobes, for example, may only shake their head at me during a conversation about conversion therapy. Although I consider it vital to still make a statement for my cause, I would not be crushed if I made no impact. However, I also believe in planting seeds. Maybe I could find an issue that we do agree on (perhaps garbage collection?) and try to build a relationship based on that issue. Politics is the art of the possible—and people do change.

Another key point about advocacy is that it requires relationships—relationships between fellow group members, other groups, legislators, and anybody else who could be involved. Today's opponent may be tomorrow's ally, so do not burn any bridges. Although your advocacy issue could be an urgent one, that does not give you permission to be harsh or abrasive. Think of your impact as leaving behind an emotional footprint. If somebody disagrees with you but still felt uplifted after conversing with you, then you have planted the seeds of a future relationship. Consider how somebody had been able to persuade you to change your mind about an issue—what happened? You were probably treated with respect instead of disdain. Thoughtful advocacy requires the emotional discipline of not screaming in the face of your opponent. Confrontational politics may prevail on the cable news shows, but that should not be the standard method for life-affirming activists.

Thoughtful activism requires patience in addition to the belief that one's legacy will live on. The historical examples of Sojourner Truth and other powerful women compel us to keep on fighting. In a recent interview, Gloria Steinem said: "The best thing to do with frustration is to turn it into action, and anger. That's the only way to relieve the pressure." Robin Morgan, another feminist with a long legacy of activism, added: "It's like mistaking a spiral for a circle: you come back at the same thing but at a different level; you see the change from before"[33].

Notes

1. Raw, L. (2009). *Striking a light: The Bryant and May matchwomen and their place in history*. London, UK: Continuum.
2. Forrant, R., & Grabski, S. (2013). *Lawrence and the 1912 bread and roses strike*. Charleston, SC: Arcadia Publishing.
3. Eidelson, J. (2017). Hotels add "panic buttons" to protect housekeepers from guests. Bloomberg News. Retrieved from www.bloomberg.com/news/articles/2017-12-13/hotels-add-panic-buttons-to-protect-housekeepers-from-guests
4. Restaurant Opportunities Center. Retrieved from http://rocunited.org/our-work/#gender-inequality-is-widespread and http://rocunited.org/2017/12/women-leadership-pen-open-letter-ny-governor-supporting-one-fair-wage/
5. Babwin, D. (2017). Sexual misconduct often part of the job in hospitality work. Washington Post. Retrieved from www.washingtonpost.com/national/in-hospitality-industry-sexual-misconduct-often-part-of-job/2017/12/10/62486bca-ddbc-11e7-b2e9-8c636f076c76_story.html?utm_term=.280ad19d23af
6. Chen, M. (2018). Millennials are keeping unions alive. The Nation. Retrieved from www.thenation.com/article/millennials-are-keeping-unions-alive/
7. Bivens, J., Engdahl, L., Gould, E., et al. (2017). How today's unions help working people. Economic Policy Institute. Retrieved from www.epi.org/publication/how-todays-unions-help-working-people-giving-workers-the-power-to-improve-their-jobs-and-unrig-the-economy/
8. Chunyan, H. (2015). Eco-feminism in Emily Dickinson's poetry. *Studies in Literature and Language, 10*:3, 63–72.
9. Gorney, E. (2017). If only I had petals, my situation would be different. *Ecofeminism in Dialogue,* 77.
10. Ruether, R. (1975). *New woman, new earth: Sexist ideologies and human liberation*. Seabury Press.
11. Carson, R. (1962). *Silent spring*. New York, NY: Houghton Mifflin, pp. 1–2.
12. Fordham, W. (*n.d.*). How ecofeminism works. How Stuff Works website. Retrieved from https://science.howstuffworks.com/environmental/green-science/ecofeminism2.htm

13. Jain, S. (1984). Women and people's ecological movement: A case study of women's role in the Chipko Movement in Uttar Pradesh. *Economic and Political Weekly*, 1788–1794.
14. Shiva, V., & Bandyopadhyay, J. (1986). The evolution, structure, and impact of the Chipko movement. *Mountain Research and Development*, 133–142.
15. American Horse, I. (2016). "We are protectors, not protesters": Why I'm fighting the North Dakota pipeline. The Guardian. Retrieved from www.theguardian.com/us-news/ 2016/aug/18/north-dakota-pipeline-activists-bakken-oil-fields
16. Indiegogo. (*n.d.*). End of the line: The women of Standing Rock. Indiegogo fundraising website. Retrieved from https://www.indiegogo.com/projects/ end-of-the-line-the-women-of-standing-rock-environment#/
17. Hult, J. (2017). Women of Standing Rock won't back down. USA Today. Retrieved from www.usatoday.com/story/news/ nation/2017/03/11/women-standing-rock-arent-backing-down/98975956/
18. Braine, T. (2016). House Democrats call for new DAPL permitting process after 2-hour forum in DC. Indian Country Today. Retrieved from https://indiancountrymedianetwork. com/news/politics/house-democrats-call-for-new-dapl-permitting-process-after-2-hour-forum-in-dc/
19. Brave Heart Society. (2016). "Obama, hear our cry": Lakota women call on president to stop violence. Indian Country Today. Retrieved from https://indiancountrymedianetwork. com/news/environment/obama-hear-our-cry-lakota-women-call-on-president-to-stop-violence/
20. Woolf, N. (2016). Native American tribes mobilize against proposed North Dakota oil pipeline. The Guardian. Retrieved from www.theguardian.com/us-news/2016/apr/01/ native-american-north-dakota-oil-pipeline-protest
21. Arasim, E., & Lake, O. O. (2016). 15 Indigenous women on the frontlines of the Dakota access pipeline resistance. Ecowatch. Retrieved from www.ecowatch.com/indigenous-women-dakota-access-pipeline-2069613663.html
22. Quote retrieved from Lincoln Studies website: http:// lincolnstudies.blogspot.com/2008/03/little-lady-who-started-this-great-war.html

23. Harriet Beecher Stowe: Activist, author, philanthropist, activist (1811–1896). (*n.d.*). Biography website. Retrieved from www. biography.com/people/harriet-beecher-stowe-9496479

24. Friedan, B. (1963). *The feminine mystique*. New York, NY: W. W. Norton, p. 1.

25. Anzaldua, G., cited in Keating, A., ed. (2009). *The Gloria Anzaldua reader*. Durham, NC: Duke University Press, pp. 27–28, 34.

26. Russonello, G. (2018). Read Oprah Winfrey's Golden Globes speech. New York Times. Retrieved from www.nytimes.com/2018/01/07/movies/oprah-winfrey-golden-globes-speech-transcript.html

27. Speech is available on many websites, including www.sojournertruth.com/p/aint-i-woman.html

28. Gabriel, M. (1998). *Notorious Victoria: The life of Victoria Woodhull, uncensored*. New York, NY: Workman Publishing.

29. Goldsmith, B. (1998). *Other powers: the age of suffrage, spiritualism, and the scandalous Victoria Woodhull*. New York, NY: Alfred A. Knopf.

30. Sherman, J. (2000). *No place for a woman: A life of Margaret Chase Smith*. New Brunswick, NJ: Rutgers University Press, p. 4.

31. The full copy of Smith's speech is available at: www.americanrhetoric.com/speeches/margaretchasesmithconscience.html

32. Gillibrand, K. (2014). *Off the sidelines: Raise your voice, change the world*. New York, NY: Ballantine Books, p. 60.

33. Ryzik, M. (2017). Celebrating global feminism with Gloria Steinem and Robin Morgan. New York Times. Retrieved from www.nytimes.com/2017/10/05/arts/gloria-steinem-robin-morgan-festival-albertine.html?hp&action=click&pgtype=Homepage&clickSource=story-heading&module=minimoth&region=top-stories-below&WT.nav=top-stories-below

34. Prin. (2015). 16 Ways to be a transgender advocate and ally. Campus Pride. Retrieved from www.campuspride.org/resources/16-ways-to-be-a-transgender-advocate-and-ally/

35. Prin. (2015). 16 Ways to be a transgender advocate and ally. Campus Pride. Retrieved from www.campuspride.org/resources/16-ways-to-be-a-transgender-advocate-and-ally/

36. What is deadnaming? (*n.d.*). Healthline. Retrieved from www.
    healthline.com/health/transgender/deadnaming#impact
37. Blay, Z. (2016). Founders of black lives matter honored among
    "Glamour women of the year." Huffington Post. Retrieved
    from www.huffingtonpost.com/entry/founders-of-black-lives-
    matter-honored-among-glamour-women-of-the-year_us_
    5818a8a2e4b064e1b4b4c8dd
38. Kehyeyan, K. (2016). The lasting impact of the black lives
    matter movement. The Odyssey. Retrieved from www.
    theodysseyonline.com/black-lives-matter-impact
39. Thorpe, J. K. (2017). What the astounding number of "Me Too"
    posts really mean. Bustle. Retrieved from www.dailydot.com/
    irl/me-too-posts-total/
40. Snyder, C., & Lopez, L. (2017). Tarana Burke on why she
    created the #MeToo movement—and where it's headed.
    Business Insider. Retrieved from www.businessinsider.com/
    how-the-metoo-movement-started-where-its-headed-tarana-
    burke-time-person-of-year-women-2017-12

10

FAILURE IS IMPOSSIBLE

INTRODUCTION

On February 14, 2018, yet another school shooting occurred. The story was sickening in its familiarity: an angry young man visited his former high school with a weapon of war. The AR-15 gun was a killing machine with bullets that tore through bodies and shredded organs. When I looked at the headlines, I felt despair because I thought that this latest shooting would not change the gun control debate. If the Sandy Hook tragedy of 2012 did not change the minds of the pro-NRA (National Rifle Association) politicians, why would the Parkland school shooting be any different?

This time *was* different, though. Only 10 days after the shooting, signs of change had already appeared. One student, David Hogg, stated that "This is not just another mass shooting. No shooting is just another mass shooting. This needs to be a turning point. This shooting was the result of a number of situations and individuals, but action can still and should still be taken to prevent something like this from happening"[1]. A 14-year-old student said that "The first couple of days I was super traumatized. . . . And then I looked at 'Never Again' and I wanted to be a part of that and to make my voice louder so that those who don't have a voice can speak through me"[2].

Soon after the shooting, the Parkland students took buses to the state capital to demand common-sense gun control such as banning the sales of assault weapons. CNN held a town hall meeting with Florida Senator Marco Rubio, who faced some tough questions. During this event, Rubio suggested that he might reconsider one gun control measure. President Trump then later indicated that he may make some changes. Meanwhile, students from all over the country held rallies in support of the Parkland students. A nationwide rally occurred the following month. With some corporate sponsors of the NRA dropping their support, public pressure has focused on the corporations who are still associated with the NRA. Perhaps the NRA brand has become toxic after Parkland.

At this early stage of this "Never Again" movement, some key lessons have already emerged. First, one would think that these students who had survived a mass shooting would have unshakeable moral credibility. The unfortunate truth is that no matter the social cause, most activists will have to be willing to be hated. Conspiracy theorists have accused Hogg and other students of being stooges of an FBI-led plot to take away their guns. Like the parents and others affected by the Sandy Hook massacre, the Parkland students have also had to cope with the absurd charge of being "crisis actors." Even a state lawmaker's aide made that assertion—an action that cost him his job[3]. Any activist, then, must be ready to face down those who would attack the messenger instead of the message.

Another key lesson is that feminism and gun control are related issues because domestic gun violence is a terrifying reality for thousands of women trapped in or leaving abusive relationships. Nearly 50 women a month are shot by their partners or ex-partners. This is not an abstract fact for me because I once had a student who was threatened by an ex-husband who would show up on her doorstep with a gun. Anytime she came to class, I would anxiously scan the hallways to make sure that he was not around. Fortunately, the police finally caught him. Domestic violence is related to mass shootings because many times domestic violence is a "warning sign in the history of the perpetrator"[4].

The third key lesson is that the Parkland students have not started something new but actually are continuing the long tradition of social activism. Their high school is named after Marjory Stoneham Douglas, the woman who helped to save the Everglades from environmental destruction. This remarkable woman started raising a ruckus in 1917, when she appeared with her colleagues before the Florida Statehouse to argue for the women's right to vote. In the committee room, the politicians just sat there without responding. "All they did was spit in the spittoons"[5].

Thirty years later in 1947, the same year that the Everglades National Park was established, Douglas published the book, *The Everglades: River of Grass*. This book "has become the definitive description of the national treasure she fought so hard to protect"[6]. For decades, she persevered not only to defend the Everglades but also for causes such as civil rights. She died at the age of 108. This quote should be an inspiration for not only the Parkland students but all activists: "Be a nuisance where it counts. Do your part to inform and stimulate the public to join your action. Be depressed, discouraged, and disappointed at failure and the disheartening effects of ignorance, greed, corruption and bad politics—but never give up" (5).

Another suffragist, Susan B. Anthony, said these immortal words: "Failure is impossible." This chapter, then, offers an optimistic vision for the next steps for feminist activism. Despite the grim news about national and international events, countless people are fighting injustice. Our reasons for hope are twofold: activism has worked before, and the resurgence of feminism appears strong. History, then, is a good starting point for the discussion of effective and thoughtful activism (Box 10.1).

WHEN ACTIVISM WORKS

Frances Perkins—"You Just Can't Be Afraid"

Perkins once wrote, "I came to Washington to work for God, FDR, and the millions of forgotten, plain common workingmen"[7]. If you support child labor laws, Social Security, workers' compensation, and 40-hour work weeks, then you can appreciate the activism of Frances Perkins. This social worker was one of the major founders of the Social Security system, which filled a drastic need during the Great Depression. The average person may assume today that these reforms in the United States just happened on their own, but they are the result of hard-working activists who faced difficult odds.

As one of the eyewitnesses to the Triangle Shirtwaist Factory fire in 1911, Perkins had stood on the sidewalk and watched the trapped girls scream and even jump to their

BOX **10.1**

DON'T BE AFRAID TO AGITATE!

Frederick Douglass, one of the greatest persons in US history, survived years of slavery before escaping to the north. His uncompromising stance against slavery often annoyed the moderates who wanted to move more slowly, including President Lincoln. Douglass's words from a 1857 speech are still relevant today:

> Those who profess to favor freedom and yet depreciate agitation, are people who want crops without ploughing the ground; they want rain without thunder and lightning; they want the ocean without the roar of its many waters. The struggle may be a moral one, or it may be a physical one, or it may be both. But it must be a struggle. Power concedes nothing without a demand. It never did and it never will. [39]

Another example of activists who were not afraid to agitate were the Pussy Riot women who openly protested against President Vladimir Putin's misogynistic policies and even went to prison. Masha Gesson, a journalist who ended up having to flee from Russia, wrote a book about them titled, *Words Will Break Cement: The Passion of the Pussy Riot* (2014). This quote is a modern counterpart to Douglass's fiery oratory. "To create, and to confront, one has to be an outcast. A constant state of discomfort is a necessary but insufficient condition for protest art, however. One also has to possess a sense that one can do something about it, the sense of being entitled to speak and to be heard"[40].

deaths. This tragedy was one reason that she founded the Division of Labor Standards and worked hard to protect the safety of workers.

Another formative experience occurred when Perkins was advocating for the women's work week to be reduced to 54 hours in the New York State Senate in 1910. She had to grab a senator before he boarded a river boat. He was a corrupt politician, but his answer to her request was a pleasant surprise: "It's all right, me gal, we is wid ya. De bosses thought they was going to kill your bill, but they forgot about Tim Sullivan. I'm a poor man meself. Me father and me mother were poor and struggling. I seen me sister go out to work when she was only fourteen and I know we ought to help these gals by giving 'em a law which will prevent 'em from being broke down while they're still young"[8]. As indicated by Illustration 10.1, Perkins had a no-nonsense manner and an unwavering determination.

After the stock market crashed and the devastating impact of the Great Depression grew even worse by 1932, President Franklin D. Roosevelt selected Perkins to be the Secretary of Labor. This anecdote shows her unshakeable determination to make big changes, not little ones:

> On a chilly February night in 1933, a middle-aged woman waited expectantly to meet with her employer at his residence on East 65th Street in New York City. She clutched a scrap of paper with hastily written notes. Finally ushered into his study, the woman brushed aside her nervousness and spoke confidently. They bantered casually for a while, as was their style, then she turned serious, her dark, luminous eyes holding his gaze.
>
> He wanted her to take an assignment but she had decided she wouldn't accept it unless he allowed her to do it her

ILLUSTRATION 10.1 Frances Perkins. Source: Library of Congress.

own way. She held up the piece of paper in her hand, and he motioned her to continue.

She ticked off the items: a forty-hour workweek, a minimum wage, worker's compensation, unemployment compensation, a federal law banning child labor, direct federal aid for unemployment relief, Social Security, a revitalized public employment service, and health insurance. She watched his eyes to make sure he was paying attention and understanding the implications of each demand. She braced for his response, knowing that he often chose political expediency over idealism and was capable of callousness, even cruelty.

The scope of her list was breathtaking. She was proposing a fundamental and radical restructuring of American society, with enactment of historic social welfare and labor laws. To succeed, she would have to overcome opposition from courts, business, labor unions, conservatives.

"Nothing like this has ever been done in the United States before," she said. "You know that, don't you?" [9]

One poignant aspect of Perkins' story is that her husband had a severe mental illness. The proudest day of her life should have been August 14, 1935—the day the Social Security Act was passed. Right before she was leaving her office for the signing ceremony, the phone rang. Her husband had left the hospital and was lost in the streets of New York. Immediately after the signing, then, she rushed to the train station so that she could look for her distraught, disoriented husband. This anecdote typifies the lives of most activists, who must balance their family and social obligations with their work as advocates.

One key lesson from Perkins' work, then, is that she did not settle for half measures but instead demanded sweeping changes. Sometimes it is wise to be bold instead of accommodating. Also when considering Perkins' successes as an advocate, we should remember her advice that still applies today: "Once you get the ear of a politician, you get something real. The highbrows can talk forever and nothing happens. People smile benignly on them and let it go. But once the politician gets an idea, he deals in getting things done. . . . Don't ever scorn the politicians. They are really the key to these situations in which we now deal" (9).

Pat Schroeder—"She Wins, We Win"

Although I never had the chance to meet Perkins, I have heard Pat Schroeder speak several times because I grew up in Denver. When Schroeder was elected to Congress in 1972, I was just a kid and had no idea of this event's momentous nature. She has been my role model for decades because of her smart and feisty personality—and because she got things done.

When growing up, Schroeder's mother had told her that it was better to read a book than to dust it. Schroeder earned her pilot's license and wanted to study aerodynamic engineering, but that was not a lady-like occupation. Instead, she studied history and applied to law school. When she started Harvard Law School in 1961, there were only 15 female and 500 male students. One professor told her that students like her were wasting "sacred space" at Harvard because "women would never use their degrees"[10]. On the first day of class, a male classmate refused to sit in his assigned seat because it was next to her. He told her that she "should be ashamed of herself for taking up a spot in the class that should have gone to a man"[11].

By breaking into the male-dominated world of Harvard, Schroeder learned how to infiltrate the "boys club of Congress"[12]. However, her parents were upset that she went to law school because they were afraid that she would never marry or have children. They were too embarrassed to tell their friends that they had a daughter in law school. Schroeder did get married and have children.

A decade later, the reaction of Schroeder's parents would be reflected in the attitude of the political experts who discouraged her from running for Congress because they never expected her to win. Her kitchen-table campaign, including the simple "She Wins, We Win" slogan, appalled these experts. They also told her that she was too aggressive. Her future female colleagues advised her that she could not make it as a congressperson because she had young children. When asked by a male colleague how a mother of two small children could serve in Congress, she said, "I have a brain and a uterus and I use both"[13]. In fact, she carried diapers around in her bag for a few years and ended up serving 25 years in the House.

Not surprisingly, the male House leadership tried to marginalize her through committee assignments. She had to fight hard to be on the Armed Services Committee because "When men talk about defense, they always claim to be protecting women and children, but they never ask the women and children what they think"[14]. The chairman did not want her or Ron Dellums (an African American) in the meetings. He gave only one chair for her and Dellums, saying that "'women and blacks were worth only half of one regular Member' and thus deserved only half a seat"[15].

Despite these obstacles, though, Schroeder emerged as a powerful Democratic leader who advocated for several progressive issues that included:

- Family Medical Leave Act, which protects the jobs of those who have to take time off for family or medical reasons;
- Violence Against Women Act, which focuses on gender violence;
- Bill banning female genital mutilation in the United States;
- Reducing Reagan's military expenditures, including nuclear arms buildup; and
- Title IX, which prohibits sex discrimination in education.

Although Schroeder's career covered a wide range of issues, the feminist credo that the "personal becomes the political" applies to her. During her second pregnancy, the medical staff had refused to listen to her, and she lost the baby. The doctor had "intimidated me and made me feel powerless" [16]while the nurse kept on telling her to "calm down" when she was hemorrhaging. During her third pregnancy, she almost bled to death. In explaining her pro-choice position, Schroeder wrote:

> Pregnancy is not a nine month cruise; it can be life threatening. I also understand that women have compelling reasons to avoid a pregnancy that could wreak havoc on their lives and the lives of their children. . . . [T]he woman is rarely mentioned by conservatives in debates about reproduction. She is just an impersonal receptor. She has no right to decide what is best for herself or any children she might have. This kind of thinking seems illogical to me. [17]

In a 2016 interview, Schroeder expressed optimism about the new generation of women who grew up with Title IX protections but still need feminism. During their school years, young women might not understand sexism—but then they'd get their first job, "and they'd come to my office and say, 'You know what happened?' And I'd say, 'Welcome to my world.' Oh, is *that* what feminism was about? . . . Somehow, they have the idea it's about not shaving your legs, not wearing bras" until they realize that feminism involves "equal pay and equal treatment"[18].

Local Successes

The triumphs of Perkins and Schroeder may be highly visible, but the small-scale successes of local feminist groups often go unnoticed. For example, the activist Michel Coconis shares this story about fighting the establishment's indifference to rape in Columbus, Ohio in 1982.

The Women's Action Collective (WAC) house, very near the OSU (Ohio State University) campus, was abuzz with activity to fight the rape epidemic. We had the rape victims' hotline sponsored by Women Against Rape (WAR), the rape awareness classes, Fan the Flames Feminist Bookstore, Committee Against Sexual Harassment (CASH), and the newly developed program to empower children against sexual assault that was being pitched to area schools. Several high profile rapes had occurred on or near OSU campus but the police barely responded appropriately. Time passed as we got little response from them. After collecting general data from the rape victims who had called the hotline, we volunteers strategized about getting the attention of the police and the justice system. We needed them to start believing these women and taking their traumatic assaults seriously. First we mapped out the locations of the reported attacks across the county. Then we posted STOP-sign type stickers or signs that said "STOP RAPE" at these locations: schoolyards, jails, churches, hospitals, homes, parking lots, banks, businesses—and even inside buses and restrooms. Fifteen volunteers distributed 356 stickers in three days, which seemingly popped up everywhere. When the local media wondered aloud who could be putting up the stickers, we sent two leaders to explain. Within a few months, the city police worked with WAR to develop strategies for intervention and training. Now, 35 years later, the Sexual Assault Network of Central Ohio and its allies within policing organizations, hospitals, and counseling all work together to bring visibility of a widespread problem and voice to the victims of sexual assault in our community. [19]

A more recent example of local activism occurred in Toledo, where the city's last abortion clinic was about to close because of the new state law. The Targeted Regulation of Abortion Providers (TRAP) law prohibited public hospitals from entering into transfer agreements with clinics. Although abortions are extremely safe, and the likelihood of a patient needing to be transferred to a hospital is nearly zero, these TRAP laws are one way to eliminate reproductive rights. On February 12, 2018, about 50 protesters gathered outside the Pro Medica Toledo Hospital to request that they sign the transfer agreement and keep the clinic open. One sign read: "They say 'No voice.' We say 'Pro choice.'" This small event resulted in Pro Medica signing the agreement that same day[20].

Of course, these two examples are a tiny fraction of the local successes all over the United States.

Whether an advocacy goal is ambitious or limited, its achievement deserves recognition and maybe a celebration. The next section provides even more reasons to maintain our hope as we carry on the fight for equality.

RESURGENCE OF FEMINISM

Fighting Sexual Harassment

In the era of the Anita Hill/Clarence Thomas case, millions of women could relate to Hill's narrative about sexual harassment. "You just don't get it!" we would exclaim in frustration to those who considered the issue to be trivial or nonexistent. The panel of male senators facing (and sometimes

denigrating) Hill symbolized the enduring power of patriarchy. As a result, Emily's List became a financial resource for
female candidates. As seen in this 1995 picture (Illustration
10.2), women have been standing up to sexism for decades.

The furor died down soon enough. In contrast, the
#MeToo movement took off in 2017 because social media
provided a venue for women to tell their own stories about
harassment and/or assault. Once-powerful men lost their
jobs and prestige for behavior that had in the past been
ignored or even condoned. Numerous debates about sexual
harassment whirled around like leaves in a wind gust. How
do we balance the rights of the accused with the rights of
the alleged victims? What is the sufficient punishment for
harassers? Should we consider all inappropriate behaviors as

ILLUSTRATION 10.2 Women outside the US Capitol in support of the
National Organization for Women's "Rally for Women's Lives" against
sexual harassment—1995. Source: Library of Congress.

a single problem or distinguish between the different levels of harm?

These debates, in addition to the serious repercussions for the harassers, demonstrated that more and more people are "getting it." In contrast to the early 1990s when Anita Hill had told her story, a cultural shift has occurred that may actually uproot the problem of sexual harassment. With hashtags and tweets and other technological advances, women can finally break the silence about their experiences. Many people now acknowledge that sexual harassment is both pervasive and serious. Even congresspersons have had to account for their actions.

With this cultural shift comes a political shift, as seen in this case study of the Ending Forced Arbitration of Sexual Harassment Act that was proposed by both Republican and Democratic senators at the end of 2017. The current law, which allows employers to force arbitration meetings on employees with complaints such as sexual harassment, deprived far too many employees from their day in court. Senator Kristen Gillibrand, a co-sponsor, stated that "When a company has a forced arbitration policy, it means that if a worker is sexually harassed or sexually assaulted in the workplace, they are not allowed to go to court over it; instead, they have to go into a secret meeting with their employer and try to work out some kind of deal that really only protects the predator. They are forbidden from talking about what happened, and then they are expected to keep doing their job as if nothing happened to them. No worker should have to put up with such an unfair system." One proponent is Gretchen Carlson, who had had to deal with sexual harassment herself despite being a famous newscaster. "Forced arbitration is a harasser's best friend." According to Senator Lindsay Graham (whom nobody would consider to be a left-winger), "To expect change without pushing for change is unrealistic"[21].

A cynic may consider such legislation to be a bandage fix for such a deeply entrenched problem, but progressives should consider working on this kind of legislation. The advantages of this approach include:

- Bipartisan support. As Gretchen Carlson notes, "Sexual harassment is not partisan because women from all walks of life and politics are targeted"[22]. Although my political views may differ sharply from Carlson and Graham, we are in agreement about how forced mediation can damage an employee's right to be heard. Setting aside differences to focus on what we can agree on, then, is an effective tactic.
- An achievable goal. Legislation can be either incremental (i.e., one small step at a time) or monumental. Either way, the goal is easily measured and has a reasonable chance of being implemented.
- Part of the bigger picture. This forced mediation bill would also affect workers in cases other than sexual harassment/assault. For obvious reasons, the National Employment Law Association (NELA) supports this bill. Its vision statement is bold: "Workers will be paid at least a living wage in an environment free of discrimination, harassment, retaliation, and capricious employment decisions; employers will fulfill their promises to provide retirement, health, and other benefits . . ."[23]. Bills like these are workers' rights bills that extend beyond a single issue. Anybody who believes that corporations have too much power would understand the long-term implications of a bill

addressing the power imbalance between worker and employer.

Women Running for Office

Political expert Carolyn Fiddler calls it "'the Trump effect'— the sudden surge of new candidates, most of them women, who said to themselves: *If that fucking schlub can be president, I can run for office*"[24]. Emily's List is the organization that provides resources for female candidates. According to its website, more than 30,000 women have signed up to run for office since the 2016 election. In contrast, only 920 women had signed up for the 2015–16 election cycle. The conventional wisdom was that men were self-motivated to run for office, but women had to be encouraged by others to run. The Trump effect has negated this belief in women's reluctance to become candidates.

Several female politicians in Virginia, for example, became national news after the election upset in 2017. They were inspired to run for office not only by Trump's presidency but also by the anti-choice legislation by the Virginia Legislature. The number of women in the House of Delegates rose from 17 to 28 out of 100. "Make no mistake about it: 2017 is the year of the woman in Virginia," stated an expert[25].

Another encouraging development is the rising number of African American women running for office—by early 2018, more than 400 had signed up to run. (The website https://blackwomeninpolitics.com has created a database for this trend.) The 2017 special election in Alabama for the senate seat pitted a progressive leader against a former judge who had been fired twice for violating federal law. Doug Jones had successfully prosecuted the KKK members who had bombed the Birmingham church in 1963, a symbolic victory over racism. In contrast was Roy Moore, a gun-toting "birther" who considered Obama to be a Muslim infiltrator and Native Americans and Asian Americans to be "reds and yellows." Moore also faced credible charges that he had harassed and assaulted teenaged girls[26]. Despite the 63% of White women voting for Moore, Jones won the election, partly because of the 96% of Black women who cast votes[27]. Inspired by leaders such as Shirley Chisholm, the first Black woman in Congress, these women have decided to seek political power.

Young Feminists

All over the world, young people are discovering that feminism still matters in their lives. One example is Lil Evans, a British woman who has started both a feminist society at her school and a Twitter group. She is only 16 years old. When asked to define intersectionality, she said: "For example, if we want abortion to be legal, we also need it to be cheap enough to be accessible to low-income women, we don't want people to be discriminated against because of their physical and mental health, we don't want it to be inaccessible because of discrimination based on race"[28].

Intersectionality, then, plays a crucial role in the young feminist organizations on a global level. These feminists are fighting for human rights despite the financial constraints and safety concerns. According to a report by the Association of Women's Rights in Development (AWID), the organizations include:

- Haus of Khameleon, a trans rights group in the Pacific that uses art to transform social attitudes. "By using feminist, human rights–based and evidence-based approaches, they address trans* issues but also other intersectional issues—ecological justice, gender-based violence, peace and security" (26).

- Salud Mujeres is an Ecuadoran group that helps women with their reproductive health. Because of severe anti-abortion restrictions, too many women are dying from unsafe abortions or being prosecuted for having illegal abortions. Fundamentalists have threatened the safety of these activists.

- Radio Udayapur is a community radio show in Nepal to help child brides learn some job skills and to challenge the practice of child marriage.

- In Eastern Europe, Giuvlipen is a group trying "to increase the visibility of the life of Roma (formerly called gypsy) women facing double discrimination through systemic racism and sexism"[29]. They primarily use theater to address the power of negative stereotypes.

In the United States, the group Young Feminists and Allies (YFA) works under the National Organization for Women to promote equality. Their work includes the issues of racial justice, trans rights, self-defense, street harassment, and building ties with Muslims. YFA also supports the "Know Your IX" movement, which aims to strengthen the students' Title IX protections against sexual harassment and assault (Box 10.2).

Iceland

In 1975, 90% of the women in Iceland went on general strike to protest gender discrimination. One woman was 10 years

---

BOX 10.2

KNOW YOUR IX

One milestone in feminist history is the 1972 amendment called Title IX, which states that "No person in the United States shall, on the basis of sex, be excluded from participation in, be denied the benefits of, or be subjected to discrimination under any education program or activity receiving Federal financial assistance." Since then, colleges and universities have had the legal obligation to provide a safe environment for all students.

In recent years, critics pointed out that colleges and universities had not done enough to fight sexual assault on campus. One successful protest occurred in July 2013, when an activist group called ED Act Now arrived at the Capitol. They presented a petition with more than 100,000 signatures, which they delivered to the Department of Education. As one student said, "There are students who don't feel safe in their homes, they don't feel safe going out at night. It's not legal and it's not morally correct that this is happening. We need to take a stance because this has been happening for so long, and schools have just swept it under the rug . . ."[41]. As a result, the White House Task Force to Protect Students from Sexual Assault was formed to investigate 85 schools for possible Title IX violations.

A setback for this movement occurred during the Trump Administration, when Education Secretary Betsy DeVos rescinded the 2011 guidelines for Title IX enforcement on campuses. Despite this action, students still have the right to demand from their schools the following:

- Prompt investigation of the alleged attack;
- Accommodations such as counseling for the alleged victim;
- An advisor of the student's choice to attend the disciplinary hearing; and
- Violence prevention training. [42]

The organization called Know Your IX is continuing the campaign for safe campuses. In addition to advocacy resources, they provide legal information and help for survivors. Because many activists are survivors themselves, it is critical for them to practice self-care as part of their activism.

old when she attended the rally with her mother. "I just remember the feeling of being among this mass of women, who were all so happy. That was a lesson for my generation . . . was that we managed to get women from all corners of society—from both the left and right, politically, and from all social classes. . . . It was a euphoric day"[30]. However, the men were less euphoric. Before the strike, they had seen it as a joke until they lost their coworkers, teachers, and other necessary people who happened to be women. "Most employers did not make a fuss of the women disappearing but rather tried to prepare for the influx of overexcited youngsters who would have to accompany their fathers to work. Some went out to buy sweets and gathered pencils and papers in a bid to keep the children occupied"[31].

Since that momentous day, Iceland has become the role model for many progressives. It has ranked number one for six years in gender equality, especially for political empowerment. The "childcare ecosystem" provides five months of parental leave for *each* parent[32]. In 1980, Iceland elected its first female president, and almost half of its Parliament is female. Because the pay gap has not fully closed, Iceland has recently passed a law making pay inequality illegal[33].

Although Iceland could not claim to be a feminist paradise, it is still advancing toward protecting women from gender violence. For instance, it has adapted the Nordic Model for prostitution by criminalizing the purchase of sex. It has also used the Austrian model for domestic violence intervention. The abuser (called "the threat") is the one who is evicted from the residence while the family members (called "the threatened") are kept safe in their homes through protection orders and support services[34].

In addition to these reforms, Icelandic women are also advocating to "free the nipple." In 2015, a woman bared her chest on Twitter as a protest against online censorship of female bodies. After trolls made rude comments, several other women posted pictures of their own nipples as a reminder that it is not controversial when men take off their shirts[35].

FINAL WORDS

Joy. That was one of the key words I found in the interview transcripts on caregivers who helped persons with HIV/AIDS. These caregivers made significant sacrifices for their care receivers, sacrifices that were barely noticed by society. One woman told me about how her husband did not make it to the toilet in time. He had stood there in the bathroom, humiliated and crying. She used gentle humor to make him smile: "Oh goodie, my mop was getting bored. Now it has something to do." As she had told me this story, her face shone with joy. She took pride in not only providing practical assistance to him but also sharing a heart filled with love. Other caregivers also spoke of how their health, finances, and social lives had been disrupted by their unpaid work. The emotional pain could be intense. One man told me about going into the garage to just let himself scream. Yet despite the difficulties, these caregivers were not merely surviving but thriving. Caregiver burden mattered less to them than the emotional rewards of doing the right thing and doing it well.

Like these caregivers, activists are caring individuals who are contributing to society. Joy should also emanate from our work because we are doing the right thing and doing it well. We are part of a larger movement that started centuries ago and will probably continue after we die.

Critics often characterize feminists as joyless, bitter creatures who focus only on their victimhood. This absurd stereotype has nothing to do with the positive, life-affirming women and men who live for hope. One hope that I cannot deny is that misogyny might be destined to collapse because it is an unsustainable system of oppression.

For example, recently Iranian women have been protesting the compulsory hijab (veil) laws. Although many Muslim women may wear a hijab as a voluntary and positive action, compulsory hijab laws can be a form of repression that goes far beyond the issue of veils. In Iran, the law also forbids women from entering certain public places and restricts their jobs and education. "More generally, it is also used to exclude anyone who disagrees with the ideology of the regime, who are branded as having 'bad-hijab.' Not adhering to hijab continues to be seen as a hallmark of opposition to the government"[36].

In December 2017, one lone Iranian woman stood up on a utility box and held her hijab high above her on a stick. This impromptu flag of personal freedom quickly became a symbol of resistance against an authoritarian government. Many other Iranian women followed her example, risking arrest for the sake of liberation. Some men also protested the hijab. Even an elderly woman climbed up a structure to wave her hijab.

Whether or not this hijab protest has any significant impact, Susan B. Anthony's immortal words, "Failure is impossible" still hold true today. Misogyny can seem like an immutable force, as solid and solemn as a mountain. However, misogyny is more like a shaky edifice on unstable ground that could collapse one day. Only time will tell whether my optimism is prophetic or foolish, but drastic changes have occurred before. The former Soviet Union, for example, was regarded as the Evil Empire that could invade the United States at any time. In the 1980s, the Reagan Administration frightened many people with its image of the Kremlin being an all-powerful force that only a multitude of nuclear warheads could stop. Yet outside of the Soviet modern cities, dirt roads and squalid poverty bedeviled the nation. Internal collapse caused by poor economic management and extreme political corruption was inevitable. However, only a few people would have predicted the fall of the Soviet Union even in the spring of 1989 when the signs became more obvious. Six months later, the "empire" did implode as the Berlin Wall came down. Two reasons for this implosion were the dirt roads (i.e., shaky infrastructure) and popular discontent (i.e., both active and passive resistance).

Like the Soviet Union, the current edifices of misogyny could be doomed to fail because of its shaky infrastructure and people's resistance. Misogyny is simply not sustainable because it defies common sense. Marxism-Leninism may have sounded logical on paper, but its communist system failed to reward hard work or innovation, so the workers did not try too hard. Also, Marxism-Leninism had created catastrophes such as the man-made famine in the Ukraine. The philosophical concepts of misogyny may also sound logical to some. Many still believe that men and women are inherently so different that they need rigid gender roles. Implementation of these roles, though, has resulted in catastrophes such as gender violence. Both Marxism-Leninism and misogyny, then, are simply stupid ideas that deserve to die out.

Indeed, the current representatives of misogynistic thinking in the United States have become caricatures who now face widespread ridicule. In 2018, a candidate for the Michigan state senate posted that it was not "sick" that men should take preadolescent girls as wives because the Bible proscribed it. The popular press quickly responded by calling him a "pig"[37]. Meanwhile, in Missouri, Courtland Sykes, who was running against a female senator, wrote this about his daughters: "I don't want them [to] grow up into career obsessed banshees who [forgo] home life and children and the happiness of family to become nail-biting manophobic hell-bent feminist she devils." One conservative columnist with the same last name posted: "Just to be clear: No relation.

At all. Thank God." After many mocking comments like these, the candidate partially retracted his post[38].

Whether or not you are as hopeful as me about the demise of misogyny, we still have work to do. We owe it to the suffragists, "women's libbers," and all those who had fought this fight before—we cannot let them down. We owe it to the young people who deserve a society that has less oppression and more open arms—we cannot let them down. And we owe it to ourselves to add our voices to the chorus of hope—and that will be our joy.

Notes

1. Andone, A. (2018). These young survivors of the Parkland shooting give voice to a nation's outrage. CNN. Retrieved from www.cnn.com/2018/02/16/us/gun-control-teenage-advocates/index.html
2. Levenson, E., McLaughlin, E. C., Gallagher, D., & Edwards, M. (2018). Parkland students: This is why we're going to Florida's capital. CNN. Retrieved from www.cnn.com/2018/02/20/us/fl-shooting-students-lawmakers-bus/index.html
3. Eltagouri, M. (2018). A lawmaker's aide called school-shooting survivors crisis actors. Within hours, he was fired. Washington Post. Retrieved from www.washingtonpost.com/news/politics/wp/2018/02/20/a-lawmakers-aide-called-school-shooting-survivors-actors-within-hours-he-was-fired/?utm_term=.bb213c2ca73a
4. Beckett, L. (2017). Domestic violence and guns: The hidden American crisis ending women's lives. The Guardian. Retrieved from www.theguardian.com/us-news/2017/apr/11/domestic-violence-shooting-deaths-women-husbands-boyfriends
5. Dreier, P. (2018). Who was Marjory Stoneman Douglas? The Prospect. Retrieved from http://prospect.org/article/who-was-marjory-stoneman-douglas
6. National Park Service. (n.d.). Marjorie Stoneman Douglas: Defender of the Everglades. National Park

Service brochure. Retrieved from www.nps.gov/ever/learn/historyculture/msdouglas.htm

7. Social Security Administration. (*n.d.*). Social Security pioneers: Frances Perkins. Social Security website. Retrieved from www.ssa.gov/history/fperkins.html

8. Perkins, F. (2011 reprint). *The Roosevelt i knew.* New York, NY: Penguin Press, p. 14.

9. Downey, K. (2010). *The woman behind the New Deal: The life and legacy of Frances Perkins—Social Security, unemployment insurance, and minimum wage.* New York, NY: First Anchor Books, p. 1.

10. Schroeder, P. (1989). *Champion of the great American family: A personal and political book.* New York, NY: Random House, p. 94.

11. Schroeder, P. (1989). *Champion of the great American family: A personal and political book.* New York, NY: Random House, p. 23.

12. Schroeder, P. (1999). *24 Years of house work . . . and the place is still a mess.* Kansas City, MO: Andrews McMeel Publishers, p. 93.

13. Women in Congress: Patricia S. Schroeder. (*n.d.*). US House of Representatives website. Retrieved from https://web.archive.org/web/20101103084757/http://womenincongress.house.gov/member-profiles/profile.html?intID=220

14. Women in Congress: Patricia S. Schroeder. (*n.d.*). US House of Representatives website. Retrieved from https://web.archive.org/web/20101103084757/http://womenincongress.house.gov/member-profiles/profile.html?intID=220

15. Women in Congress: Patricia S. Schroeder. (*n.d.*). US House of Representatives website. Retrieved from https://web.archive.org/web/20101103084757/http://womenincongress.house.gov/member-profiles/profile.html?intID=220

16. Schroeder, P. (1999). *24 Years of house work . . . and the place is still a mess.* Kansas City, MO: Andrews McMeel Publishers, p. 107.

17. Schroeder, P. (1989). *Champion of the great American family: A personal and political book.* New York, NY: Random House, p. 33.

18. Kennerly, B. (2016). Former Congresswoman Pat Schroeder still bold, blunt. *Florida Today*. Retrieved from www. floridatoday.com/story/opinion/columnists/britt-kennerly/ 2016/05/24/former-congresswoman-pat-schroeder-still-bold-blunt/84763986/

19. Email correspondence from Michel Coconis dated January 20, 2018.

20. Reiter, M., & Patch, D. (2018). ProMedica authorizes patient-transfer agreement with Toledo's last abortion clinic. *Toledo Blade*. Retrieved from www.toledoblade.com/local/2018/02/ 12/Protesters-urge-ProMedica-St-Luke-s-to-sign-agreement-with-Toledo-s-last-abortion-clinic.html

21. Graham, Gillibrand announce bipartisan legislation to help prevent sexual harassment in the workplace. (2017). Website of Senator Graham. Retrieved from www.lgraham.senate.gov/ public/index.cfm/press-releases?ID=CAF74791-2E1C-4026-8BD0-3774292BC858

22. Parker, T. J. (2017). Gretchen Carlson introduces "essential" legislation that would void forced arbitration agreements. WCPO website. Retrieved from www.wcpo.com/news/ gretchen-carlson-introduces-essential-legislation-that-would-void-forced-arbitration-agreements

23. National Employment Law Association (NELA). (*n.d.*). Vision statement. Retrieved from NELA website: www.nela.org/

24. Walsh, J. (2017). Democrats have a problem. Can these women fix it? The Nation. Retrieved from www.thenation.com/article/ democrats-have-a-problem-can-these-women-can-fix-it/

25. Schneider, G. S. (2017). Is it finally blue? Democrats speed Virginia's transformation—thanks to Trump. Washington Post. Retrieved from www.washingtonpost. com/local/virginia-politics/democrats-speed-virginias-transformation---thanks-to-trump/2017/11/08/a352a39e-c447-11e7-84bc-5e285c7f4512_story.html?utm_term=.540721a2f10b

26. Martin, J., & Stolberg, S. G. (2017). Roy Moore is accused of sexual misconduct by a fifth woman. New York Times. Retrieved from www.nytimes.com/2017/11/13/us/politics/ roy-moore-alabama-senate.html

27. Aggeler, M. (2018). There's now a database of black women running for office in 2018. The Cut. Retrieved from www.thecut.com/2018/01/new-database-of-black-women-running-for-office-in-2018.html

28. Cochrane, K. (2014). Teen spirit: Young feminist heroes. The Guardian. Retrieved from www.theguardian.com/lifeandstyle/2014/mar/29/fifth-wave-feminists-young-activists

29. Association of Women's Rights in Development. (2016). Brave creative resilient: The global state of young feminist organizing. AWID website. Retrieved from www.awid.org/sites/default/files/atoms/files/frida-awid_field-report_final_web_issuu.pdf

30. Cochrane, K. (2011). Is Iceland the best country for women? The Guardian. Retrieved from www.theguardian.com/world/2011/oct/03/iceland-best-country-women-feminist

31. The day the women went on strike. (2005). The Guardian. Retrieved from www.theguardian.com/world/2005/oct/18/gender.uk

32. World Economic Forum. (2014). Gender gap report. Retrieved from http://reports.weforum.org/global-gender-gap-report-2014/economies/#economy=ISL

33. Kottasova, I. (2018). Iceland makes it illegal to pay women less than men. CNN Money. Retrieved from http://money.cnn.com/2018/01/03/news/iceland-gender-pay-gap-illegal/index.html

34. Cochrane, K. (2011). Is Iceland the best country for women? The Guardian. Retrieved from www.theguardian.com/world/2011/oct/03/iceland-best-country-women-feminist

35. Sanghani, R. (2015). #FreeTheNipple: Women in Iceland bare their breasts on Twitter. The Telegraph. www.telegraph.co.uk/women/womens-life/11498799/FreeTheNipple-Iceland-Women-bare-their-breasts-on-Twitter.html

36. Mirdamadi, M. (2018). Why Iranians are really protesting compulsory veiling laws. Informed Comment. Retrieved from www.juancole.com/2018/02/iranians-protesting-compulsory.html

37. Reverb, J. (2018). Senate candidate's horrifically perverse sexist Facebook posts revealed. ReverbPress. Retrieved from http://reverbpress.com/politics/

senate-candidates-horrifically-perverse-sexist-facebook-posts-revealed/

38. Rosenberg, E. (2018). GOP candidate says feminists have "snake-filled heads," hopes daughters don't become "she devils." Washington Post. Retrieved from www.washingtonpost.com/news/powerpost/wp/2018/01/25/gop-candidate-says-feminists-have-snake-filled-heads-hopes-daughters-dont-become-she-devils/?utm_term=.a296f7e9b149

39. Douglass, F. (1857). Speech retrieved from www.libraryweb.org/~digitized/books/Two_Speeches_by_Frederick_Douglass.pdf

40. Gesson, M. (2014). *Words will break cement: The passion of the pussy riot*. New York, NY: Riverhead Books, p. 15.

41. Ramanathan, K. (2013). Student activists demand stronger punishment for colleges that fail to address sexual assault. Think Progress. Retrieved from https://thinkprogress.org/student-activists-demand-stronger-punishment-for-colleges-that-fail-to-address-sexual-assault-1810e03d754d/

42. The Know Your IX website is www.knowyourix.org

INDEX